AMBITIONS OF THE DEPRIVED

AMBITIONS OF THE DEPRIVED

EMEKA VINCENT EGBUONU

KNOWLEDGEBIDDERS

This book is for the next generation.

Summer, Malachi
Tochukwu, Nnenna and Onyinye

'Do not allow the voice of self-doubt and fear to play louder than the voice that helped create the ambition in the first place'.

CHAPTER ONE

It was late in the afternoon and the splash of puddles could be heard all over the market as crowds surged for the best deals.

'Bunch of bananas for a pound, love.'

The market stall sirens merged with the cultural sounds of reggae rhythms across a grey sky. Hubbub ensued as multi-lingual conversations darted diagonally across the square; mothers scolding their children, old ladies examining fruits, and Junior, working his way through the masses, struggling upstream, examining his local environment.

Dalston. East London. The source of deprivation, low education attainment, and a vast supply of social houses. Families scraping pennies together to survive, working hard; their wages entered a bag full of holes. Low pay, unemployment and discontent. This was home.

Junior walked through Ridley Road market, careful not to step on the toes of passers-by; squinting to ensure his new Nikes didn't get abused in the process. He cursed inwardly as yet another person stalled in front of him to peer at the fish displayed. Side-stepping just in time to avoid crashing into the back of him, Junior continued his journey.

Nearing the top of the market, which would lead him to the main road, Junior saw a young mother who looked no older than nineteen. She had long dark hair, her skin pale white, coloured slightly by the bruises on her face. Skin covered in a faded pair of denim jeans, a sad-looking grey hooded top and beat-down shoes; she looked unkempt. Her soundtrack the screaming child in the pram; she looked tired of the tune. Ignoring the screams, she continued pestering the butcher to let her off the pound she was short of. Junior sighed, glanced back in disbelief and continued to the bus stop ahead.

The dancing raindrops falling against the bus shelter were drowned by the thumping bass entering Junior's ear drums. He was desperate to escape the arguing and shouting that surrounded him. Volume turned up to maximum, his head bobbed to the beat. Across the road, 'Demand living wage not minimum wage' was scrawled in passionate black graffiti against the concrete wall. He nodded in silent agreement.

Clambering on to the packed bus, Junior's discomfort could only manage three stops before his finger found the bell and he escaped into the cold air. The weather was miserable; like a child who had lost his dummy, the clouds bawled repetitively. Even so, Junior decided to take his chances. It was supposed to be summer. Mid-June and the temperature refused to rise above a breezy fifteen degrees.

Briefly checking the time, his leisurely pace quickened and his inner sat-nav diverted to a side road shortcut. Momentarily, his attention was captured by the contrast of Lawford road. Generous-sized terraced houses boasted expensive cars in every driveway; even the birds seemed to favour the large trees spaced evenly along the road. His eyes found his reality, 100 yards away – a desolate sight of tower blocks, tiny windows and cracked paintwork. Symmetrical yet obscene. With a last glance, he took in the beautiful distraction before commencing to the council estate overflowing with last week's bins, litter and badly spelt graffiti.

Junior reached his destination with moments to spare. The Lion's club, a local refuge for aspiring young boxers. Randomly painted in pink, the two-storey building was home to the statue of the lion on the side. As old as his granddad, this club had survived seven decades, a landmark in the local community. Although it used to be specifically for boys, it now accommodated all young people in the area. They came to box, to train and reach professional status. Junior's friend, Jamie, was a regular at the club and Junior was here to support him. He knew his other friends, Samuel and Jason, were probably discussing his lateness as he approached the entrance. Typical.

Junior's hands met his pocket as he tried to find change for the sub fee to get in. He signed his name and smiled at the lady behind the desk, still unable to locate any money in his tracksuit. She tutted at him, slowly losing her patience.

'Junior, you always do this. Why don't you sort your money out before you come in?'

Junior smiled as he responded. 'I'm sorry, I think I dropped some coins as I was running here. Is it okay if I can owe you?' The woman looked at him while she checked his name in the database.

'Seems like you now owe us five quid,' she said. 'Please make sure you bring it next time you come.'

'No worries, I will,' Junior replied with a relieved look on his face.

He quickly made his way into the main hall where the fight was due to take place. He could taste the energy in the atmosphere as he walked in, overwhelmed by the number of unknown faces. The hall was decorated with handmade banners and signs; the people holding them chanted and laughed. The place was in high spirits. It seemed as if the whole community had trekked to the club to support the young amateur boxers. As Junior attempted to locate his friends, the announcer strolled into the middle of the boxing ring.

'In the blue corner,' he declared, 'we have Jack "the deadly blow" Porter from Bermondsey in South London.' Parts of the crowd began to boo at the sound of his name, but simultaneously a larger roar erupted from his supporters. Looking around the ring, the announcer waited for the noise to subside before continuing.

'And in the RED corner,' he boomed, 'we have Jamie "the Menace" Marker from New North Road, the next rising star out of Hoxton.' The end of the announcement was barely audible over the loud shouts, chants, stomping feet and crazy noise the people made. In the midst of the commotion, a chant was raised and avalanched around the hall.

'Stand up if you love Jamie! Stand up if you love Jamie!'

His work complete, the chubby announcer crawled out of the ring awkwardly, barely squeezing through the ropes. Jamie and Jack strutted to the centre of the ring signalling the big fight was imminent. Junior was now desperate to find a seat; scanning the crowd again, he located Jason and Samuel at the other end of the hall. He moved towards them, leaving behind him a trail of angry spectators.

'Get out of the way,' one shouted.

'Move, idiot. You're not transparent,' shouted another. He ignored them.

'Look who finally decided to show up,' Samuel said to Junior as he stood up to touch fists with him. Jason barely acknowledged Junior's presence; he was totally focused on the fight taking place.

'Jamie looks in really good shape,' Junior commented. 'Look how ripped his arms are. He has even worked on his core. Just look at those abs.' Samuel laughed.

'Just like your abs, don't you think?' he said sarcastically.

'On a serious note, Jamie has seriously been working out,' Jason said. 'He has gone from twelve and half stones to eleven stones. He is really serious about making it pro.'

The boxing match had reached epic levels. The third and final round commenced and, even though Jamie seemed to be in control, the competition was extremely tight. Emotions were tense and the crowd were supporting at the top of their lungs.

They had seen Jamie knock out bigger contestants, yet they were anxious to see it again. The expression on Jamie's face oozed passion and desire, his concentration working through his veins, evident in every well-planted blow. The clock was ticking. Only minutes left and Jack had Jamie cornered. A couple of inches between them, but Jack's height gave him a slight advantage.

Jack's supporters were urging him on, encouraging him to go for the knockout. Jack leant into Jamie, throwing long jabs. They were no match for Jamie, whose light footwork enabled him to manoeuvre past the assault with ease. Biding his time, Jamie faked left as the wild swing of a right hook came from Jack. Noticing this prime opportunity, Jamie launched a devastating right hook on Jack's face, flooring him completely.

The crowd were on their feet, clapping, jumping and screaming victoriously. The chant echoed triumphantly around the hall. Junior, Samuel and Jason all stood up simultaneously and joined in on the chorus.

'Stand up if you love Jamie!'

Samuel suddenly stopped singing.

'Did you see how he kept his composure and knocked him out?' he cried.

'That was nothing short of amazing,' replied Junior with a big smile on his face. 'Most importantly, look at all the love he is getting from everyone.' Beside him, Jason's expression went from jubilation to one of sadness.

'What is the matter, Jay?' Samuel asked. Jason stood up and waved at Jamie, who was taking his headgear and gloves off. He then turned to Samuel and Junior.

'It's a shame his dad is unable to be here and watch his son, it's just sad. I know it must be affecting him on the inside.' At that exact moment, the announcer climbed back into the ring.

'Your winner, and still undefeated in the amateur ranks, Jamie "the Menace" Marker!' The crowd began shouting with joy, but grew silent as Jamie addressed the crowd.

'First and foremost, I would like to dedicate this win to my dad, who is fighting cancer. His hardest challenge to date.' Jamie stopped with one hand over his eyes, trying to stop the tears, which were already freefalling from his eyelids. Regaining his composure, he continued.

'To those that have supported my family and me, I am so grateful and I thank you all for your support. The support you have shown me today has been amazing and I will never forget where I came from. Finally, I would like to thank my mum, who couldn't be here due to work commitments, and also my three good friends, Jason, Samuel and Junior. I consider them my brothers. Thank you all very much.'

The serious nature of his speech touched the whole room and gained him a standing ovation, even from his opponent's supporters.

A few hours later, Jason, Samuel and Junior met up outside Jamie's council flat, a two-minute walk away from the Lion's club. They chatted amongst themselves as they waited for Jamie to appear. Sitting on the cracked wall inside the square, they reflected on Jamie's victory, ready to go and celebrate at the local youth club.

Twelve storeys high, old and depreciating, the tower block looked ready for the scrap heap. Brown dirty stains ran across paint stripes that were once cream. From the wall, the friends could see Jamie's single-glazed bedroom window on the tenth floor. The frame was decorated with rust. The light was on.

Inside, Jamie grabbed his jacket, checked his face in the mirror, winked at his reflection and left. Entering the lift, the stench of urine arrested his nostrils and Jamie struggled to breathe. Disgusting. He couldn't understand what was so appealing about a lift that people had to queue to leave their liquid waste all over it. Maybe it was territorial. Like animals.

Before he had finished this thought, he'd arrived on the ground floor and escaped the pee pit. As he pushed his body weight against the large metal blue door, he was met by Samuel's voice.

'Bruv, how long do you need to get ready? You are acting like a girl.'

Jamie quickly replied with a big smile on his face. 'I don't usually take this long, but the house was in a state and I didn't want my mum to come home and start cleaning up. You know she works a long shift at the hospital, I just want her to come home and rest.'

Samuel's voice went from a high pitch to a calmer tone. 'I hear that, bro. Things must be hard right now.'

'Yes, they are,' replied Jamie. 'That's why I'm going to this CV writing workshop at the youth project, so I can see if I can get some work to help support my mum.'

The four of them started making their way to the youth project. 'Elevate' was a local hangout spot for most of the young people; great facilities, good company and amazing, dedicated staff. It was a Friday night and most people were now on their way home. Others were already preparing for a night out on the town. The street was quite busy, the sun had already set and the rain had stopped.

'So,' began Jamie, 'what have you guys been up to all day, apart from coming to see me fight?'

Samuel was quick to reply. He was the loudest amongst the four friends, and he always had something to say. He could not go a day without using his sarcastic banter to irritate people.

'I finished college early today, so I went round to that girl's house. The one I met the other day. What's her name?' Samuel started playing with the little hairs he had on his chin as he tried to remember her name. Junior rolled his eyes.

'You mean Rachel? The same girl you met at that party last week?' A cheeky grin appeared on Samuel's face.

'Yes! Rachel, that's the one,' he shouted. Junior shook his head, unsurprised by Samuel's antics with the ladies.

Samuel considered himself an artist when it came to the ladies, painting pictures with his words, drawing them with his creativity. A smooth talker, certified charmer, it was true. The ladies loved him. Jason kept a straight face the whole time.

'I couldn't be bothered to go to college today,' added Samuel. 'It's Friday and my main teacher said he wouldn't be in, so I didn't go.'

Junior jumped in. 'I didn't have any lessons at college today, either. My plan was to stay at home, but my mum left me a list of things to buy from Dalston, in the market. Highlight of the day was watching Jack's face as he plummeted to the ground from your blow, Jay!' Junior turned to Jamie who was walking a few steps behind him. 'It was epic! How far do you want to go with this boxing? You seem to be knocking guys out for fun.'

Jamie heard the question but was distracted by the passing traffic as they crossed a busy main road and headed to the park. Quickest way to the youth club. The rain from earlier had caused the grass to become muddy and, in the dark, there was no way to avoid the squelch underneath their feet. They tiptoed delicately, light-footed as ballet dancers across the muddy patches of grass.

'The way things are now, it's just really tough,' said Jamie. 'First my mum and dad separating, now my dad is fighting for his life at the hospital. I just want to achieve something that would bring some proud moment to my family. Boxing is what I know best. What are we in, June?'

'Yes,' Junior replied. Jamie nodded and continued.

'Next month, 6th of July, is a big day, because we will find out if London will host the 2012 Olympics—' Samuel abruptly interrupted him.

'The Olympics! You do know that is seven years away, right?'

'Yes, I know. Can I finish?'

'Go ahead, bro.'

'My plan is to try and make the Beijing Olympics in 2008,' continued Jamie. 'But if not, then by 2012, especially if London wins the bid. I will definitely work hard and make sure I'm in the Great Britain team for that year. You know what? Once I win gold in 2012 I will then turn pro.'

Jason was ahead of them all as they were exiting the park. He looked back.

'I'm happy you have a plan,' he said in a calm voice rather than his usual angry tone.

'That's more than I can say for myself and these two clowns,' Samuel laughed.

'Who are you calling a clown?' Jason said. 'But on a serious note, if anyone can make that dream happen it is you, Jay. Besides, you deserve it.'

Jamie looked deep in thought when he replied.

'Just because you deserve it, it doesn't mean you will get it,' he said. 'You have to work hard.' His voice started to tremble just as it had when he was giving his speech after the fight. This time, the sadness that overcame him was more controlled. 'My dad has worked hard all his life, now he has cancer. Did he deserve it...? NO!'

The mood was now despondent. Like a dark cloud, it overshadowed the group of friends as they continued on in silence. Their neighbourhood was dismal. Concrete slabs, a maze of tower blocks and low-rise estates. Graffiti was territorial and splashed everywhere. 'NN1 Family', New North Road.

Despite the relational vandalism, it didn't feel like a family on the streets. The residents all had their own struggles; often proud, some working hard, but never reaching financial freedom. Others worked their way to the Jobcentre, resulting in welfare, surviving on benefits. There was an attitude divide, the hard workers often despising those that took advantage of the system. Criminal activity was rampant, by those who needed extra money to survive and those who longed to live a luxurious lifestyle.

In the distance, a familiar pattern of blue lights flashed in their direction. Zooming down the street in an intimidating silence, the friends suspected trouble. Police. A daily occurrence in New North Road. Screeching to a stop, just opposite the group, four officers bundled out of the vehicle in record time. Faces stern, thunderous expressions headed towards them. Randomly ambushed, Junior, Jamie and Samuel looked confused. Jason, irritated and annoyed, carried on walking, acting uninterested. The senior police officer in charge shouted.

'Stop right there, you! The one with the blue and white hoody. STOP!' Jason stopped walking and looked back at the officer.

'What is the problem, officer?' he shouted back in his deep voice. The police officer replied, calmer now.

'First of all, can I have you all against the wall? My name is Sergeant Stone and these are my colleagues, PC Webb, PC Paisley and PC Vasques. We have a description of some lads who have stolen some phones from the area.'

'So what the hell has that got to do with us?' Jason shouted. 'Let me guess, we fit the description of the guys that did it.'

'As I was saying,' replied Sergeant Stone, 'we have intelligence, so we are on patrol making sure we respond to that intelligence.'

Jason was not satisfied with the reason the police officer was giving in regards to stopping them. His temper was starting to rise; his short temper often got him into trouble.

The police officer continued. 'We will have to search you all, to make sure you don't have any stolen or prohibited items on you.'

'What do you mean, search us?' Jason shouted. Junior interjected.

'Jason, calm down, man. Don't give them a reason to arrest you, seriously.'

'Junior is right,' Jamie said, looking at Jason. 'Don't give them the satisfaction.' Jamie turned to the police officers. 'Look, just do what you have to do, but I can tell you – we do not have anything on us.'

'Then you'll have nothing to worry about,' Sergeant Stone replied sarcastically.

The officers started searching all four boys. Pressed up against the wall, they watched and felt hands patting them down. Embarrassment filled the countenances of Samuel, Jamie and Junior as they realised they were prime entertainment for the multitude of partygoers across the street.

Jason was filled with aggression. Hating the violation he was experiencing, he made sure his feelings were made known as he maintained eye contact with the officer. With every passing second, the vein on the side of his temple pulsated in anger; his hands were screwed into fists and his jaw clenched tighter. At 5'11, he was the tallest of his friends and he refused to be intimidated. Not by the police. Not tonight. Fingers were pointed at them from pedestrians, drivers and people on the top deck of passing buses. A typical sight, four young men being searched by the police. They must be guilty of something.

Eventually, the search was over. Sergeant Stone stood back with a dissatisfied look on his face.

'You are no longer detained as we have found nothing,' he said reluctantly. 'Thank you for your cooperation, lads.'

'Thanks for nothing,' the boys all shouted. As they made their way towards the old community hall, they all muttered about their experience with the police. Conversation peaked as they leant against the side of the building, backs against professional graffiti artwork. Black and red-painted words shouted 'Inspire our youth'.

'Of course it has everything to do with race!' said Jason angrily.

'I agree with Jason,' Samuel replied. Jason was sitting on a low brick wall; he jumped off, raising his voice.

'I get stopped all the time, whether I'm in a group or by myself. Ask Jamie how many times he has been stopped on his own.' Samuel looked at Jamie.

'Go on then, tell us how many times,' said Samuel.

Jamie looked embarrassed. 'Just once, I think.'

A huge grin sprung across Jason's face. 'I rest my case, bearing in mind we are all from the same area. None of us are in a gang, selling drugs or robbing people. But they still harass us for no reason.'

Samuel started laughing.

'What is so funny?' Junior asked.

'I was just thinking,' said Samuel. 'I have a new code the police can use to describe people. Instead of IC3 male, which is for a black suspect, right?'

'Yes, I think so.'

'Well, next time they can refer to me as brown chocolate suspect. Junior, you would be a dark chocolate suspect...' They all started laughing; even stone-faced Jason could not help himself.

'Jamie would be that white chocolate suspect,' continued Samuel. 'As for Jason, I'm not even sure. How would you describe mixed race?'

'Refer to Jason as that caramel suspect,' Junior quickly responded. The group cracked up. Junior was never the quickest with banter so, when it was a success, it took them all by surprise.

They headed inside the youth project. The hall was buzzing with young people. Some were perfecting their skills on table tennis, the ping pong rallies broken up by a sudden slam shot and resulting cheers. Others were by the pool table, putting their maths lessons to good use as they angled the balls to sink their shot. The four boys were regulars at the youth club and walked through greeting staff and friends alike. A few people patted Jamie on the back, congratulating him on his win earlier.

A large group of young people surrounded the TV, causing a commotion around the PlayStation 2. It was tournament time – game of choice, Pro Evolution Soccer. Sixteen players and the prize was a fifty pound JD Sports voucher. Looking at each other with confidence, Samuel and Jason quickly signed up. Nothing like a new pair of trainers.

Jamie, on the other hand, undeterred by the competition, focused on attending the CV writing workshop. It was important business. He managed to convince Junior to be a part of the workshop even though he was not planning on looking for work.

Patricia commanded the room to be quiet; she had an announcement to make. Patricia Browder was one of the founders of the Elevate youth project. She was highly respected in the area by the young people and their parents. She was in her late forties and helping young people was in her blood. She did it because she actually cared about the progress of the children that were in her care. She was dark-skinned and of Guianese origin; her accent was still there, but was now tinged with Cockney.

'This is Malachi Richards,' she announced. 'He will be taking the CV writing workshop today. He will also be engaging in different projects of his own. So make sure you all make him feel welcome.'

Malachi stood strong, his chocolate brown skin shining under the fluorescent lights. He looked around, sizing up the faces and then moved to the computer room to run the workshop.

Two hours passed and the CV writing workshop was in full swing. Shoulders curved over keyboards, hands frantically typing and editing their Microsoft Word documents. Outside, the tournament was getting heated as it entered the final stages. Jason had been knocked out by a thirteen-year-old boy and was not best pleased. He sulked his way to the music system and turned the volume up to zone out his humiliation.

Samuel's face was screwed in concentration as he ordered his players around the pitch with the dance choreography of his fingers against the PlayStation controller. He had made it to the final round; his competitor, known as Face, was an older boy in the area with a hard reputation. He wasn't to be messed with.

As Samuel glanced over at Face, he noticed a new tattoo on his left hand. In toughened font, 'NN1 Family' was printed just underneath his knuckles. Samuel knew the type of people who represented New North Road. Even though they had neutral respect for each other, he knew you did not mess about with them. They were dangerous.

A crowd was forming now; the score was 2-2, with only a few minutes left. The mood was tense. Jason was playing a track by a rapper called Immortal Technique. Samuel scored a goal and he stood up with a clenched fist, thumping it high into the air. His excitement caused him to demand Jason to repeat the track. Samuel, also high on adrenalin, shouted out a line from the track.

'I've got mad skills, but unused like fallopian tubes on a dyke.'

Face was irritated that he was losing, but he couldn't deny the lyrical finesse and joined in with Samuel, also urging Jason to turn up the music.

'You young boys won't even know what that line means,' Samuel said.

The final whistle on the game blew, making Samuel the tournament champion. Face was gracious in defeat; he stood up and shook Samuel's hand. He then walked out to have a cigarette with his close friends Martin Oke – also known as 'Runner' – and Mo Ahdeem, though people knew him as just 'Mo'. All three were respected in the area.

Jamie and Junior came out of the workshop. Jamie looked very tired but was feeling optimistic about his chances of getting a job. Junior yawned.

'That was a very long two hours,' he said. 'But it was really powerful. I feel inspired!'

Malachi followed them out of the workshop to address all the young people before they left. Some of the youngsters were commenting on his appearance. He was six feet tall and quite toned, his biceps bulging through his dark blue shirt. His short, black hair and beard were freshly trimmed. He had a deep voice that got the attention of everyone in the room. When he started speaking, they all listened.

'My name is Malachi Richards. As Patricia said earlier, I will now be a regular volunteer here. I will be putting on a project to help you guys in whatever it is you aim to achieve.'

Face, Runner and Mo walked back into the building while Malachi was still talking.

'I am twenty-eight years old,' he continued. 'I grew up in this area so I understand the struggles you have to face each day. I am here to make that journey easier—'

'How exactly are you going to do that?' interrupted Face, looking directly at Malachi. 'You think helping people with their CV will make a difference. Look at where we live! No one cares about us. Are you going to give us jobs?' Jason and Samuel looked at each other wondering what would happen next.

'No, I am not in a position to provide jobs,' Malachi responded respectfully. 'But what I can do is help give you guys the information that will help you, so you do not have to rely on anyone.' Face had a cheeky grin on his face.

'Listen bro, heard it all before. Yet another person with a hero complex. You can't save us all, mate. This is how we were meant to live.' Face, Mo, and Runner walked out, slamming the door shut behind them. The room went silent. All eyes were now on Malachi.

'I am sorry they feel that way,' he said. 'Like I said, I can provide a unique way to look at life. From now on, I will be here helping with CVs. But most importantly, I will be setting up a fortnightly mentoring session called YAM.' The room burst into laughter. Malachi did not have a clue as to why they were laughing. Samuel was the first to speak.

'YAM! So wait, are you going to start up a cooking lesson on how we should eat yam?' More laughter echoed around the youth project. Malachi responded, an embarrassed smile on his face.

'When I say YAM it is the abbreviation of Young Ambitious Minds. This session is purely optional and it will start in two weeks' time.' With that, the young people filtered out of the club.

Jason, Samuel, Junior and Jamie walked back through the park, conscious that this was where they had been stopped by the police just a few hours before. As they all lived in opposite directions, this was their last chance to discuss the events of the evening before making their solo journeys home. Samuel piped up first.

'Soooo... what did you lot make of this Malachi guy?'

'He seems like a genuine guy,' Jamie said. 'He was really patient with me during the workshop.'

'Yeah, he seems like he has a lot to share, especially about ambitions and success,' Junior agreed. Jason threw his can of coke into the bin.

'I think I agree with what Face and them lot were saying,' he said. 'What can he really change, though?'

'Well, after spending two hours with him today, I think we should at least hear him out in the YAM sessions,' Junior replied.

'I agree,' Jamie said. 'Alright guys, I'm off now. Mum's probably waiting for me.'

'Yeah, me too,' said Jason. 'Catch you lot later.'

'Peace!' they shouted and, with that, the two boys walked off.

Once they were out of earshot, Samuel grabbed Junior by the arm.

'Jay, can I please stay at your place for the weekend? As much as I love my aunt for taking me in, I need some respite from that house.'

'Yeah, that's cool, man,' replied Junior. 'You know my house is really small though, right! I mean, look at me. I'm eighteen and I still share a room with my little brother and sister. My sister sleeps on the top bunk and my brother and I sleep head to toe on the bottom bunk.'

'Yeah, I know, I know,' said Samuel. 'But right now I'm so desperate I am ready to sleep anywhere – the sofa or even the floor. All I need is a pillow!'

Relieved that his residency was settled, Samuel walked with Junior back to his flat. Outside, the building was well-maintained; it had been freshly renovated. The yellow brick walls were cleaned to look like new, but traces of the brown dirt were still noticeable if you looked close enough. All the flats in this block had two bedrooms, yet you wouldn't think it as they all contained large families residing in small quarters. Overall, it was extremely overcrowded and cramped.

Mr and Mrs Okoli could not afford to mortgage a bigger home. They worked hard to look after their three children and Junior played a big part in looking after his siblings when his parents were working. Junior's parents were both of African descent. His dad, Francis Okoli, was born and raised in Nigeria and had then come over to the UK in the 80s. His mother, Gladys Okoli, was from Ghana; she'd arrived in the UK in the 80s also. Proud of their culture, both parents still maintained their traditional accents and attempted to communicate with their children in their native tongues. Their children, however (British-born and raised), were unresponsive to anything besides English.

Junior walked into the living room with Samuel. His siblings were watching television.

'Where's Mum?' he asked.

Matthew, the thirteen-year-old, replied. 'She went on a sales call. I think one of her clients wanted to buy some makeup stuff.'

'Didn't she only just finish work at seven?'

'Yeah, she did, but you know how she is with the home sales job.'

Junior gave his little sister, Gloria, a hug. She was only ten years old and he was very protective of her. She responded warmly to his gesture, hugging him back tightly. She had missed him. Over his sister's head, Junior took in the state of the living room with a sigh. The evidence of Gloria's imaginative play was scattered all over the beige carpet. Toys, dolls, puzzles, activity books arranged sporadically, a welcome colour in contrast to the plain cream stripy wallpaper. Pressed against him, Gloria's stomach rumbled loudly.

'Have you two eaten?' Junior asked.

'No!' Matthew shouted as he picked up all the clothes off the floor in the corridor. Junior shook his head in disbelief.

'I am going to make something for all of us to eat.' He then turned to Samuel. 'Samuel, do you want some tuna and pasta?'

'Yes, please. I'm famished!'

Dinner successfully gobbled up, Matthew and Gloria were stuffed and relaxing in the bedroom. It was a Friday night so they had more leeway about their bedtimes. The clock announced it was 11pm and Junior began worrying about his mum.

As he picked up the phone to try and call her, he heard the front door slowly creaking open. Arms lumbered with two large suitcases, Junior's mum entered the house looking exhausted. This was unnatural, as she always took pride in her appearance; but tonight was a definite exception. Noticing her shoulders sagging under the weight of the bags, Junior and Samuel rushed over to help.

Samuel politely greeted her. 'Good evening, Mrs Okoli.'

She smiled at him. 'Good evening, my dear. How are you?' Her voice sounded drained.

'I am fine, thanks,' replied Samuel. Junior looked at his mother, his face filled with concern.

'Mum, you need to take it easy. You came back from work at seven, went out again and now you're coming back at this time.'

'Junior, my dear, if I do not work hard we cannot survive.' He knew she was right. Junior respected his mum for the hard grafting she had put in to keep a roof over their heads, but when he looked around the flat it hardly seemed worth the effort. He needed to do more to help.

The thoughts plagued him as he heated some food for his mum. She ate, and then retreated upstairs to bed.

In the bedroom, Junior and Samuel were getting a major leg workout, manually pumping up the inflatable bed. Junior knew things must be bad for Samuel to want to stay at his house so badly.

'What is really going at your aunt's place?' he asked.

Samuel stopped. A cloud overshadowed his face and his expression became instantly dejected. He hesitated before replying.

'I love my aunt so much, really I do,' he said. 'You know she has done a lot for me ever since I left my dad's place, four years ago. And I appreciate her very much. Honestly. She didn't have to take me in. But, at the same time, I feel like an extra. Like a burden. And I just wish I had my own family.'

Samuel paused. He took a deep breath before he continued. 'You know what happened with my mum, and then having to live with my dad after that. It was the hardest two years of my life. Sometimes, living there with her husband and my cousins gets too much for me. I just need some time.' Junior placed his hand on Samuel's shoulder.

'You are welcome to stay here anytime.'

'I appreciate that, bro,' said Samuel. 'It's good to have real friends you can count on. You, Jason and Jamie are like family to me.'

Not long after their conversation, Junior and Samuel fell asleep.

CHAPTER TWO

The following day, Jason went to meet up with Jamie. Jamie had phoned him early in the morning, interrupting his beauty sleep. Jason wasn't best pleased, but he knew that times were difficult for Jamie, so it must be important. Jamie was on a certified mission. The CV workshop had ignited in him a desire for success and he was determined to secure himself a job. Armed with twenty copies of his CV, their destination was the West End, one of London's biggest shopping districts.

Jason took the stairs up to the tenth floor to Jamie's flat. Even though it was a long climb and he was barely awake, he refused to enter the disgusting metal machinery they called a lift. He knocked and Jamie opened the door. Jason looked out of breath. Jamie shook his head at the state of his friend.

'I don't know why you don't just use the lift.'

'Have you seen your lift?' Jason responded, still trying to catch his breath.

'I just try not to touch anything,' replied Jamie. 'I even use a pen to press the buttons.'

'That's effort. I'd rather take the stairs. Anyway, is your mum home?'

'Yes, she is in the kitchen.'

'Good morning, Mrs Heale,' Jason shouted.

'Morning, sweetheart,' she replied as she came out from the kitchen. She went over to Jason to give him a hug. 'Are you okay? You look like you have been running a marathon.'

Jason had finally caught his breath 'I am fine, Mrs Heale. I just ran up those stairs.'

'I told you to call me Claire.' Jamie's mum, Claire Heale, was a very soft-spoken woman, petite in stature, rocking a short blonde bob that framed her pale face well. Next to Jason, she looked tiny and had to stand on her tiptoes to hug him. She was flustered, rushing to get to work on time; she was packing away her rubber gloves, hospital ID in her bag.

'Jamie, are you going to see your dad today?'

'Yes, Mum.'

'Well, tell him I will be round to see him tomorrow. I finish work late tonight and I will be too tired to go.'

'No worries, Mum. Have a good day at work. I love you.'

'I love you too, sweetheart. Bye, Jason.' She closed the door and left.

Outside, someone had reminded the sun of the season and brilliant rays of sunshine poured delightfully through the windows. The children on the estate had wasted no time in enjoying the weather; their laughter could be heard throughout the block as they congregated in the large football cage located in the centre.

Football was generally the sport of choice for most of the young boys and their shirts were a rainbow of different colours against the cage, painted with famous Arsenal football players. As Jason and Jamie passed the cage, they declined offers for a match and engaged in banter with a few of the boys before making their way to the station.

The weather had an impact on the West End, Jason and Jamie mere specks in the growing crowd of shoppers. CVs in hand and a strategy in mind, they attacked the shops with fierce determination.

Weaving in and out, scanning the floor for management, repeated conversations and the same responses.

'Sorry, we currently have no vacancies.'

However, nothing would deter Jamie from his goal, urged on by the impact a job would have on his mum and the household. Although internally Jason was becoming impatient after the first three hours, he refused to complain. He knew why Jamie wanted a job so badly and he was willing to support him.

Shops were closing and Jamie began to realise this might take longer than he initially anticipated. His face showed disappointment but he still maintained optimism. With that task complete, they made their way to the University college hospital to see Jamie's dad.

Tom Marker was a man of great reputation in his community. Popular, respected and humble, he was known for his integrity and love for his family and friends. He was loyal and dependable, willing to go out on a limb for those he loved. The news of cancer sent shock waves through the community; they couldn't believe someone like Tommy M would have to suffer this fate.

Knowing his love for his son Jamie, they all surrounded Jamie with support, attending his matches, giving him encouragement, being there when his dad couldn't. The divorce had hit Jamie hard. Having come so unexpectedly, some of the wounds had yet to be healed. Jamie knew, though, that he was lucky. Despite separating two years ago, his parents still loved each other. His mum was supporting his dad and their relationship made it easier to deal with the situation.

As they approached the oncology ward, Jason had no idea what to expect. He noticed Jamie looked overcome with sadness and respectfully kept silent. He didn't know what to say, anyway. This was the first time Jason had visited Mr Marker in the hospital. He was scared.

They entered the room and Jason couldn't help but notice the change in Mr Marker's appearance; he was a shadow of his former self. Life seemed to have left his body, leaving behind a wispy, weak replacement. The full head of hair, once proudly groomed, was gone and Jason noticed his face and body was thinner; every bone was noticeable. Jamie had become used to seeing his dad this way; for Jason, however, it was a lot to take in. Mr Marker spoke faintly.

'Jamie, how are you, son?' Jamie went over to his dad and gave him a hug.

'I am fine, Dad. How are you feeling?'

'I've had better days, son. Jason, come over here and stop acting like a stranger.' Jason still looked shocked by Mr Marker's appearance and realised he was staring. He quickly tried to shake it off.

'Hello, Mr Marker. Sorry, I just didn't know what to expect.'

'It's okay, son. Others have reacted much worse.' Jamie's dad was the one who had got him into boxing. He trained Jamie up until he became ill.

'So son, how did your fight go yesterday?' A cheeky grin appeared on Jamie's face as he boasted.

'I knocked him out in the third round, Dad. Just like you taught me. Tire them out, then aim for the KO.'

'Yes, you should have seen him,' added Jason. 'He was a beast in there.' Mr Marker tried to laugh, but began to cough uncontrollably. His voice was starting to fade.

'I am proud of you, son. Keep it up.'

The two boys stayed with Jamie's dad for a while. They talked and laughed until the nurses told them it was time to go.

Jamie liked spending quality time with his dad because, deep down, he knew his days were numbered. He still had hope that the chemotherapy would help send his dad into remission. When it was time to call it a night, Jason and Jamie both headed back to their neighbourhood. Once there, they parted ways.

Jason lived literally two minutes' walk away from Jamie. Unlike the other three, Jason lived in an affluent street; houses boasted large front gardens, exquisitely maintained flower beds and inviting patios. Houses his friends could only dream about. Jason knew this. He was an only child of two loving parents, yet he lived in a four-bedroom house with two large reception rooms, two bathrooms and a conservatory. Expensive wallpaper hung in every room, decorated with fine art collections from various auctions across the country. The smallest TV set in the house was fifty inches wide, and they had seven!

Jason lived a life of luxury, never having experienced the hardship of his friends. He didn't know what it was like to experience the emergency of the electric key, or struggle to make a meal out of the leftovers in the fridge. He wanted for nothing. He was completely and utterly spoilt by his parents, who used materialistic things to substitute for emotionally connecting with their son.

His dad was Tony Burrell. His family heritage was St Lucian, but he was born and raised in East London. Together with his wife, Susan, a white English woman, they worked hard to build and maintain a successful upscale restaurant in central London. With an exceptional work ethic, but not much else, their parenting was based on monetary provision. Jason understood the privileged position he was in and was always careful with his spending when in the presence of his friends. Although he had plenty, and his friends knew this, they had never asked for a handout and Jason respected them for that.

Before long, Jason's parents arrived home from a hard day's work at the restaurant. Mr Burrell slouched into the house, looking extremely tired. In slow motion, he removed his woolly hat, revealing his shiny bald head.

'Hi Mum, hi Dad. How was your day?' Without a word, Mr and Mrs Burrell walked past him, barely acknowledging his presence, and went straight upstairs.

'It's been a really long day. We'll catch up with you tomorrow,' his mum responded under her breath.

Jason sighed inwardly, wondering why his parents never had time for him. Tomorrow would never come. He guessed success came at a price, but sometimes he envied his friends who had close relationships with their parents. He was used to the emptiness in his home, the lack of communication and understanding, but it bothered him sometimes. Money couldn't fill the gap.

A few weeks later, Jamie, Jason, Junior and Samuel were playing football in the cage in front of Jamie's flat. As usual, the heated topic was football. Junior and Jason were both major supporters of Arsenal and were tag teaming the debate, gaining strength and confidence from each other. Samuel supported Manchester United, while Jamie's heart belonged to Tottenham. Given their differences, competition was rife and any win amongst them was an opportunity to even the score.

At this point, Junior and Jason had boasting rights as, two months previously, Arsenal had beaten Manchester United on penalties to win the FA cup. Samuel couldn't withstand the barrage of abuse as it had been on-going since the win. He believed they had lucked out, that he had the better team.

Jamie listened with interest as the banter continued between his three friends; being a Tottenham supporter, he didn't have much to contribute seeing as his team were not contenders for silverware. He saved his banter for arguments regarding Arsenal and Tottenham. The North London rivalry was not to be played with. They all took this particular game seriously. The match was in full swing, two on two, each one wearing their team's replica tops. Jason and Jamie. Samuel and Junior.

'What is the score?' asked Samuel.

'4–3 to us,' Jason yelled back. Samuel looked confused.

'Are you okay?' he said. 'When did you score the fourth goal? It's three all, bruv.'

'Look, I am telling you, it's 4–3,' Jason insisted.

Junior intervened. 'Let's just call it 3–3, and we'll play next goal win.'

'I agree with Junior,' said Jamie. 'Let's just finish this. I want to go upstairs and watch the announcement for the host of the 2012 Olympics.'

By a stroke of luck and an impressive goal, Samuel and Junior eventually won the game. Jason felt cheated, believing they had been robbed as they were winning the game. His feeling was not shared by Jamie, who was glad the game was over. His focus was on the outcome of the host for the Olympics. If London won, it would give him an extra push in training. To win gold on his home turf was the ultimate dream.

Bursting into his living room, Jamie rushed to turn on the TV, anxious and excited. The other three followed suit, eyes glued to the screen. The room lit up with the crowds from the shortlisted cities: London, Madrid, New York, Paris and Moscow. Samuel was distracted momentarily by his big toe poking through his over-worn socks. He scowled, hoping no one would notice. Jamie's mum was very particular about shoes in the house, even though it was covered in oak wooden flooring. Samuel could understand if it was cream carpet. Knowing what teenage boys were like, Mrs Heale was always prepared with air freshener to keep the house smelling fresh.

Samuel turned his attention back to the TV. It was almost time for the announcement to be made. Union Jack flags filled the screen as the camera zoomed in to the thousands of supporters congregating at Trafalgar Square. With three cities eliminated, only London and Paris remained. The anticipation increased. Jamie could barely hold his emotions, desperate for London to get the vote.

Silence filled the room as they waited impatiently for the news. The cameraman flicked between areas of London. The atmosphere was the same everywhere, filled with hope and expectation.

The stage was set; many of the delegates from the International Olympic Committee were there, standing behind the IOC president, Jacques Rogge. They were all dressed in sharp suits. Singapore was the venue for the occasion. As Jacques Rogge took to the stage, Jamie shouted for his mum to come; his right fist was clenched, tapping the open palm of his left hand. Jacques Rogge opened the envelope.

'The games of the 30th Olympiad in 2012 are awarded to the City of London!'

In that moment, Mrs Heale walked into the room. Jamie quickly ran to her, knocking down the side table that was behind him. He embraced her, overjoyed. His mother was tiny in comparison, her head only managing to rest on his chest. Samuel, Junior and Jason could not help but get excited with Jamie. The emotion was contagious. They shared in his joy and rejoiced with him, knowing how much he had wanted it.

'I need to call Emma,' cried Jamie. 'Oh my gosh, I am so excited.'

'How long has she been away?' Junior asked.

'She's been gone about three weeks now. She's due back in a few days.'

Emma was Jamie's long-term girlfriend. Having been in a relationship since they were at school, they were made for each other. Since she said yes to his schoolboy charm, Jamie has not looked at another girl. He never needed to. He adored Emma, and was happy she wanted to be with him. Especially since the stress of his dad's illness, Emma had been a rock of support. Just what he needed.

Samuel and Jason had different views on how to treat girls. Never wanting to be tied down to one girl in case they missed out on someone better, they regularly juggled three girls at a time. Confident in their abilities to impress the ladies, they enjoyed the variety they had. Junior, on the other hand, was also single; but with less confidence than the rest, he often felt intimidated by girls he found attractive.

'Dinner is almost ready,' said Jamie's mum. 'Do I even have to ask if you boys are hungry?' Without hesitation, Samuel stood up from his seat and yelled toward the kitchen.

'I can eat, Mrs Heale. I'm not sure about these guys here, but all this anticipation and waiting for the announcement has got my stomach rumbling.'

Claire Heale was always very nice to Jamie's friends. She knew what type of people they were and she approved. She'd reverted back to her maiden name Heale after the divorce with Jamie's dad.

With dinner on the table, they decided that this would be their little celebration for London winning the chance to host the Olympics for the third time. Jason had let slip some of the spaghetti from his fork and it now stained his white T-shirt. As he was cleaning the stain, he looked over at Jamie who was sitting opposite him at the dining table.

'Looking at all those computer-generated images of what East London will look like during and after the games has got me excited,' he said. 'Do you really think all that money will be spread out to fix areas like ours?'

'Here we go again,' Samuel muttered.

'I truly hope so,' Jamie replied, ignoring Samuel. 'I just hope it won't be built on false promises. Look at where we live. It's not the greatest; but for me, it is the people who live here that make it bearable.'

'Thank you very much, Mrs Heale,' Junior said while rubbing his hand on his belly. He was the first to finish. 'That was really good.'

'You're welcome,' replied Claire. 'Do you want seconds?'

'No, thank you. I'm stuffed!' Junior then turned to the other boys. '2012 is a long way away. That is seven good years. A lot needs to be built and done before we can see long-lasting changes. The way I see it, Hackney and Newham should see mass regeneration because the site is literally on our turf.'

Jason grinned. 'We will just have to wait and see. I have my doubts. I truly believe that the people in charge do not care about places like this.'

Jamie coughed. 'Well, on that note, you lot need to get out,' he laughed. 'I'm being serious. You've finished off my mum's cooking. Now I need to rest as I have training early tomorrow morning.'

Over the next few days, Jamie's training attitude reached new levels of determination. His coach had never witnessed the intensity Jamie displayed in any other amateur boxer. Jamie was on fire. The first to arrive at the gym and the last to leave, he pushed his body to the limit, constantly aiming to outdo the previous workout. Fourteen days between Jamie and his next big fight meant every second counted. He wanted to be on top form and increase his stamina, flexibility and range. His days consisted of the ring and Emma. Back from her college trip to Paris, Jamie used any free time he had to spend in her company. He had truly missed her.

While Jamie was sweating it out in the gym, Samuel and Junior had been sweating over textbooks in the library. Long hours of revision and intense cramming for final exams had left them both exhausted. As they were the only ones from the group that attended college, they studied together to keep each other motivated.

Jason had enrolled into college also, but had spent the last few months taking a sabbatical from education. He truly believed he was making the right decision, but his lack of attendance finally resulted in expulsion. His laid-back approach to his studies was largely due to his easy access to finances from his parents and not feeling that he had to work hard.

Thankfully for Samuel and Junior, the academic year was ending, exams were over and it was time to relax. They met up on the last day of college to celebrate their freedom.

It was a bright Friday afternoon, the sun had awoken in a blaze of glory, reflecting the general attitude of the community. Everyone seemed to be in a good mood, and smiles were frequently exchanged between strangers as spirits lifted. Samuel and Junior were destined for the local bowling alley, a short bus ride from their area. As they jumped on the bus, they noticed the outside humidity meshed with the inside heat, causing a greenhouse effect. Passengers fanned themselves, windows were opened and the dress code appeared to be the bare minimum. Beach weather.

'Seriously, why is it so hot?' said Samuel. 'At this rate, I will end up your colour and you will probably end up looking like crude oil.' He cracked up as he started laughing uncontrollably. Junior tried not to laugh but couldn't hold it in.

'So what are you trying to say?' he replied. 'I keep telling you lot I am happy being this dark chocolate. The girls love it.'

'If you say so, Junior,' Samuel chuckled.

They arrived at the bowling alley in record time. The air-conditioning welcomed them as they entered, and they appreciated the cool. Inside, the place was buzzing. Samuel scanned the room and noticed the variety of girls; he licked his lips, rubbing his hands together in glee. Three games in, the score was tied at one game each: this was the decider. Winner takes all. It had been a tight competition and Junior only needed a spare to win the game. Anxious, Samuel watched with baited breath. He had been trash talking for the last twenty minutes.

Junior, composed and ready, aimed and released the bowling ball with finesse. STRIKE! He had won. With inward satisfaction, he turned to look at Samuel and smiled. Not one to take losing lightly, Samuel suggested a game of pool to even the scores. Balls racked up, cue in hand, Junior was about to break. He paused and looked up at Samuel.

'What are we going to do this summer?'

'Not too sure,' replied Samuel. 'We can see what the youth project has on for the summer. I know they normally have trips on. Hopefully, we can go on a residential with some girls.'

'Samuel, it's your shot! You're reds,' Junior snickered.

'What is so funny, eh, dark chocolate?' said Samuel.

Junior used the pool stick to point at the girls Samuel was looking at.

'You can't help yourself, can you?'

Samuel grinned. 'You know me well. Let me show you how a brown chocolate brother does this.'

He strutted over to the two girls who were at the other end of the room. Swagger initiated, his confidence visible from head to toe, he was about to turn on the charm. As he approached the girls, he took in the beautiful creatures in front of him. Easily the prettiest girls in the room, their simple style (white T-shirts and mini denim skirts) allowed focus on their faces. Radiating gorgeousness, they chatted amongst themselves before being interrupted by Samuel's arrival.

He introduced himself and complimented both girls, who giggled, tossing back their long braided hair. Ten minutes passed before Samuel remembered Junior, waiting impatiently at the pool table. He brought the girls to meet Junior before disappearing with his favourite of the two.

'I will be back,' he said over his shoulder. 'Dion challenged me to a game. Keep Ngozi company.'

There was an awkward silence between Junior and Ngozi. Junior thought she was very attractive; he wanted to impress her, but his tongue seemed frozen. He shuffled uncomfortably, looking down at his trainers, unable to make eye contact.

Ngozi thought his awkwardness was kind of cute. He seemed different to his friend; less showboating, more genuine. She wanted to find out the story behind his eyes, so she broke the silence and started talking. Junior responded shyly, but after a few minutes they were talking freely and he became more relaxed. They decided to go into the private karaoke lounge and spent an hour pretending to be RnB singers, dancing and being silly.

'That was fun,' Ngozi said.

Junior smiled. 'Yes, it was. To be honest, I have never actually done that before.'

'I love karaoke,' replied Ngozi. 'My girls and I do it all the time.' She returned the smile.

Junior felt confident enough to hold her hand as they went to the bowling section to look for Samuel and Dion. As he reached for her hand, Ngozi blushed, enjoying the feel of his palm against hers, their hands intertwined.

'Are you planning on going to uni?' asked Ngozi.

'Yes, all the universities I applied for are all outside London,' replied Junior. 'Not sure what I plan to do in the future. In my household, university is the only option.'

By now, they had been joined by Samuel and Dion. Dion had a big smile on her face.

'I told your friend he would lose to a girl. Look at him now. No words.'

Samuel chuckled. 'Babes, I let you win.'

'Whatever! Ngozi, are you ready?'

'Yes,' replied Ngozi hesitantly, wishing she could spend more time alone with Junior.

'Okay, let's go,' said Dion.

Before they left, Samuel and Junior exchanged numbers with the two girls. Junior had a glow on his face; his wide smile stretched from cheek to cheek.

It was almost the end of July and the heat had been constant for the last week. On this particular Saturday evening, however, the heavens opened up, filling the sky with depressing grey clouds. The wet weather had caused the sun lovers to retreat to safety, leaving the streets empty. Jamie was on his way back from the cinema with Emma. They had just watched the new Johnny Depp film, Charlie and the Chocolate Factory. Jamie had not been particularly interested in the film, but was persuaded to go see it by Emma.

'Did you enjoy the film?' Emma asked.

'Nope,' Jamie muttered.

'What was that?'

Jamie turned his head away from her and smiled, knowing better than to repeat himself. He pressed the lift call button at his flat.

'Next time we go to the cinema, I think I should pick the film.'

'Okay, Jamie,' Emma mused.

Jamie walked into his flat, thinking about a horror movie he could antagonise Emma with for their next date. His mum was just coming off the phone. Her hand struggled to put the phone down as her eyes flooded with tears, which fell onto the wooden floor.

Jamie froze. This scene had been played out in his dreams, like déjà-vu. His heart pounded through his chest as he tried to remain calm. He feared the worst, didn't even want his mum to speak, wished he could rewind time and stay outside the front door. Emma sensed something was wrong. The momentary silence between the three of them seemed endless. She grabbed Jamie's hand and squeezed it in support. Jamie forced himself to walk towards his mum.

'Sweetheart, your dad has lost his battle with cancer,' she said. 'I am so sorry.'

Like a burst pipe, Jamie's emotions erupted in a downpour of tears as he embraced his mum. His shoulders sagged under the weight of the news, his knees buckled and he could barely stand. His dad's face in the photos hanging on the wall smiled down on them both as Jamie's arms tightened around his mum. Emma was in pieces. Her face was soaked with tears, a thin black mascara line trickling down her pale cheek.

The room was silent. No one spoke, as the three of them just held each other in comfort. Jamie's mother, and Emma were both of similar height, and both their heads rested just below Jamie's shoulder. Jamie's face was straight, but the tears continued to roll down his cheeks.

'I was preparing myself for this,' he said at last. 'But now that it has happened, I feel empty inside.'

'Son, your dad was a good man,' said Claire Heale. 'Even though our marriage did not work, he always did his best to make sure we were alright. I will always love and remember him for that.' Jamie looked down at his mother.

'The last conversation we had was about becoming a man,' he said, his voice thick with emotion. 'At the start of the year he gave me his old boxing shorts for my eighteenth. I told myself I would only wear them if he went into remission and recovered.'

Emma looked him in the eye as she wiped the tears from his face.

'Now you can wear them with pride and in remembrance,' she said.

Claire Heale, now the head of the household, it was her responsibility to call the other members of the family and give them the bad news. It was a difficult evening for her: dialling, repeating the news, receiving condolences.

Jamie avoided the phone. He couldn't bear to hear people offering their support. He didn't want to speak to anyone. Instead, he reflected on his childhood through the pages of old photo albums with Emma and his mum. Hours passed and they mused over the family's history; laughed as they remembered old times. Emma was happy to be there and Jamie was glad she was.

The following week was the funeral of Mr Tom Marker. The church service took place at a local catholic church. Sombre for the occasion, people dressed in black and sat in every pew, or stood in the aisles when there was nowhere else to sit. In every corner people stood; it seemed the church couldn't contain all those who wished to pay their respects. The mood melancholic, the people mournful; the organist and priest led a bittersweet service.

As they all made their way to the grave, Jamie was engulfed by love, hugs and words of condolence. He was amazed at the number of people who had showed up. Among them, Samuel, Jason and Junior stood in well-tailored black suits. They surrounded him as the coffin was lowered into the ground. Soars of cries ascended into the sky as black balloons were released. Jamie took hold of his mum's hand as he said a few words to those gathered around.

'My dad was a very strong individual and he hardly ever showed his emotions. He told me that, to be a man, you must learn how to be in control of your feelings.' Jamie's voice started to tremble as he spoke; he was fighting back the tears. 'My dad wanted me to be successful. I am not one who excelled academically and he accepted me for who I was. But I want to live my life knowing that I am going to make him proud. Thank you all for being here with us.'

With a Tottenham Football Club jersey in his hand, he threw it on the coffin. He then picked up a handful of dirt from the ground and watched it fall into the grave. Mr Marker had been a lifelong supporter of Tottenham FC and he always said he'd want to be buried with the club's shirt. It was this same loyalty that Jamie had inherited for Tottenham FC.

Jamie, Samuel, Junior and Jason, along with other male family members, picked up shovels and began heaving dirt into the hole. Around them the mourners' voices joined in spiritual hymns, while fresh flowers were thrown. Jamie looked up briefly, wiping the sweat from his brow and saw Emma holding his mum. His eyes circled around him and saw the closest people to him. He felt his dad's presence and felt at peace.

Eventually, after leaving the graveyard, close family and friends congregated at the local community hall, to eat and celebrate the life of Tom Marker. The opportunity for speeches arrived and Jason stood first to address the crowd.

'Hi, everyone. I would like to thank you all for being here on behalf of Jamie and his family. I would like to say that Mr Marker was a great man. When I first moved here and met Jamie, he would always give us advice. He trusted our judgement even though we would sometimes get into mischief.' Jamie smiled at his mum. Jason continued. 'Jamie is the person he is today because of his dad's great influence and the character he was.'

Samuel, standing next to him, also said a few words.

'It has been a great pleasure for me to have known Mr Marker. Like Jason said, he has guided us and he will continue to guide us. I know what it is like to lose a parent.' Tears started trickling down Samuel's face. 'When my mum died, I was only thirteen. The pain of knowing she would not be there when I woke up in the morning was unbearable at times. That pain has never disappeared, but with time and the love and support from friends and family you learn to move forward. So, Jamie, you know we are here to support you through thick and thin.'

Junior then stood up, took a deep breath and began his speech.

'I would like to say Mr Marker did not like me and Jason much because we were Arsenal fans. He would ban us from entering his house if we had our Arsenal tops on.' The crowd laughed. 'On a more serious note, Mr Marker had had a great impact on my life. He was someone I could call an inspirational figure. He had his fair share of bad times, but he got through it. He built his own business and supported his family and, for me, that is a real life inspiration and I will never forget him.'

The hall was filled with a hundred people; they were all simultaneous with applause as Junior finished. Jamie walked over to his friends and gave them all a hug.

CHAPTER THREE

August had arrived. It was a few weeks after the funeral and summer was in full swing. Every morning, the weatherman gave excellent news of heat and sun, and green spaces quickly filled up with sun worshippers. Clothing and traffic cones signified makeshift goal posts as football matches took place on the field. Swings and slides were full with screaming children, sandcastles erupted in the pit as Barbies and action figures joined forces.

The seductive sound of the ice cream van, the personification of Pied Piper, drew children from all four corners of the park, their parents frantically chasing after them. Blankets outstretched under large willow trees; couples enjoying picnic baskets and good conversation, combined with embraces and snogging.

On a metal bench, in the middle of the park, Samuel sat, ob-serving the scene around him. His eyes caught the attention of a family of four in the distance, mum and dad playing with two young boys no older than eight. As they played catch, Samuel witnessed the joy plastered on all their faces. Samuel's heart broke as he thought about his mother and how happy they used to be when she was alive. He remembered being small, coming to the park with his mum; her watching him play. Good times. He sat for hours recalling the memories, soaking up the sun, deep in thought.

Eventually, he left the park, en route to his aunt's house in Hoxton. The scenery changed from trees and flowers to boarded-up council properties and grey cement pavement slabs. The local betting shops were overflowing with their daily flurry of gamblers, while young people transferred drugs and money, all seeking a get-rich-quick escape from their reality.

As Samuel approached the house he stopped, looking for his keys. They lived in the middle of a local council estate. Felicity Brown and her husband, Gary Brown, had purchased the three-bedroom house a few years ago from the council. Felicity had two children, a sixteen-year son and a fifteen-year-old daughter, both of whom Samuel got on with. Locating his keys in his jeans, Samuel opened the door and quickly realised no one was at home.

The house was well-furnished and loved; baby photos of his cousins hung proudly against the beige walls. Feeling his stomach grumble, Samuel headed to the kitchen to prepare a meal to shut his stomach up. The kitchen was a mess. Plates were piled high in the sink, the oven hadn't been cleaned and dirty pots had been discarded on the stove. Rolling up his sleeves, he got to work. He never shirked away from housework; it was always a good opportunity to show his aunt he appreciated living there.

On his knees, getting acquainted with the inside of the oven, Samuel heard keys in the front door. By the sound of the footsteps, he realised it was his Aunt Felicity. She entered the kitchen with a sigh, dropping her bags and leaning her slim frame against the door. Arms unloaded, she brushed her long, brown hair out of her eyes and saw Samuel hard at work. Her exhaustion transformed into relief.

'Thank you very much, Samuel,' she said. 'I was dreading coming home to do all that cleaning after a long day of teaching'. Samuel looked up and smiled.

'It's not a problem, I'm just happy to help.'

Felicity Brown was a teacher at a local secondary school, so was very interested in the progress of her own children and Samuel when it came to education. Samuel finished cleaning and went to sit down with her in the living room.

'Would you like something to drink?' he kindly asked her.

'That would be lovely. When you've finished doing what you're doing, please come in here. I want to speak to you about something important.'

Samuel was anxious about what could be so important and wondered how the tone of her voice could go from one of exhaustion to dramatic concern. He returned and handed her a cold glass of water.

'There you go. Aunty, why don't you take a break? You have been teaching all year round. Now it's the summer break and you still decide to teach summer school. Why?'

Felicity sighed. 'Well, my dear, we need the extra money to keep up the mortgage payments and pay all our bills. I would love to just rest, but sometimes that is not the viable option.' Samuel shook his head in disbelief.

'You work so hard, you deserve a break.' His aunt smiled at him as she sat up from the sofa.

'Don't worry about me, Samuel. I'll be fine. Have a seat, please.' The mood suddenly shifted and Samuel sat, deeply concerned, as Felicity put her glass down and looked at him. She had a serious expression on her face.

'Your eighteenth birthday is in a few days and your dad has tried to reach out to you again. I really think...' Inhaling deeply, Samuel fidgeted with his shirt sleeve before butting in abruptly.

'Aunty Felicity, with all due respect, I do not want to talk about that man.' She leaned over and took his hand.

'Samuel, please, just hear me out. Your father has been trying to reach out to you for over two years. I feel it is time you sat down with him and talked. Especially now you are turning into a man.'

Tears started to roll down Samuel's face; he leant back in a desperate attempt to stop them from falling. His voice was filled with anger.

'I have learnt to be a man without him,' he replied. 'After what he did, I cannot forgive him.'

'You must learn to relieve yourself from all this hate you are carrying with you,' said Felicity. 'Your brother has moved on, you should too.' Samuel's nose flared in anger. His eyes dried up immediately as he became instantly defensive.

'I was thirteen when all this happened,' he shouted. 'Mark is a good ten years older than me. Not all of us can be in control like he is.'

Realising she had hit a nerve, Felicity put her arm around Samuel to comfort him. Moments passed before she spoke again.

'I won't rush you. When you are ready to make contact with him, just let me know and I will make it happen. Your mum is still smiling down at you from up there. She must be so proud of you, as am I. You have just finished college and have applied to universities. You're doing very well.' Samuel replied with a croaky voice as a smile started to appear on his face.

'We get our A Level results in three weeks,' he said. 'Hopefully, if I get some decent grades, I will be able to go to university and start a different chapter in my life.'

They continued the conversation, discussing Samuel's aspirations and future goals. Samuel was glad he had his aunt to talk to, and that they were home alone. He often felt pushed out by his aunt's husband and was unable to be himself. Knowing the sacrifice they had both made for him, he was always respectful; but that didn't change the fact that he knew Mr Brown didn't want him in the house.

Later that week, on Saturday morning, Samuel awoke. He hit his head on the top metal frame of the bunk bed. Dressed in nothing more than his boxers, he searched for a top to wear. His eyes were still burning him. He hadn't had much sleep, as he'd been up all night talking to different girls on the phone.

'Happy birthday to you, happy birthday to you, happy birthday dear Samuel, happy birthday to you.'

Samuel could hear singing, mostly soft voices with the odd, husky voice trying to blend in with what sounded like his aunt and his cousin, Ebony. The chorus of singing continued as they all walked into the room.

His aunt shouted out to him. 'I hope you are decent, Samuel?'

Samuel was shocked. 'Yes, I am.'

They gave Samuel his birthday cards and a cupcake with the number eighteen on it.

'Andre,' Samuel called out to his cousin as he was walking out of the room.

'Yeah?' he replied.

'Please don't sing for me again. It's just weird with your deep voice. How come you have a deeper voice than me and you are barely sixteen?' They both laughed.

'Don't worry about my voice,' replied Andre. 'This voice gets me all the girls. You know I get more girls than you, right?' Samuel smiled and pushed him and Ebony out the room.

'In your dreams,' he muttered.

However, Samuel's aunt had another surprise for him. She pulled out a card from the plastic bag she was holding. She looked him in the eye, took hold of his hand and gave him the card.

'This card is from your father, Samuel. He remembered your birthday and wanted me to give you this. Do with it as you please, but please remember our conversation from the other day.' With that, she left Samuel alone, closing the door behind her.

Samuel stared at the card for a few minutes. He contemplated opening it, but couldn't bring himself to do it. The sight of it infuriated him and he chucked it on the top bunk. His eyes filled with rage; he no longer felt like celebrating his birthday. The sound of his ringtone jolted him out of his thoughts as he reached to find his mobile. It was Junior.

'Happy birthday, bro! You have finally joined the eighteen club.'

Samuel's voice was toneless. 'Thanks.'

'What's wrong?' replied Junior. 'You don't sound happy at all.'

Samuel hesitated. 'I'm okay, JR man. Just need to process some things.' Junior was not convinced, but he knew his friend well so he did not want to push him.

'Okay,' he replied. 'Well, I'm going to Dalston market for my mum quickly, and then I will come over. If you want to talk, you know I'm here for you.'

'Yeah, I know,' said Samuel. 'Thanks man, see you in a bit.'

Standing up, he grabbed his dad's birthday card from the top of the bunk bed and walked over to the built-in wardrobe. Opening the door, he threw the card in and shut the door after it.

Over the next few hours, the house was filled with Samuel's ringtone. As soon as he finished one call, his phone would start ringing again. Girls, mostly, ringing to wish him a happy birthday. He felt loved. The attention from all his friends had improved his mood and he was no longer thinking about his dad. He was ready to have a good time.

Soon, Junior arrived at the house. They sat together in the garden soaking up the mid-afternoon sun. There was a slight breeze in the air that made the weather even more enjoyable.

'Have you spoken to Jason or Jamie today?' asked Junior.

'Yeah, I did,' replied Samuel, sipping on a cold can of Coke. 'They both called me after I spoke to you earlier.'

'Are they coming around today? What is the plan for your big eighteenth?' Junior asked, sounding very excited. Samuel had his hands on his head.

'Argh, brain freeze. That drink is too cold. Well, Jason is going through some drama at home with his parents, Jamie has no cash and anything he does have he is using to help his mum out. To be honest, I don't have much money, either.' Junior's excitement had now disappeared.

'That's too bad,' he replied. 'I was even going to use my last payment of EMA college money to go out tonight.'

'Don't worry about it,' said Samuel. 'We can celebrate another time. Save your money. Plus, I have one chick who wants to take me out to dinner then back to hers for a movie night.'

Junior smiled. 'I take it this is not Rachel. One day, you will meet a girl that will be your match. She will tie you down and you will not see it coming.'

'Not me, bro,' replied Samuel laughing. 'I will leave all that love shit to you sweet boys. Look at you – only a few weeks and you are already all lovey dovey with that girl, Ngozi.' Junior responded proudly.

'Yes, I like her. There is nothing wrong with being with one chick. Not everybody wants to be rotating four or five girls at a time.' Samuel and Junior continued talking and laughing until Samuel eventually went to get ready to go out on his birthday date.

Junior returned home. Sometime later, his dad arrived from a twelve-hour shift on a construction site. He was a security guard who worked long shifts, often seven nights in a row, one day off and then back to seven nights. Due to his work schedule, all Mr Okoli wanted to do once he was at home was rest. He barely saw his children, let alone had time to raise them. As the enforcer in the house, he was called upon for disciplinary duties; to keep his children in line when they misbehaved. Junior wanted his younger siblings to have a better relationship with their dad than he did.

'Hi, Dad. How was work?'

His father looked up, disgruntled.

'It was fine.'

'Okay....' continued Junior, hesitating. 'Anyway, Dad, the reason I wanted to speak to you is because Matthew and Gloria would like to see you more and spend time with you. You are always busy working.' Junior's dad cut his eye at him and laughed sarcastically. Mr Okoli still had a strong Nigerian accent when he spoke.

'Listen to me carefully,' he replied. 'How do you think we pay for the food in this house? Or the electricity? Or the clothes you are wearing? Please do not disturb me. I do not have the time for this nonsense.'

Junior replied with a penetrating voice. 'I understand that, but what is the point of making or having money if you are not around to share it with the people you love?'

His dad stood up.

'Shut up!' he shouted. 'I told you to stop disturbing me. Go and warm up the food your mother left for me.' He sat back down. As Junior walked out of the room he heard his father mutter to himself. 'Will love pay the bills? Stupid boy!'

Junior went to the kitchen to prepare the meal for his dad. He was angry but, out of respect, he would never dare to lash out and bark back at his father. Junior managed to suppress his feelings, as he always did.

Over time, Junior and Ngozi got closer. Junior was infatuated with her; she was a constant source of comfort to him, and he could talk to her about anything. Her personality was full of good qualities and they had great fun together. Sophisticated dress sense, a beautiful smile and long braids, Ngozi was gorgeous. Not like any other girl, Junior knew. He wanted to treat her like a queen and often arranged date nights out.

One Friday evening, he took her to the cinema. When the film was finished, they came out of the theatre hand in hand, excited and talking about the film with big smiles on their faces. At the bus stop, Junior saw the volunteer youth worker, Malachi, from Elevate Youth Club. Malachi instantly recognised Junior and shook his hand.

'How are you?' Malachi asked.

'I'm fine,' replied Junior. 'Just trying to enjoy what is left of the summer.'

'That is good. I'm still running my sessions at the youth project. I have not seen you and your friends for a while now.' Junior kept looking behind Malachi to see if the bus was coming.

'To be honest, things have been pretty hectic for everyone,' Junior told him still looking distracted. 'That is why no one has been there.' Ngozi coughed.

'Excuse me!' she said. 'Junior is so rude. Well, if he is not going to introduce me, I guess I will have to do it myself. Hi, I'm Ngozi.' Malachi laughed.

'I was actually waiting for him to do that,' he replied. 'I guess he is a bit distracted.' Junior looked slightly embarrassed.

'I am sorry,' said Junior. 'This is Malachi. He is volunteering at the Elevate youth project.'

'Oh, okay,' Ngozi said. 'Unfortunately, I've never been. What do you do there?'

'I have been running my Young Ambitious Minds session now for over a month,' replied Malachi, 'and recently no one has been coming. Junior, I'd like you to at least come to one session. If you don't find it useful, then you don't have to come back.'

'I have been meaning to pass through,' said Junior embarrassed. 'I will definitely come to one of your sessions.'

'I'll remind him as well,' Ngozi said.

As the 149 bus arrived they said their goodbyes. They sat at the top of the bus. There was burning heat coming from underneath the seat hitting Junior's leg.

'I don't get why they keep the heaters on during the summer but refuse to put them on in the winter,' he moaned. Ngozi laughed.

'You would think it would be the other way around. Anyway, that Malachi seems like a nice person.'

'I have only met him once. But yeah, he does seem like a good guy.'

'Well, I think you should go to his session and get a feel of what it is like. You never know, it might be something you enjoy,' Ngozi suggested.

Meeting Malachi had reminded Junior of the youth project. He decided it may be worth a try, knowing Ngozi would want him to at least attend one session.

So, the next week, he decided to drop in to one of the sessions, and he was glad he did. He had been worrying relentlessly about his exam results, as his future depended on them. Malachi showed him a perspective he hadn't seen before. His words penetrated into his anxiety and removed it. Junior left inspired and optimistic about his future.

A Level results day approached with a bang, as anxious students across the UK discovered their fate. Junior and Samuel met up, excited about their future prospects. Jamie joined them for moral support, also fired up about the day's significance. Jason, having dropped out of college, left his house under the pretence of going to collect his results only to make a diversion to a girl's house instead.

After joining the masses already queuing, Junior and Samuel finally received their envelopes. They stood outside the large modern building, watching other people rip open their future, observing the various responses; elation, despair, surprise, disappointment. Samuel's nerves flared up.

'No need to worry,' Junior assured him. 'I have a good feeling we both did enough.'

'I hope you're right, JR,' replied Samuel. 'Because if this is not what I'm expecting, then I have no idea what the future will be for me.'

Junior began to tear the sealed slip of the envelope. He slowly pulled out the two pieces of paper that were inside. He looked at them both and jumped up in the air and yelled.

'Yes! Yes! Two Bs and a C! I got Bs in English and Politics. In media I got a C.' Junior quickly realised that Samuel was yet to open his envelope.

Jamie looked at him. 'Mate, just get it over and done with. I'm sure you did good.' Samuel was hesitant, but he opened the envelope and pulled out the yellow and white pieces of paper from inside.

'Where do I even see my grades?' he said. He stared at the papers in bewilderment. 'This is so complicated.' Junior took both papers from him.

'You got an A, B and a C!'

Samuel's eyes opened wide. Junior continued to read out the results. 'You got an A in law, B in media studies and a C in business studies.'

Samuel stared at him in disbelief. He grabbed the papers from Junior and, when he saw the results with his own eyes, he jumped up and punched the air in jubilation.

'I can't believe I got an A in law,' Samuel uttered. Jamie touched fists with both Samuel and Junior.

'Congratulations, you both deserve it.'

'Thanks, Jamie,' Junior replied with a big grin on his face.

'So, what is the plan now?' asked Jamie. 'Does this mean you are both guaranteed to get into uni?'

'We're not guaranteed entry yet,' replied Samuel, 'but these results go a long way to making that happen.'

The three friends left the college and headed back to their neighbourhood. When they got there, they saw Face, Mo and Runner. The three of them were coming out of one the main gambling shops. As they walked past them they acknowledged each other by bumping fists.

Face and his boys were part of the NN1 family (local boys from their area who involved themselves in territorial wars and low-level crime). Samuel, Jamie and Junior knew them all but did not associate themselves with those types of activities. Their relationship was based on a passing hello.

Face turned to Samuel.

'You owe me a rematch.' Samuel looked confused.

'Rematch for what?'

'C'mon man,' replied Face. 'You beat me in the final of the football game tournament in the youth club.'

Samuel laughed. 'You need to go and practise before you come and challenge me again.'

'Cocky!' Face said, smirking. 'Keep talking. Anyway, I am gone. Bless.'

Samuel and Junior both went home to show off their results, while Jamie went to boxing training.

Later on that evening, Jason's parents were waiting for him to come home with his exam results. They had both made time in their busy schedule to get home early to be there to support him, but Jason was nowhere to be seen. His dad had been calling his phone consistently but without success. After a while, they began to worry about his whereabouts.

Meanwhile, on the other side of the estate, Jason was relaxing at a girl's house. She had provided him with a welcome distraction from the impending doom he was sure to face when he got home; however, her mum had been giving him the impression it was time to leave.

Reluctantly, Jason left, deciding to take the long way home. Despite being away all day, he still hadn't figured out a way to tell his parents the truth. He dreaded their reaction, but knew it could not be avoided. The decision to drop out of college was his, and now he had to face the music.

As Jason's house came into view, he paused, wondering if there was another way to escape his fate. Options exacerbated, he opened the front door and walked in. His mum and dad were both in the kitchen. Mrs Burrell ran to meet him as he walked into the living room, a look of concern on her face.

'Is everything okay, sweetheart? We've been worried sick.' Jason kept his head down, not able to look her in the face. When he replied, his voice was barely audible.

'I'm fine, Mum.'

'Where the hell have you been?' shouted Mr Burrell, storming into the living room. 'Don't you know how to use a phone?' Jason kept quiet, unable to speak. He knew he was in a very vulnerable position.

'Where are your exam results?' his dad asked. Jason was mumbling something to himself, eyes focused on the floor. Courage had left him and he was struggling to find the words. His dad was ranting, asking rhetorical questions, looking to the heavens, pacing up and down the living room. After a few minutes, Jason eventually found his voice. He took a deep breath.

'Mum, Dad, the truth is... I didn't finish college. I was not engaging in the subjects I picked... So I stopped going.'

'What?!' Mr Burrell shouted. 'What do you mean you *dropped out?*' He clenched his fist, eyes bulging out of his head, red with rage. Jason stood his ground, no longer afraid of what his dad could do to him. His biggest concern now was the disappointment he had caused his mother. She was unable to speak. She looked dejected, her face gloomy with despair.

'Jason, why didn't you come and talk to us?' she asked. Jason's dad was now pounding up and down. His temperature rising with each word Jason uttered, he was quickly losing control. Jason, noticing his dad's anger, turned to his mum.

'I tried to speak to you and Dad so many times, but you were both always busy working...' Lightning flashed before Mr Burrell's eyes. Out of nowhere, he darted towards Jason and grabbed him by his shirt, lifting him inches from the floor.

'So you want to use the fact that we work hard as an excuse?' he shouted.

'Tony! Tony!' Jason's mum wailed. 'Let him go before you hurt him.'

'Hurt him? Hurt *him*? He's hurt *us*! Why are you always so quick to come to his rescue? You've spoilt this boy rotten! Look at him now, for Christ's sake! Are you satisfied?'

Mrs Burrell knew there was an element of truth to her husband's outburst. She had always bought Jason whatever he wanted. Inwardly, she blamed herself for Jason's inability to focus, his lack of work ethic and drive.

'Mum, I'm not sure what I want to do yet,' began Jason. 'But being at college, especially doing those subjects, it just wasn't for me.' Again, his dad interrupted him.

'You must go back to college in September and finish your studies. That is how we do it in this family.'

'I am NOT going back to college!'

Mr Burrell, in exasperation, walked into the kitchen to get a glass of water. Removing himself from the situation allowed space for his temper to calm a little. After a few minutes, he returned to the living room.

'So, you're a man now? You're going to be eighteen in a few months. So, you want to make decisions like a man? In that case, you must support yourself like a man.' Jason's mum stood up from the chair and walked towards her husband.

'Tony, what are you saying?'

'What I am saying, my dear, is that if your son wants to be a man, then so be it. I will no longer support him. He must leave my house today!' His wife shook her head several times.

'No! No! Tony! No! You can't kick my baby out on the streets. Where is he going to go?'

'That is the problem right there, woman. You baby him too much. Just look at him. Useless.' Jason's eyes filled with tears but he refused to let them flow.

'I will get my stuff and I will leave.'

'Please, Tony, do not let him walk out of this house,' Jason's mum wailed. 'We will lose him forever.' Mr Burrell, however, was not interested in what his wife had to say. His face was blank, emotionless. Jason went upstairs to pack his things. His dad shouted up at him.

'Make sure you only take clothes. Any electronic devices, your PlayStation, your Mp3 player, leave them here. I worked for those.'

Jason could not believe his dad was responding like this. He had no plan. All he knew was he could no longer live in the same roof with that man. Jason's mum was downstairs, weeping at the fact that her family was being torn apart.

'Tony, please reconsider,' she begged.

'Listen to me carefully, Susan. I have said all I have to say on this matter. If you want him to stay, tell your son to reapply to college and apologise to us. Until then, he is no longer welcome in this house.'

Jason came downstairs, one suitcase in each hand. With an inner strength, he kept his composure, refusing to show his dad how hurt he was.

Dropping the bags by the front door, he walked over to his mum. Wiping away her tears with his hand, he hugged her, kissed her cheek, and then left.

Jason decided to go to Jamie's house. He knew it was his best chance to get a place to stay. Samuel was living with his aunt and he knew it would not be appropriate. Junior's house was already overcrowded and there wouldn't be any space. When he got to Jamie's house, Samuel and Junior were both there. Jason told them everything. They were shocked that his dad had taken such drastic actions. Jamie was more than happy to accommodate Jason in his house, subject to his mum's approval.

'It will only be for a few days,' said Jason. 'I will go to housing at the council and tell them I'm homeless. They will probably give me a hostel.'

'Mate, it's not a problem,' said Jamie. 'You are welcome to stay for however long you want.'

'Thanks, I appreciate that,' replied Jason.

Samuel nudged Junior. 'You were saying something about that Malachi guy's sessions before Jason came in.'

'Oh, yeah,' said Junior. 'Basically, I've been going to his sessions for the last two weeks. They are really inspiring. The guy really knows how to motivate people. He also has contacts that can help you progress.'

'Sounds really interesting,' replied Samuel. 'When is the next one?'

'Tomorrow,' said Junior. 'You lot should definitely go. It will be worth it, trust me.'

Samuel and Junior then said their goodbyes and left. Jamie told his mum about Jason. She was worried about him, but agreed to let him stay on a short-term basis. Ideally, she wanted him to make amends with his parents.

Time passed. Seasons changed and the summer disappeared. It was the middle of September and darkness was creeping in to early evenings. Junior had convinced Samuel, Jamie and Jason to go along to Malachi's Young Ambitious Minds sessions and they had attended for the last two weeks.

During their first session together, Malachi was able to get them to open up about their lives. He was the type of person who you could trust. He did not ask them to trust him, but the way he spoke, with so much confidence, was enough for them to believe in what he was saying.

Malachi was a very confident and charismatic individual; he believed in the young people and wanted to make a real difference. His strong physical presence and his deep voice made the things he was saying pack more weight. After that first session together, they all continued to go along with Junior. They were building a strong and healthy bond with Malachi.

It was a wet and windy Friday evening. Jason was still living with Jamie. They both left his house, en route to the youth project. Samuel and Junior were already there by the time they arrived. Inside, the youth project was really quiet. The early session, which normally had the younger age group, was empty. The rain had kept most people indoors. Malachi welcomed them in from the rain.

'It is good to see you all managed to make it, despite the terrible weather,' he said cheerfully. 'Come in and get settled so we can get started.'

'Yes, the weather is terrible,' replied Junior. 'But some things are more important.'

Malachi smiled. 'I love your enthusiasm.'

They were bundled into a separate room where the sessions were held. A cosy size, it could hold a maximum of ten people at a stretch. Malachi took out a large piece of paper and wrote 'Ambition'. He turned to the group.

'Can anyone tell me what the true meaning of ambition is?'

Samuel shouted out. 'It is when you want to achieve something. Like a goal, or an aim?'

Malachi nodded to him. 'I like your answer,' he replied, 'but I am looking for one word in particular.'

Junior and Jason looked at each other, trying to think about what that word might be. As the room fell silent, Malachi explained.

'The word I am looking for is *desire*.' He yelled out the word again. 'DESIRE! You see, for me the word ambition only has true meaning when you include the word *desire* in it. This is the difference between success and failure.'

The four friends were listening carefully, registering every word he said. They were determined to learn from him. The way he spoke made them want to grasp every word. Malachi continued as he paced around the room.

'The desire to want to achieve some type of distinction, be it fame, wealth, power or knowledge. You see, there are steps you need to take when you have a definite goal you are working towards. Identify your long-term ambitions, then break them down into short-term targets.'

Malachi told them to get out pens and paper and start writing about what they would like to do with their lives. As the session was coming to an end, Malachi gave them something to think about.

'When I was your age, my best friend and I made a pact. We called it the ambition pact. This was based on real friends that wanted to succeed, no matter what. In this pact, if one was starting to go off-course, the other had to do all he could to help him achieve his goal. For me, it was one of the best decisions I ever made. I would not be here today if it was not for my best friend. We refused to be defeated, regardless of the obstacles. If one failed, we both failed.'

Samuel, Junior, Jason and Jamie were all taking notes and writing down most of what he was saying. Jason's eyes were glued to Malachi's lips. He was often drifting off, day-dreaming about what he could achieve if he truly put his mind to it. This particular session had them all thinking, but Jason especially. As the session ended, Malachi gave them some final instructions.

'To finish up, I want you all to think about the ambition pact. Then, next week, hopefully we might have some ideas of what you want to achieve. We will also discuss the five main causes of failure.'

After the session, on the way home, all four boys were deep in thought about what they had learnt. There was no laughing or joking about; their mood was sombre. It had been raining for most of the afternoon, but now it was relentless. They were all soaked from head to toe as they scattered in all directions to their respective homes.

The following week, the four friends returned to the youth club for another session with Malachi. They were all excited.

'I hope you all have an idea of what your ambitions are,' Malachi began. 'Before we start, I want you to know that I appreciate

your time and you allowing me to have an input in your lives.'
Jamie was the first to stand up and speak; he was confident and
composed.

'For me, I have always had an idea about what I want to
achieve. My desire is to win a gold medal at the London 2012
games, then become a professional. My ultimate aim is to allow my
mum to retire early.'

Samuel stood up next. 'For me, I had to think hard and long
about this. I think I studied law for a reason; one I didn't know
until last week's session. When I was younger, before my mum
passed away, she would always tell me that I would be a top
barrister some day. I am very interested in the law, so my desire is
to achieve the dream my mum had for me. I can then show my
appreciation to my aunt for taking me in.'

Junior stood up with a smile on his face.

'I want to do something similar to what you do, Malachi. To
inspire the younger generation. I had terrible teachers at school,
who did not really care whether we passed or failed. I want to be in
their position and help break the negative cycle of under-
achievement in our area. My desire is to become a teacher that
makes a difference inside and outside the classroom. I also want to
be a role model for my younger siblings.'

Jason was last to speak. As he got up, he seemed unsure of
himself; however, when he began to speak, he was very confident.

'At the moment I am homeless. My parents have money but
my attitude towards my dad broke us apart. I am the type of person
that cannot work for someone for a long period of time. So, I want
to follow in my dad's footsteps and build my own business. My
desire is to outdo what my dad did and create a thriving business. I
am not sure in what field yet; my journey begins now.'

Malachi gave them all a round of applause.

'You see?' he said. 'When you say it out loud, you speak it into
existence. Growing up in similar circumstances to you all, I have

seen it and lived it. I do this job because I want to be part of the solution, a solution that creates more successful young people. Now, there are five things that will cause you to fail: procrastination, over-indulgence in sexual activities, egotism, doubt and fear of failure. The reason I am telling you this is because we live in areas some might call deprived. People believe that anyone who comes from here cannot achieve greatness because, apparently, they are all criminals and live off benefits. Forget that stereotype! Don't let anybody tell you you can't, not even yourself. Understand that you are great and you will achieve greatness. So this is your pact; the ambitions of the deprived.'

The four friends agreed to help each other achieve their aims, regardless of what obstacles came their way. The plan now was to always stick together.

A few weeks later, all the boys' situations had changed. Junior and Samuel were preparing to go to university. They had both been accepted by their chosen univerities after having achieved good results in their A Levels. Samuel was heading to Brunel University, Middlesex, to study law. This was his chance to finally leave his aunt's house and be independent. He was looking forward to experiencing the whole university lifestyle, especially living on campus. Junior chose the University of East London to study English. Being only a short journey from his home, Junior decided he would commute.

The good news continued. After months of trying, Jamie finally got a job. He was working as a waiter in a restaurant. Although the job wasn't the greatest, he was happy to be able to contribute to the bills, and take some pressure off his mum by working. He knew his mum had been struggling to cope since his dad had passed away, as his dad had always provided for the family. Now Jamie was the man of the house and he was determined to fill his dad's shoes.

Even Jason had progressed; he had managed to move out of Jamie's flat and into a hostel some twenty minutes away. Jason was still in the process of figuring out how to achieve his new ambitions. Due to the distance now between them, Jason didn't see his three friends as much as he used to.

The weather was getting colder; withered autumn leaves littered the streets. Junior was on his way back from the youth project. He was dressed in his usual manner – a grey, zip-up hoody and blue distressed denim jeans to match. Headphones plugged in, he was enjoying the music selection of his iPod when he bumped into Face, Mo and Runner. They were walking along the New North Road, just off one of the many estates that surrounded the area. Junior stopped to acknowledge them. In usual fashion, this greeting was more of a passing hello. Face looked at Junior.

'Yo cuz, where did you get them trainers from?'

'From some new shop down Brick Lane,' replied Junior. 'I think it's called Kazmattan.' Face started shaking his head and rubbing his two hands together.

'I'm gonna go get that. Looks sick, fam.'

'You should go there as soon as possible,' said Junior, 'because these ones are selling out fast.' Runner joined in the conversation.

'Yes fam, I'm definitely going to buy that as well.'

'What's wrong with you?' shouted Face. 'You can't be copying everything I wear, man!'

Junior touched fists with all of them before walking off in the opposite direction. Seconds later, he heard a loud scream. Junior turned around and saw Face, Mo and Runner punching someone on the floor. Shock gripped him, but only momentarily; he knew the type of boys they were. He stopped for a moment, a few yards away from the commotion. The boy was shouting.

'Please, please, help me...'

'Shut up, you prick!' said Face. 'You think you can come around New North Road and nothing would happen to you?' Runner motioned to Face.

'Yo Yo, leave him now,' said Runner. 'Let's move off.'

The three of them then ran towards where Junior was standing. Face shouted at him as he ran past.

'Yo fam, you better move off before the police come.'

Junior ran with the three of them, parting ways at the end of the road. Unable to stop, adrenalin pumping, he sprinted all the way home. When he got there, he could barely catch his breath. Junior's mum saw him first.

'Junior, what is the matter?'

'Nothing, Mum. I was just running.'

'Okay,' she replied, accepting his explanation.

Junior went to his room to check to see if his student loan papers had been sent. His mind now focused on his studies and his future, he concentrated on filling out applications for student grants.

The following day, Junior went to meet up with Samuel and Jason. They were on their way to the local park to play football. They realised that, in less than three weeks, they would all be busy with their new ventures. Time was running out and they wanted to spend as much time with each other as possible. While they were playing football and talking, Jamie arrived from work, looking smart and professional in a white shirt and a black waistcoat. He started to change.

'Did you lot hear about what happened on New North Road yesterday?' he asked.

'What?' asked Samuel.

'Someone was beaten up and stabbed.'

Junior looked shocked. Although he'd been there, he didn't know the boy had been stabbed.

'Is the guy okay?' asked Jason.

'Mate, he didn't make it,' replied Jamie. 'I saw a yellow board appealing for witnesses. It's now a murder investigation.'

Junior walked away from his friends, pacing up and down the football pitch. He had his hand over his mouth. The other three walked over to him, concerned.

'Are you okay?' Samuel asked. There was no response from Junior.

Jason, Samuel and Jamie all looked at each other. They were confused and did not know why Junior was acting this way. This was not the first time someone had been shot or stabbed in the area. They all knew what some of the people in the area were capable of. As sad as it was, it came as no surprise to them. Junior spoke softly, constantly rubbing his hand over his face.

'I was there when it happened. I know who did it.'

'Seriously?' Samuel shouted.

'Keep your voice down, man,' Junior hissed. 'I was going home from the youth project when I bumped into Face and them other guys he is always with. I was talking to them briefly. As I walked off, I heard a scream so I looked back to see what was happening.'

Jason interrupted. 'You mean they killed someone...'

'Let me finish,' Junior said. 'So they were beating him up, stamping on him. It was like they were literally in front of me. Then, afterwards we all ran off.'

Samuel, Jamie and Jason were shocked and could now understand why Junior had seemed worried.

'Mate,' said Jamie. 'The police are probably looking for people like you to come forward and be a witness.' Junior quickly stopped him from continuing.

'Me! Be a witness? Never. Are you forgetting where we live? It is not about snitching on people.'

Jamie hesitated, unsure of what to say next. Samuel spoke up.

'No way are you telling the police anything. Do not get involved. Let the police go and catch them themselves. Plus, Face and those others know you saw them as well.'

'Exactly,' Junior replied. 'I cannot believe this has happened. Why did they have to stab him, though? He was already on the floor taking a beating.'

'Those guys are heartless,' said Samuel. 'They rep the area like they own it.'

'I feel sorry for the family of the guy who got killed,' said Junior. 'So sad, man.'

They all carried on playing football for a while, but Junior's head was no longer in the game. After hearing the tragic news, his biggest worry was that he would be called to be a witness. But he'd made it clear he was not ready to do anything of the sort. The fact that he had seen someone being killed was very difficult for him. He was unable to process it all properly.

Over the next few days, Junior tried to forget what had happened, but the images kept flashing into his head. He tried to remind himself that he would be starting university very soon, but nothing would block out those images. Junior told no one else about what had happened. Even when he was with Ngozi, he kept it to himself. When he was spending time with her, his attention was elsewhere.

It was mid-October, two weeks since the incident, and Junior was now in a better place. Only a week to go before he'd be starting university. Preparation for it was now complete. His student loans and grants had all come through and he was ready to start his new path in life.

One evening, Junior was at home with all his family. For the first time in a long time. Normally, his dad would be at working, as would his mum. He was always left in charge of looking after his two young siblings, who were dependent on him. He loved being able to support his brother and sister, but felt that nothing he did could replace the love of their own father.

Junior had never said 'I love you' to his dad and his dad had never said it to him. He believed his dad was incapable of showing any emotions. He was past the stage where he wanted that affection for himself, but he did not want the same thing to happen to his siblings.

There was a loud knock on the door that evening. Mr Okoli looked up, wondering who would dare to knock on the door at this time. The knock was then repeated. Junior's dad walked up to the door. As he went to open it, Junior heard loud voices.

'It's the police, open up.' Mr Okoli opened the door. There were three uniformed officers and two plain-clothes officers, both wearing suits.

'Is Junior Okoli here?' one of the officers asked with an aggressive tone.

'What is this about?' Mr Okoli asked. Junior then came to the front door.

'Are you Junior Okoli?' the police officer asked again.

'Yes,' Junior replied. He instinctively knew this was about the murder incident. One of the officers pushed past Junior's dad and grabbed Junior by the hand.

'What the hell is going on?' he shouted.

'Junior Okoli, I am arresting you on suspicion of murder. You do not have to say anything, but it may harm your defence if you do not mention when questioned something which you later rely on in court. Anything you say may be given in evidence.'

Junior's parents watched helplessly as their son was dragged out of the house like a common criminal. Handcuffs were forced onto his wrists and he was stuffed in the back of a police van.

'You have the wrong person,' cried both his parents, but the police refused to explain.

Mrs Okoli was in tears, the weight of the events forcing her to her knees. She was desperate to comfort her son, to let him know everything would be alright.

She attempted to get past the police. They violently shoved her aside, warning her she could also be arrested.

Hiding behind her father, Junior's younger sister watched the commotion in confusion. She had never seen police this close up and knew that her brother must have been involved in something terrible. She loved her brother and was scared that he would be hurt. Looking up at her dad's face, she asked to be held, but her dad was too busy shouting to hear her. She ran and hid under the living room table.

The police handed a warrant to Junior's father. After searching the whole house, they then came out with some of Junior's clothes which they had placed in a big see-through evidence bag.

Junior kept screaming. 'I didn't do anything. You have the wrong person.' However, his cries were unheard as the neighbours congregated, pointing in hushed criticism at another young black criminal.

CHAPTER FOUR

It had been a sleepless night in Junior's household. Puffy face, eyes bloodshot, Mrs Okoli was distraught. Part of her brain held on to the slim hope that this couldn't be real, that last night never happened.

Deep down, her soul ached in reaction to the truth. Her son, who she had carried in her womb, raised in her arms and watched over, had been snatched from his refuge: in front of her. In front of her daughter. How could this happen? They were not a family of troublemakers. She had made sure Junior was kept away from the foolishness she witnessed around the estate. Her son was not a thug. And definitely not a murderer. The word alone caused her body to tremble. It wasn't her son. It couldn't be.

Disbelief had shaken the foundation of the house. Junior's sister was in hysterics and Mrs Okoli had to deal with it all herself. Her husband had left earlier that night. A call had come regarding a shift at work that needed covering. Focused on the extra money, he had left, leaving his wife shattered and vulnerable.

'For better, for worse,' she repeated to herself as she dragged her sleep-deprived body down the stairs.

Unimpressed that her husband had left her alone, Mrs Okoli knew she had to pull herself together. There was work to be done.

She caught a glimpse of a photo which pictured a younger, beaming Junior, front teeth missing, tie pulled to the side, proudly smiling in his school uniform. She remembered the look she had given him when he had brought home the pictures, wondering how her son could leave the house looking pristine and end up so ruffled twenty minutes later. Her mind went over the scene from the previous evening and she gasped as she recalled her son's face as he was dragged by the police. Gaining strength, she grabbed the phone from the kitchen counter.

Minutes turned to hours; the phone was stuck in limbo, playing the most annoying music known to man. Determination had gripped Mrs Okoli and she would not stop until she knew what had happened to her son. Eventually, she managed to get through to a police officer who gave her the bare minimum: Junior was in custody at a local police station, not yet questioned regarding the crime. Armed with this news, she proceeded to ring friends and family, seeking help and advice about what to do next. She inwardly cursed her husband for accepting an extra shift at such a critical time.

Exhausting her options, she decided to change her approach. She picked up her mobile phone and scrolled down looking for Samuel's number. She could not find it.

'Matthew, do you know Samuel's number?'

'Yes, Mum, hold on.' Matthew was good with numbers, a gift that came in useful, especially now. He searched for Junior's phone for a few minutes before realising it had been taken by the police. Relying on his memory alone, he eventually managed to recall it and gave it to his mum.

She dialled Samuel's number and he answered within two rings.

'Hello, Samuel, this is Junior's mum.' Her voice was distressed and Samuel instinctively knew something was wrong.

'Good morning, Mrs Okoli,' replied Samuel. 'Is everything okay?'

'My dear, everything is not okay. Junior has been arrested.'

Samuel sprung up from his bed.

'Arrested! For what?'

'The police came here last night,' said Mrs Okoli. 'They said he is a suspect in a murder investigation.'

Samuel had lost his voice. Shock gripped his tongue.

'Samuel, Samuel, are you there?'

Memories of what Junior had told them flashed through his mind as he quickly realised Junior was not being called as a witness, but a suspect. Dang! This was major. Moments passed before Samuel spoke again.

'Yes, I am here,' he said. 'I'm just shocked to hear this. Junior has never been in trouble. How can they just arrest him like that?'

'Samuel, did Junior tell you anything that might have happened for the police to suspect him?' The difficulty of the situation intensified; although Samuel had information, he knew he couldn't reveal anything.

'No, he didn't tell me anything,' he replied. 'I will call the other guys and see if there is anything we can do, or at least find out.'

'Okay, my dear,' said Mrs Okoli. 'I will speak to you soon.'

Wasting no time, Samuel immediately called Jason, Jamie and Malachi. Disbelief echoed through every response as he explained the situation. They decided to meet up in the evening and discuss the next steps. Samuel, Jason and Jamie were aware of what Junior had seen and knew this meant trouble. Malachi was not privy to this information; as a result, he was completely baffled by what had happened.

A few hours later, Samuel met up with Jamie and Jason. They made their way to Junior's house to check in on Mrs Okoli and see how she was coping. When they got there, only Matthew was at home.

'Where are your mum and dad?' Jamie asked.

'My mum got a phone call from the police station,' replied Matthew. 'I think she's gone there to find out what's happened to Junior.'

'How is your sister? Is she okay?' Samuel asked.

'No, she's not,' said Matthew. 'She keeps crying and asking for Junior. She doesn't understand what is going on. I keep trying to explain to her, but she just keeps crying.'

Samuel went inside to speak to Gloria, Junior's little sister, while the others waited outside. Gloria was hiding under the dining room table clutching a teddy bear. Her face worn with tears, her shoulders heaved under the weight of her thoughts.

Samuel managed to pry her from her refuge and sat her on his knee. Wiping her tears with the sleeve of his hoody, he hugged her tightly. Although he'd had no experience in what to say at times like this, he spoke to her from the heart, promising her things would be better and that everyone was working hard to get Junior back home.

Gloria looked desperately into his eyes, seeking reassurance and comfort. The contact was so intense Samuel couldn't hold eye contact for very long. Pain reflected through her deep, soulful eyes and moved him emotionally. He had adopted Gloria years ago in his heart, treated her like his own sister and hated that he felt so unable to protect her from this misery.

'Matthew, make sure you look after your sister,' said Samuel, as he went outside to the others. 'We're going to find out what's going on.' He rubbed Matthew's head affectionately.

The boys left, heading towards Elevate in order to meet Malachi. They entered and saw him on the phone. He had been calling lawyers and trying to collate more information about Junior's predicament. Noticing them, he hung up and approached them.

'How are you boys feeling?'

'Not great, mate,' Jamie replied.

'Mmmm, I can imagine,' Malachi replied. 'I was talking to a friend who is a partner in a small law firm that deals with criminal cases. Her name is Victoria. She said she would see if she could represent Junior. Before you guys arrived, I was on the phone to a journalist from the *Hackney Gazette*. She told me that four people have been arrested in connection with a murder that took place on New North Road a few weeks ago.'

Samuel looked at Jamie and Jason, shaking his head in disbelief.

'So that means that Face and the rest of the gang got arrested as well?'

Malachi interrupted. 'Hold on. You know who else got arrested?'

Jason, Samuel and Jamie all looked at each other, contemplating whether to talk. Junior had entrusted them with the information and sharing it could backfire. Despite this, they all felt Malachi was trustworthy; it was better to get it out in the open.

Samuel nodded at Jamie, who began to reveal the details behind the arrest. Malachi was quiet throughout, analysing the information carefully. There was no longer any confusion as to why the police had targeted Junior. Malachi explained to the boys that this situation was not good. He picked one of the colourful chairs and sat down gingerly.

'The reason I say things do not look good for Junior is the fact that he was seen with these other guys. Plus, and most importantly, he was running away with them after they stabbed the boy.'

Jason responded. 'Surely they can investigate and find out that he was not involved?'

'As you said, Junior will not snitch on Face and his crew. This will make it harder to explain why he was there and why he ran away. Let's wait and see if they charge him with the murder. Hopefully, it won't get to that stage. Victoria is a great lawyer and will be happy to represent him. She would advise him accordingly, as long as he gives her all the information she needs.'

The next day, Junior was sitting expectantly in the police station interview room awaiting his solicitor. Sleep had cheated on him and his face showed extreme exhaustion, while his mind weighed up his options. All night he had gone over the scene in his head, knowing he was innocent, that he hadn't been a part of it. His eyes would then rotate around the cage he was in and doom would overshadow him. Usually so optimistic, this negativity was an unwelcome change for him. He didn't know how to react. His mum had called him and he had lied, assuring her that he was coping, that everything was fine. He didn't want to worry her, but inside he was broken.

He sighed and placed his head in his hands. Just then, Victoria, his solicitor, strolled into the room, confidence oozing from her. She was tall for a woman (almost six foot), slim and well-dressed; her walk meant business and she suddenly had Junior's full attention. She was slightly darker than Junior; her complexion reminded him of smooth, dark chocolate. Sexy. Flicking her long, black hair over her shoulders, she smiled at him, instantly putting him at ease. Experienced in dealing with murder cases, she had an interest when Malachi called her. Observing her new client, she approached the table.

'Hello, Junior, I am Victoria Sutton. I will be representing you from now on.'

'Hi, it's good to meet you.' Junior stood up to shake her hand.

'I have been reading the notes from the duty solicitor,' said Victoria. 'I can see that your first interview was a no comment interview. That's good.'

'Yes,' replied Junior, 'I was advised to do so. But doesn't that make me look guilty?'

'No. It ensures you do not say something that may later incriminate you in court.'

Junior clenched his left hand into a fist and started tapping it repeatedly with the open palm of his right hand. He was nervous. Despite his anxiety, Junior took a liking to Victoria straight away. He felt he could trust her, especially since it was Malachi who had referred her to his case. Knowing that his friends on the outside were still supporting him made him feel better.

'Junior,' said Victoria, 'I need you to tell me exactly what happened. Once I have all the information, I will be able to know how to proceed if they decide to charge you. I will advise you on what we should do, but ultimately we will follow your directions.'

Junior looked at her and then looked down at the metal table that was in the middle of the room, contemplating whether to tell her the whole story. He decided to tell her the truth – part of it, anyway. He omitted the fact that he actually saw them beating up the boy. He told her he had been talking to Face, Mo and Runner, that he had walked away and eventually they ran towards him, so he ran as well.

'The reason I ran is because, around my area, there is a lot of violence. Different areas have conflicts with each other. So when I saw Face and the rest running with intent, I just instinctively ran as well. Around here, you run first and ask questions later. For all I knew, someone could have been trying to shoot them.'

Victoria scribbled notes in her expensive leather-bound note-book as Junior spoke. Outlining the events, he explained his movements after leaving the other boys. Skipping over the crucial factor that he had witnessed them beating up the victim, he continued. Convinced she would try and get him to testify against them, he kept the information to himself. Snitches didn't live long in his area. No brainer. If she knew, she would have a duty to inform the court and he couldn't risk it.

An hour passed and Junior felt Victoria had brought a glimmer of hope to his dismal situation. She was willing to fight his corner, and he needed that.

'I will be back in a few hours,' she said at last, putting her papers away in her briefcase. 'I need to go and find out if they are going to charge you. Sit tight.' She stood and shook his hand. Junior thanked her before she left.

A few hours had passed and Junior was once again waiting for his solicitor's arrival. As promised, she arrived, but there was a difference in her step. The atmosphere shifted and Junior's optimism quickly faded.

'Junior,' began Victoria, 'there is no easy way to say this, so I am just going to say it. You are being charged with murder, along with three others.' Junior covered his face with his hands, shocked into silence. Their conclusion confused him. Silence reigned for a few minutes as Victoria let Junior digest the fact that he had been charged with murder.

'So, what happens now?' he said at last.

'Well, you will have a preliminary hearing at a Magistrate court within forty-eight hours, and then it will be referred to a Crown court.'

Junior, still in disbelief, rubbed his hands over his face. 'What exactly will happen at court?'

'You will be asked how you want to plead,' explained Victoria. 'A timetable for a trial will be set out, dates for trial, dates for prosecution to prepare its case and evidence and the same for the defence. What is important is that we could also apply for bail on that same day, if you want me to. I would need to prepare and give the court twenty-four hours' notice.'

'Please, do what you can,' replied Junior. 'I am losing my mind being caged up in here like an animal.'

As Victoria predicted, the case was referred to Crown Court. Junior appeared at court early in the morning, driven by the police. As the court was in session, Junior saw the other co-defendants. Anger burnt within him as he reflected on how their actions had ruined his life. He was not a criminal. Before giving their pleas, Junior was hopeful that the crew would accept responsibility for their actions and exonerate him. His knees weakened as, one by one, they pleaded not guilty. Not Guilty! How could they possibly do this to him, tarring them all with the same brush when he was in fact innocent?

Blood boiling within him, Junior noticed a smirk from one of the other defendants. He was enraged, but could do nothing about it. His attention returned to the proceedings. The trial was set to begin in nine months. Where Junior would spend that time would depend on the Judge, a wrinkly, old, white man with a stern look of disapproval. His hopes began to diminish.

Standing strong, Victoria presented a case for Junior to be granted bail. Her experience shone as her arguments echoed around the room. She highlighted his exemplar record – no prior convictions, attempting to convince them he wasn't a flight risk. Promising the Judge that, should he grant Junior bail, he would be monitored weekly in appointments at the police station, she concluded her case.

In the public gallery, Junior's friends and family sat, grief-stricken. Anxiety fell on Junior as he awaited the outcome. He found no comfort in the faces of his supporters. The pain in his mum's eyes hit him forcefully, cracking his heart in the process. He projected a fake smile, desperate to look together. It didn't last long.

Despite Victoria's compelling case, the Judge denied Junior bail, declaring he would be remanded in custody due to the seriousness of the crime. The words spun around Junior's head as he struggled to process them. Surely this couldn't be real? Nine months. In jail. For a crime he hadn't committed. Words failed him as his mouth hung open in shock. He barely had time to wave goodbye to his family and friends before he was led away by security. Victoria managed to speak to Junior before he was transported to the prison.

'I am so sorry you have to go through this,' she said. 'I will try my best to build a strong case for you. I will seek for a second autopsy and, from there, I will begin to build my case week by week.'

'Thank you,' replied Junior.

Now emotionally attached, she gave Junior a hug before he was put in a security van.

A week passed and life continued. Samuel was looking forward to starting his new life at university. Packing was the most difficult part; he looked at the mess around him – jumpers, jeans, T-shirts and underwear were strewn across his room. Time was running out; he was due to leave that evening. With a militant attitude, he got the job done.

He had some people to see before he departed. Ngozi was one of them. Since Junior's arrest, he had felt a duty of care towards her and had been checking in on her regularly. This would change once he went to university and he wanted to say goodbye personally. They agreed to meet up at the local park.

She was late, as usual. Samuel busied himself with his phone, playing snakes on his battered Nokia. Clocking her approaching, he readied himself to engage in a barrage of banter, but was stopped in his tracks. Her face a picture of fury, she was shaking, waving a newspaper.

'Hey. Are you okay?' said Samuel.

'No! Look at this.' Ngozi held up that week's edition of the *Hackney Gazette*. 'They are talking about Junior like he is in a gang.' Samuel took the newspaper and read the headline.

'Four gang members charged for local boy's murder.' Samuel was reluctant to read the article, but forced himself. The words converted into rage as they entered his body, causing an explosive physiological responsive. The compressed feelings stacked up with each paragraph until he could no longer contain his emotions. He threw the newspaper on the ground.

'How can they write that about him?' he shouted, clenching his fists. 'They don't even know him.' Ngozi was sobbing, her voice faint as she spoke.

'Nine months on remand in prison. Junior is not the type of guy that should be in prison.'

The article had ruined Samuel's plans for his meeting with Ngozi. He struggled to keep his composure. They spoke about

Junior and the effect of the media – the negative portrayal of black males, the stereotypical comments and views.

'I need to go,' said Samuel at last. 'Malachi is picking me up and taking me to uni. I need to let off some steam. We will catch up later. Tell Dion I said hi.'

'Okay,' replied Ngozi. 'Take care, Samuel.'

Samuel couldn't leave without catching up with his friends. Realising he was running out of time, he ran over to Jamie's house. Jason was also there. Although the boys had still remained close since Junior's arrest, things had changed. Laughter and banter was missing from their interactions, the mood downcast and solemn. Every time they met up it felt unnatural, strange, almost a betrayal to have fun without him.

Samuel said his goodbyes, bittersweet, and left. He hurried back home and grabbed his suitcase from the room. His aunt and cousins ambushed him as he tried to make a swift exit. Malachi was outside waiting for him.

'Samuel, make sure you behave yourself when you get there,' his aunt Felicity said, hugging him. 'The most important thing is to stay focused on your studies.'

'Yes, Aunty.' Samuel was now itching to leave, but the good-byes were not over yet.

'Did you ask your brother to see if he could drop you off?' she pressed.

'No, I didn't bother,' replied Samuel. 'Mark is always too busy; he is living his own life now.'

Samuel hated it when his aunt talked about his brother; it remind-ed him of how far apart they were. As far as he was concerned, an older brother he couldn't count on wasn't worth mentioning. That was his cue to leave. Samuel hugged his aunt and cousins. He said goodbye to Gary, his aunt's husband, but he barely acknowledged him. Finally, once outside, he apologised to Malachi for the wait, chucked his suitcase into the boot and jumped in the passenger seat.

An hour later they arrived at Brunel University. In Malachi, Samuel couldn't have asked for a better companion for the journey; he had uplifted his spirits with their conversation. He was now excited about starting his degree.

After saying his goodbyes to Malachi and waving him off, he paused momentarily, reflecting that Junior should have been starting this journey with him. As he looked around the campus, he wondered what Junior was seeing at that exact moment. Taking a deep breath, Samuel grabbed his bag and wondered around, looking for student registration. He collected the keys for his apartment and dragged his luggage to Isambard Complex.

It was a nice set-up; sharing with five other people, they all had their own rooms, with a common room to socialise. The kitchen was big and spacious, with two fridges; the whole place was painted cream. Samuel's room was not that big, but for the first time in four years he had a place he could call his own. Eager, he started unpacking his things. Junior crossed his mind again as he realised they would be sleeping in a similar confined space – the difference being that he was free. Trying to keep positive, Samuel attempted to shake the melancholy off and focus on the university experience.

In Hackney, Jamie was struggling to keep up with his training schedule. Since he'd started working, the shift patterns had impacted his routine and the constant changing was hard to maintain. Boxing was his ultimate goal and passion, but he knew the extra income was helping his mum. This knowledge spurred him to continue, despite the effect it was having on his training.

It was Saturday and Jamie was preparing to go to the Lion's club for a special opportunity. A professional boxer had heard about his talent and wanted to meet him and train with him. Jamie was excited; he couldn't stop talking about it.

'Mum, have you seen my other gym bag?' he called out.

'No,' his mum called back. 'When was the last time you used it?'

Jamie rummaged through all his things in his bedroom. He lifted the mattress and pulled everything from his wardrobe out onto the bedroom floor. He suddenly stopped and sat on his bed.

'Darling, did you find it?' asked his mum from the landing. There was no response, so she shouted at him again. Concerned, she walked into his bedroom and saw Jamie slumped on the bed looking dejected.

'Darling, what is the matter?'

'I remember where my other gym bag is now.'

'The one that has the gloves in that your dad gave you?'

'Yes,' said Jamie. 'I gave it to Junior to take home after I finished a session and was called into work. It is probably still at his house.'

Mrs Heale knew this was not about the bag, or the special boxing gloves; this was another reminder Junior was in prison. She had been very sympathetic over Junior's ordeal and did not believe he had been involved. Time had passed and she'd witnessed first-hand how Junior's incarceration had affected her son. He hadn't been the same; she'd tried her best to console him, but often to no avail.

'I will go and pick it up later on this week,' she said kindly. 'While I am there, I will check on his brother and sister.'

Finally ready for training, Jamie headed towards the front door. His phone rang. It was his manager at work; someone had called in sick at the restaurant and they were understaffed. He demanded Jamie come in immediately. Throwing his bag on the floor, Jamie stomped up to his bedroom looking for his uniform. Yet another occasion where he would miss out on training due to work.

'Jamie, what is the matter now?' asked his mum.

'I've been called into work again. This is becoming a joke.' Claire Heale was also preparing for her cleaning shift at the hospital. She shook her head, saddened that her son had to work so they could keep up with payments.

'What about your session with that trainer you were going on about?'

'Well, I am just going to have to call him and cancel,' replied Jamie. 'If I don't go to work they might tell me not to come back.' His mum walked into his room and saw him ironing his uniform; she took his hands and gave him a big hug.

'Jamie, I do not want you to lose track of what you are trying to achieve in boxing. If working is going to destroy that, then I would like you to stop.' She said it because it was the right thing to say, but she also knew that his contribution was necessary and they would struggle without it. Jamie kissed his mum's forehead.

'Mum, I love you. I know I need to work. Our situation is only temporary. Boxing can wait.' They both left for work together.

Jason was becoming accustomed to living alone – not that his accommodation was anything to be proud of. A run-down, dirty hostel; old, mangy carpet lined the hallway, a minor distraction from the cracked, peeling paintwork. Guarded twenty-four hours a day to ensure no late-night guests, the place was hardly welcoming. This was a huge step down from what Jason was used to. At times, he missed his parents' luxurious house. He often fantasised about his double bed and flat screen TV. All it would take was an apology to his dad. However, he refused to do so; he needed to prove to himself he could be successful on his own.

At times, he missed not being close to his friends and loneliness plagued him. Fortunately, he found consolation in Sian Keys, a girl he met in the local neighbourhood. He'd approached her and they instantly connected. Although Jason was confident in himself, he was ashamed of his living conditions, so wouldn't bring girls back to his hostel.

One Saturday evening, Jason was with Sian watching a film at her place. Her house reminded him of his parents' house – spacious, well-decorated, expensive technology in every room. He held her close on the cream, leather sofa as they watched the movie. Content.

'What did you think of the film?' he asked, once it was over.

'It was amazing,' said Sian. 'That ending was not what I was expecting.'

'I kind of knew something was up with that guy who was lying on the floor the whole time,' Jason replied as he moved her closer to him. She did not resist his advances, placing her head on his chest.

'Seriously, who comes up with these things?' she added. 'How could they make him cut his own foot off? That was just grim.'

Fuelled by passion, Jason looked lovingly at Sian and kissed her intensely. This was a well-used tactic; knowing his advances would have her swooning over him, he turned on the charm. As he predicted, Sian soon fell head over heels for him, wanting to be in his company all the time.

He used her emotions to his advantage, allowing her to fall deeper into his spell. Complimenting her, making her feel special, sending her cute text messages; Jason was no amateur. Although he had other girls, he made Sian feel as if their relationship was exclusive of anyone else. She had money and, before long, was buying him gifts and giving him cash. This continued for a while, with Jason enjoying the excess he received for playing the role of boyfriend. He knew how much she liked him and manipulated her consistently.

A few weeks later, Jason had left his phone open and Sian delved into it. His phone was filled with sexual messages to other girls, naked pictures and erotica. Soul-destroying reality. Hurt and humiliated, she slapped him, broke his phone (which she had paid for) and told him to leave. Jason was upset, but only because he had been caught; he had enjoyed the ride.

Back to square one with empty pockets and a seducing smile, he decided to bite the bullet and sign on. He hated that he had reached this place in his life – on fifty pounds a week, a slave to the system, jumping through hoops to survive.

On the loathsome Metropolitan line from Uxbridge, Samuel sat; he was finally returning home from university. The journey was long. With his iPod keeping him company, he reflected on the changes that had taken place in his life. He felt somewhat distant from Hackney now, although it was still his home. He had moved on.

Anticipating the change in scenery and familiarity of his neighbourhood, nostalgia attacked him. Longing for home, he counted the stops on the map, still bobbing his head to his music selection. Eventually, after a few tube changes, engineering work he hadn't accounted for, diversions, and a bus ride, he was home. His aunt and cousins were excited to see him, having missed his presence in the house. He was overwhelmed by the response; he hadn't been away that long, yet it pleased him that he had been missed.

After dumping his bags in his old room, he used the opportunity to visit Junior's family. Gloria almost knocked him to the ground when she saw him. He grinned, spinning her around the room and laughing. Acceptance. He was a welcome older brother substitute and took the role in his stride, spending the whole day keeping the young ones entertained.

Mrs Okoli watched him, pondering on how similar he was to Junior, yet how their lives were so different. It grieved her to acknowledge her son was in prison instead of here with them, rampaging around and creating havoc in the home. She wanted her son back. Mid-thought, the doorbell rang; she snapped out of her daydream to answer it. It was Jamie. She greeted him with a smile and a hug, appreciating immensely the extent to which her son's friends had supported the family.

That evening, Central London was packed with miserable commuters desperate to get home. Interaction minimal, except for the agitated pleas of 'Move down!' on the tube platforms. Squashed into sweaty carriages, the morning's deodorant depleted, a musky scent greeted new passengers as they piled on.

Their destination Tower Hill, Samuel, Jamie and Jason were en route to meet Victoria at her office. Malachi had arranged it so they could all hear the latest developments in Junior's case. They all arrived at the same time; Victoria was waiting for them at the reception. Jamie marvelled at the view of Tower Bridge from the window.

'How is everyone doing?' Victoria asked.

'Fine,' they replied in unison.

'Great. Follow me.' She led them to the glass elevator and up to the fifth floor to her office.

Grabbing chairs from around the room, they sat opposite her large desk, which was covered in piles of paper and documents. They made themselves comfortable as she offered them tea, coffee or water. Sitting in her leather computer chair, she straightened some papers and began.

'Let's get straight into it. As you all know, I requested a second autopsy of the deceased. The reports show that he was killed with a single stab wound to the chest, which punctured a lung and caused internal bleeding. Junior is pleading not guilty and, ever since he was charged, I have been building his case slowly.' She looked down at all the pieces of paper that littered her desk. She carried on speaking, but this time she was more composed as she found the notes she was looking for.

'The prosecution case will be centred on the fact that Junior was part of the attack.'

'How can they do that?' interrupted Samuel. 'Junior is not part of the madness that happens on the streets. He was planning on going to uni.'

'Their case is based on witness testimonies putting Junior at the scene of the crime,' replied Victoria. 'He was seen talking to the other defendants as the attack happened, plus he was also seen running away with them. Now, Junior said he had nothing to do with it, as he was merely talking to them briefly. The case is hard because we now have to prove that he had no prior knowledge of the attack and that he was not involved. The notion of joint enterprise has been used in this case.'

Jamie and Samuel looked at each other, confused by what she meant. Malachi interjected.

'I think you will need to explain to them what that means.'

'Yeah, joint enterprise. What is that?' asked Jamie.

Victoria put all her notes down and looked at the three boys. 'Joint enterprise is a form of secondary liability for someone else's actions. So, effectively, each participant is equally liable regardless of his or her level of input in the offence. In cases such as this, it can be a wink, or encouragement to attack someone. All this is a part of joint enterprise.'

Samuel snapped.

'That is seriously messed up. How can they prove things like that in court? It makes no sense. How can I be responsible for someone else's actions?' Victoria nodded her head in agreement.

'Unfortunately, Samuel, that is the law,' said Victoria. 'The case I have to now build for Junior is based on his past and building up a positive character. This shouldn't be difficult based on what I have heard about him. But, ultimately, it will be down to the Jury whether they see him as guilty or innocent.'

'Is there anything we can do to help?' asked Malachi.

'Not right now,' she replied. 'If I need anything, I will contact you.'

Thanking Victoria for her time, they filed out of her office, reflecting on what she had said. It didn't look promising, but they were pleased she was on the case. Her demeanour and attitude was positive and it was evident she was putting in a lot of hard work to help Junior. Although they had little understanding of certain elements of the law, she was patient and willing to explain the law and procedure to them.

As they waited for a taxi, Malachi discussed the Young Ambitious Minds sessions with Jason and Jamie, encouraging them to attend. Noticing a change in Jason's attitude, he tried to delicately broach the subject, reminding them of their goals and aspirations. Jason was ambivalent, poker-faced, giving nothing away but a dismissive silence. He was unresponsive to any mention of Junior. Malachi was worried about his current state of mind; he seemed depressed.

Giving them a last pep talk, he hoped he had made an impact before they parted ways.

Days turned into weeks, then months. The New Year had come and gone, but little had changed. Freezing weather conditions bit at the noses and toes of the community and earmuffs, scarves and woolly hats struggled to keep body parts insulated. Snow boots trod down icy pavements and young and old alike hid thermal clothes under their garments.

Samuel took refuge in the top floor of the university library, shivering at the sight beyond the windows. Surrounded by bulky hardback books crammed with small print and impressively long words, he proceeded to unpick the topic. Joint enterprise.

Since the meeting with Victoria, Samuel had been eager to find out all he could on the subject. Instead of partying and drinking in the Student Union Bar with his classmates, Samuel spent his free time here in the library, seeking knowledge. The more he learnt, the angrier he became; the force of a 300-year-old doctrine irritated his core. Researching past cases and asking Law lecturers for more information, he noticed a pattern: the law was primarily used on youth violence and gang culture. He rubbed his temples with his index fingers in small, circular motions as he glanced at the bland clock on the wall. Time to call it a night.

Exiting the library, Samuel passed the on-campus chip shop and heard his stomach rumble. Fumbling in his pockets, he realised he had no change. Disappointed, he hurried back to his room. A bunch of letters with his name on greeted him. He flicked through them quickly — TV licence, phone bill, student loan and a hand-written envelope. It was from his aunt Felicity, he knew instantly by the perfectly-formed cursive script. Wondering why she wouldn't just call him, he ripped it open. Inside was a smaller envelope addressed to him at his aunt's address. He realised it was from Junior and his aunt had forwarded it to him. Sitting down, he started to open the letter when one of his flatmates ran into his room.

'Yo, Samuel?'

'What's the problem, Femi?' Samuel replied with annoyance.

'You need to come with me. I need a wing man. Those girls from the other hall, at the other side of the campus, told me to come round. I can't go there alone. I beg you, come with me.'

Samuel smiled. 'Femi, that's all you know. Did your dad send you to uni to chase girls or to get a degree?'

'Fam, this is uni,' replied Femi. 'You have to enjoy every part of it, and part of it is getting sex. Which I am getting tonight, with or without you. So, what are you saying? You rolling?'

'Not tonight, Femi, man. I have something important I need to do.'

Femi looked at him sideways and shook his head.

'Your loss, fam. Wish me luck.' He laughed and walked out of the room.

Finally alone, Samuel locked his door, sat on his bed and un-folded the letter.

To Samuel, Jamie and Jason,

Life sucks right now. In the last three months I have experienced every negative emotion known to man. At times I think it's all a dream, but every day I wake up to this hell hole. Not having anyone to talk to about it is the worst part. I feel so alone. I know you guys want to know how I'm coping, so I'm gonna attempt to give you the rundown.

So the morning of the bail hearing I had convinced my body we would be walking out of the court room with family, back to normality, back to Mum's home-cooked dinners and my room, my bed, my clothes. I didn't even allow myself to ponder on being locked up for any longer. Sure, Victoria tried to warn me about my odds, but I pushed it all aside, confident the Judge would have mercy on me. I saw you lot in the court room, appreciate you all for being there.

As I stood in the docks I saw my mum and my heart broke in two. Never in my life could I have expected my mum to be in court because of me. I am not that kind of guy. She put so much effort into raising me, protecting me from the evils of the street. I can't imagine how she felt watching me being ripped out of our house like a common criminal. All I wanted to do was run into her arms and hug the pain out of her eyes. I listened to Victoria make her case for me and I thought it was strong. Plus, it was true. First offence, that's not even an offence because I didn't even DO it! With every sentence she uttered I thought my wish would be granted. Yet, when the Judge spoke, my world shattered! NINE MONTHS! Might've well been a life sentence. I'm innocent! The tears from my mum's eyelids were daggers to my heart. I was broken.

You lot know what my mum's like, she's a strong black woman. She doesn't cry. I felt so weak and helpless, wanting to reach out to her as Security twisted my arms and handicapped me. She doesn't deserve this, to be ridiculed, tormented, torn by this experience; plagued by my captivity, broken by the accusations against me. Imagine what the neighbours are saying, the responsibility she feels, and the humiliation she's had to endure.

They think her son is a murderer. One of the most serious crimes ever. How is she supposed to handle that? I can't even put into words how it feels.

As my wrists adjusted to the metal restraints, my thoughts continued circulating frantically. The constant stop-start action of the van meandering through the London traffic made me want to heave the disgusting contents of my stomach onto the Security guard I was handcuffed to. Some chubby blonde woman with rotting teeth and the breath of sewerage. Urgh. I couldn't wait to be free from her.

The journey was long, but eventually I was forced out the van in the dark and shoved into a depressing building. A camera flash shocked my eyes into a blurred focus. I'm sure my mug shot looks hideous. The intrusion continued as I was forced to strip naked, squat and cough while prison officers inspected my body. I felt violated. I'm sure they took longer on purpose just to vex me.

After I had been branded with a number and given clone clothes, I was given a long lecture about surviving inside. I tried to pay attention but I was pissed off; I shouldn't have even been there. Had to accept it wasn't their fault and just try to get through my time quietly.

One phone call. Just one. Had to call my mum, but somehow I wish I hadn't. Her voice travelled from our living room right to my heart and I was crushed by her silent tears. All the prisoners were locked up; that was my fate. My room was a tiny rectangle of living space filled with a bed, toilet, sink and a small TV. Home.

23-hour lock-up; one hour social. 23 hours! Animals get more freedom. They get fed better, too. The foolishness they described as food is ridiculous. Mushy, bland, lumpy crap. But to survive I had to eat, forcing myself to keep it down. Six days passed before I was moved to the main prison. It's so much worse, feel like I've been downgraded from 2★ to -5★ accommodation. My cell mate is cool, though, at least I haven't had to beat him up, and we can spend our lock-up time talking. Don't think I would've coped if I was all alone. Took me a few weeks to get into the rhythm. Living off cereal, small talk and press-ups. What a life.

Every day is a step towards getting out of here. Six months. It's still ages but I'm hoping after the trial I will never have to step back in this filthy, rotten, hell hole. I'm not even going to entertain any other scenario. I'm coming home. My mum told me recently on a visit that you guys have been checking in on her and helping out with my bro and sis. I really appreciate you guys for that.

You lot better be making the best of your freedom. Want to hear how you've reached your goals and ambitions. Don't waste it. Tell Malachi I said hi. I wrote Ngozi her own letter. I'll try send a visiting order for you all soon.

Well that's it. Make sure you write me back.

Bless, JR

After reading the letter, Samuel was overcome with emotion. He wasn't used to feeling so attached, but with the details of how Junior was doing it answered a lot of unknowns and made the situation real. Sitting on his bed, he looked around the room and tried to imagine not being able to leave, but it was unimaginable.

Reading week was approaching, a perfect opportunity to share the letter with everyone. He headed back to Hackney. Knowing the guys would be at the Y.A.M. session, he diverted to the Elevate youth club. Jamie had been attending religiously, while Jason drifted through as the wind took him. Luckily, they were both there.

Surprising them, Samuel entered loudly, causing them all to turn around. Pleasure lit up every face and they greeted each other in affectionate man hugs.

'It's good to see you,' Malachi said. 'How have you been?'

'I am okay,' replied Samuel. 'Just trying my best to get through this first year.'

'That's good, keep it up.'

'I know you have been all over them uni chicks,' Jason shouted. 'I hear they are the freakiest kind.' They all laughed; even Malachi could not help but smile.

'That is all you know, Jason. Girls, girls, girls,' Jamie said.

'Not at all, Jay,' Samuel insisted. 'Mainly been on my studying thing.'

Jason rolled his eyebrows sarcastically. 'If you say so, you act like I don't know you.'

'Forget all that,' replied Samuel. 'Like I told you guys on the phone, Junior sent us a letter. You lot need to read it.'

They circled around, reading in unison. Laughter disappeared with each line and they all reflected on Junior's situation. After a few moments, Malachi continued with the session.

'You all need to challenge yourselves and elevate beyond mediocrity. You have to believe that, whatever barriers and obstacles are in your way right now, you can overcome.' As he spoke, he looked directly at Jason before he continued. 'It is all well and good to have an ambition, but you will need to plan and work hard for it to become fruitful. We all know about Junior's situation; all we can do for him now is to be there for him and his family. Most importantly, we need to have hope.'

After the session, Samuel, Jamie and Jason spent the weekend catching up with each other. They normally spoke on the phone every now and again, but it felt good being together again. However, things were just not the same, as Junior's absence was truly missed by them all.

CHAPTER FIVE

Calendar pages fell from the wall as the months passed. The weather changed; bulky winter clothes were exchanged for a lighter catwalk dress code. Sunshine drenched nature in beauty as the trees blossomed in response, while branches were decorated with the joyful song of resident birds. Typically, the London heatwave was short-lived, soon to be replaced by the familiar grey. A shift of dull, bland landscapes; colourless, miserable, as if Mother Nature was mourning the incarceration of her son Junior.

He remained bound in the walls of his fate, crossing off the days, longing for freedom. Nine months had passed since he had last seen his bedroom walls, tasted his mum's breakfast or argued with his friends over whose football team was better. They had gone to see him, but only once and he missed the banter, the carefree attitude. His thoughts were plagued with the potential doom that awaited him at his trial, only interrupted by his cell mate, David.

A South London resident, David was as hard as the tattoos that were etched up his arm. His tone bellowed with self-confidence, a persona that earned him respect from the other prisoners. Despite his intimidating presence, David was a thoughtful, reflective person and he and Junior had spent many hours in contemplative conversation.

They had a lot in common, had similar upbringings and connected on a number of levels. Junior was surprised at their relationship; had they met in any other situation, they would probably never have spoken.

It was recreation time; Junior and David were competing at pool in the social area. As usual, Junior had the upper hand; David was distracted by the intense table tennis match occurring in the corner. It was a serious match; fights often broke out over disagreements over scores. A natural athlete, Junior had skills at table tennis, often giving his peers a run for their money at the youth club. Here, however, he didn't want to get involved.

'Yo David, it's your shot.'

'Sorry man, those guys are hitting some great shots on the table tennis,' said David. 'You should go and show them how it's done.'

'Too much hype over there for me, man. I like to play a low-key game when no one is around. Plus, I do not want to show anyone up.' Junior kneeled down, looking under the pool table.

'What are you looking for?'

'The chalk.'

'You're not going to find it,' said David. 'What you need a chalk for? Who do you think you are? Colin Hendry? Bruv, just take your shot.'

Junior grinned. 'Either way, you're going to lose.'

The game went on and Junior was left with the black ball; he was one shot away from winning the game. The only thing in his way was one of David's yellow balls.

'Take note,' Junior mocked.

'Whatever man,' said David. 'Just take the shot.'

Junior lifted his pool stick right underneath the white ball. Generating enough lift, he jumped the white ball over David's yellow ball, effectively hitting and potting the black ball. Junior smiled at David.

'That's three in a row. I'm tired of beating you.'

David looked defeated but tried to shake it off; in honesty, he was used to losing to Junior. It was now almost 8pm so they returned to their cells for lock-up, commenting on David's constant losing streak on the way. Banter flowed naturally and they continued mocking each other, laughing at the other's pain.

It wasn't home, couldn't compare to spending time with his friends outside, but Junior was grateful for the friendship. It kept him sane and grounded against the stringent rules of the prison and time away from his family. Some of the other prisoners weren't adjusting so well; they were unable to cope with the environment, fighting against authority, other prisoners, or against their own inner demons. The inner anguish expressed itself through aggressive attacks, pounding themselves all the way to isolation.

Fights were commonplace on the wing. Caged animals growled; predators premeditated assaults on their prey, waiting for them to become isolated from the pack. Weakness was unacceptable and many of the inmates had something to prove. Disputes that had caused them to get arrested continued in the confined space with bloody consequences. Territorial clashes, postcode wars, enemies became neighbours and there was nowhere to hide. Paranoia clouded judgements and often perceived fear of attack led to fights that hadn't been on the cards before. Gangs fought for honour, for respect, for authority. Often, wars on the streets affected relationships inside, and wars inside affected relationships on the streets. An ongoing cycle of violence that Junior had no desire to be a part of.

Inside their cell, Junior and David waited for the officers to complete their checks and head counts before sealing the door shut. There were also random spot checks on particular cells to ensure there were no prohibited items inside. Tonight, Junior's cell was selected. A middle-aged, balding man with bloodshot eyes entered and began turning the room upside down. Junior's blood boiled as he watched the guard ransacking their room. Disappointed, he left ten minutes later, finding nothing.

'I actually can't stand being here anymore,' shouted Junior. 'It's actually pissing me off.'

Unable to control his emotions for the first time in a long time, Junior snapped and continued where the prisoner officer had left off. He began trashing the room, overturning the bed, furious. David quickly intervened as he tried to calm Junior down.

'Yo fam, take it easy. Look at it this way – you only have two weeks before your trial. Based on what you told me about your case, I don't see how they will find you guilty.'

His anger unleashed, Junior slumped onto the bottom bunk, breathing heavily. Calmer, he looked around at the destruction and began picking things up from the floor.

'I hear what you are saying,' he said, 'but I can't help but think about the worst-case scenario of what could happen at my trial.'

'Look, you can't allow yourself to think like that,' replied David. 'Look at me, for instance. I am here because I was guilty of moving drugs. I knew exactly what I was doing. So, when I was caught I pleaded guilty and accepted it. But you need to stay positive and believe you will be okay.'

'I hear that,' said Junior. 'I was even going to ask you, why take the risk of selling drugs and all that shit? When you know you could get caught and be put in here.' David was helping Junior tidy up. He stopped for a moment and leaned back on the sink.

'Junior, look at it this way. For me, I was never great in school. After a while, my school shipped me off to a pupil referral unit. From there, I was kicked out permanently. All because I fell behind in my work and I did not want to look stupid, so I started messing around instead of looking dumb. Started acting up till my mum got sick of me and I found company and acceptance with the older lot from the blocks. They gave me white to sell; from there, I started making money.

'Eventually, I started building up my own line, till I got caught. Before that I was making crazy money. Paying the bills at my mum's, taking care of my family the best I knew how. My mum knew what I was doing, but she could not say no when I was able to ease her stressing about when we were gonna pay the next bill. So, to answer your question; yes, it was worth getting five years because I was able to help my mum the only way I knew how. Other guys were in it for the girls and chains and watches. I was about being smart and stacking. I've been in here for a year now. I will be out in about a year and a half; still have my money stashed. I will be nice.'

Junior looked at David and saw in him the same type of drive and ambition that he and his friends were pursuing. David's methods were different, but his intentions were the same.

The cell was now tidy. Junior took off his grey jumper and put a white vest on. The window could not open wide enough for them to get enough air in. Junior picked up a book and put his head on his pillow.

'So David, when you are out, would you carry on selling white?'

'I doubt it,' replied David. 'I say that now, but the way things are you never know. Look how many guys have been in before for the same shit.'

Junior laughed. 'Loads of them. I don't get it, though. Do they enjoy being in prison or something?'

'Junior, it's not even funny. The reason why they go back to being on the streets is because it's all they know. Some guys will try the jobs route, but who really wants to give you a job when you have a criminal record? Plus you are black. So some keep trying and would be willing to stay broke and go straight because they do not want to come back here. Others will go back to what they know and, more times than not, will get caught for the same shit and the cycle continues, fam. It's fucked out here.'

Junior was trying to process everything David was saying to him. David continued on his rant.

'To be honest, guys like you should not be in here. You had the right idea, trying to make it the legit way before all the shit happened to you. Like I said, stay positive and you should be fine.'

Silence fell and, before long, Junior heard David snoring. He chuckled to himself as he concentrated on finishing the chapter he was on before calling it a night.

There was only a week left before the trial; Junior was focused on his case and felt optimistic. Knowing it was the final hurdle, he knuckled down to prison life, certain he would not be returning. Education sessions filled his schedule during the day; literacy and numeracy levels were low among the prisoners. Not Junior, though. As a university student prior to incarceration, he had no trouble with basic skills. Yet, he signed up as a way to escape the torture of being in his cell all day. The work was way below his capabilities and bored him, so he turned his attention to assisting other students. He enjoyed it, allowing himself to reveal more of himself to the others. It was an awesome opportunity to test his skills in the teaching profession he aspired to.

One day during an English lesson, Junior realised that one of the guys he'd been helping with his work was not there.

'Where is TK?' Junior asked. The teacher in charge of the class responded.

'He's been released. He was found not guilty in his trial.'

Junior's cheeks stretched upwards as he gave a huge smile. The news had hit a unique positive spot for him. TK had been on remand for murder and had claimed to be in the same situation as Junior. They had united over their predicament while on remand, discussing the joint enterprise perspective: guilty by association. TK, however, was aware of his friend's capabilities and the fact he had simply witnessed the murder.

Based on this, Junior believed he stood a major chance of being acquitted. The news couldn't have come at a better time; he relaxed for the remainder of the week, certain his worries were soon to be over.

Samuel was relaxing at home. First year over, he had moved back in with his aunt for the holidays. To be honest, he had struggled with the workload, not fully able to concentrate on the changing lectures and modules. Preoccupied with Junior's case and studying on the joint enterprise, he had failed to expend the same passion on his studies.

Samuel's friends couldn't understand how he bad barely scraped through when he never took part in the rave scene, spending every spare minute cooped up in the library. The letters that accompanied his module result were so far down the alphabet it was distressing. However, Samuel had convinced his family everything was fine, hiding the truth beneath his university jumper in his suitcase.

He adjusted to the routine of his home quickly; it was as if he'd never left. His aunt was still inundated with work, his cousins knee-deep in school work. With no work to do, Samuel focused his attention on acquiring the pink plastic that would assure him full driving status. He desperately wanted to experience the freedom of the road and was determined to do so in record time. One evening, Samuel was helping his aunt Felicity prepare dinner.

'So, Samuel, how was your driving lesson?' she asked.

'It was okay,' he replied. 'I just need to improve on my reverse manoeuvres.' Samuel got the cutting board from the cupboard; he took out the onions and started dicing.

'I am sure you will master that shortly,' said Felicity. 'You young boys are quick to pick up these things. It took me three attempts to pass my test. Countless hours of driving lessons. Look at you, you've barely done twelve lessons and you are talking about booking your test.'

'I want to make sure I pass my test by my birthday in August,' said Samuel.

'Well, you have two months to go, I am sure you will do it by then.'

Samuel smiled. That smile quickly turned into tears as the onions arrested his eyes and released water bombs onto his cheeks.

'This is why I hate cooking with onions,' he moaned.

'Well, you asked me to teach you how to cook, so when you get back to university you can start making decent meals for yourself,' replied his aunt. 'Onions will always be a part of that process.' She laughed and handed him some tissue.

'I'm sure I'll get used to it,' he sighed, frantically dabbing his overflowing eyes. 'I have to learn, though. I ate nothing but junk food this year.'

'I am glad you asked,' said Felicity. 'I should've taught you earlier, but it's never too late. I'm sure your wife will appreciate your culinary skills when you're trying to impress her!' she laughed. 'We ladies love a man that can throw down in the kitchen.'

Samuel laughed, walking over to his aunt by the sink, taking mental notes of each step.

'So, Samuel, you need to make sure the chicken is washed and cleaned thoroughly, then we can start adding our spices and a small amount of salt.'

As she showed him the ropes, Samuel was struck by how similar his aunt was to his own mother. He loved this private time with her; it felt like he had been transported to his imaginations of what his mother-son interactions would have been like. He treasured the moments they spent together and the quality of time she invested in him.

Meanwhile, Jamie had been investing his time in his work. While Samuel had struggled to make the academic grade, Jamie was struggling to meet his athletic goals. Training had been put on the back burner and his physique no longer showed the hours spent sweating at the gym. Flab began to settle on his waistline and his fitness level began to decline. All due to slaving away at Cavanagh's, where he worked tirelessly.

He became bitter about his circumstances and the imbalance took a toll on his relationships. Boxing was still his heart's desire and he continued to pursue it, though not as intensely. An opportunity arose for a fight and Jamie jumped at the chance. He needed to prove himself, for his own self-esteem and to kill the rumours that he had lost his prior talent.

It was Friday and Jamie was pacing around York Hall in Bethnal Green, nervous about the fight. Three times as large as his training club, he was slightly intimidated, but determined to conquer. Samuel and Jamie's girlfriend, Emma, were sitting amongst the crowd, rooting for him.

The fight began and Jamie looked uncomfortable; his balance off, his moves clunky. His opponent loomed over him at 6 ft 2 and took advantage of Jamie's poor start, breaking through his defence, hitting powerful jabs. After the second round, Jamie's stamina began to falter and he knew he needed to do something special if he was to win the fight and remain undefeated.

'Come on, Jamie,' his trainer muttered. 'This guy is there for the taking. Side step the jabs, his defence with his left arm is weak, that is where you need to catch him.'

Jamie nodded his head in acceptance, and looked over his shoulder to where Samuel and Emma were sitting.

'Come on Jamie, you can do it!' shouted Samuel.

Jamie stood up purposefully from the stool, pumped up for the last round. Despite his mental preparation, the pattern of the round was the same as the previous two and time was swiftly running out. Constant punches landed on Jamie's face and Samuel and Emma were worried. It was now or never. With thirty seconds left on the clock, Jamie saw an opportunity open up. His coach was right about the weakness of his opponent.

As the 6-foot fighter opened up his body for a left hook, Jamie side-stepped to the right and faked a right hand jab. As his opponent went to dodge the punch, Jamie caught him with a devastating left hook. Jamie had knocked him out with only a few seconds to go. The crowd erupted; they had been waiting for a knockout. Jamie heard the crowd's reaction but refused to process it; he could not accept the applause. It was undeserved. Frustrated, he removed his headgear, anxious to leave, the displeasure showing on his face.

'Yo Jamie, what's wrong?' asked Samuel. 'I thought we were going to stay for the main event?'

'I'm not in the mood for this right now,' replied Jamie. 'That was such a shit performance. If it hadn't been for the knockout, I would have lost that fight.'

Emma interrupted. 'These things happen, Jamie.' She grabbed his hand, trying to reassure him.

'I've hardly been training,' he said. 'I've put on too much excess weight and I am not as sharp as I used to be.'

'You just need to find the balance and you will be back to your best,' Samuel insisted.

'Anyway, let's not talk about it anymore,' Jamie said, changing the subject.

'What happened to Jason?' Samuel asked. 'I was expecting him to show up. I haven't seen him since I've been back from uni.'

Jamie shook his head.

'Mate, Jason's got his own issues right now. He told me he would make it. He did say he will go to Junior's house with us tomorrow, to go see his family before his trial starts next week, but who knows.'

Samuel looked concerned. *Hmm, I hope he makes it*, he thought before heading back home.

The following day, Samuel, Jamie and Jason met up to go to Junior's house. Jason did not look his normal self; he looked tired and unkempt, his clothes unbranded and washed-out. His friends noticed the change and were surprised at how much had changed.

'So Jason, I see your phone works, but you don't know how to text back or return my phone calls,' Samuel said in a sarcastic tone.

'Bruv, calm down, it's not that deep,' Jason snapped back. 'I've been busy trying to sort myself out.'

'That's why I have been trying to call you, to see how you are doing,' said Samuel. 'Cuz, sometimes we have to go through some shit and it's how we react to those things that prove how strong we really are.'

Jason looked incensed. 'Please do not quote me all that Malachi bullshit. I stopped going to his sessions. All that advice isn't doing shit for me. So save it for someone else, uni boy.'

Samuel looked at him and smiled. He was trying to understand what had happened while he had been away at university. Jason, the friend he thought he knew, had changed.

'You two need to leave it out. Put your claws away,' Jamie said mockingly before they entered the house. Mrs Okoli's face brightened when she saw them and she proudly introduced them to the other guests.

'How are you boys doing?' she asked.

'Fine,' they all responded

'So Samuel,' she continued, 'you must be finished with your first year at university?' Jason cut his eye at Samuel when she asked him about university. Samuel noticed it, but did not react to it.

'Yes, I have finished,' said Samuel. 'It has been a very difficult year for all of us.'

'I am proud and happy that you are all doing well.'

Jason muttered under his breath. 'If only she knew.'

Junior's mum took them into the living room. There were

many people cramped up inside. Some were sitting on the sofa and plastic chairs, while others had to stand.

'What is happening today?' Samuel asked.

'My dear, most of these people are from church. The pastor told everyone to come here today so we can pray for Junior before the trial starts.'

The pastor then invited everyone in until there was no space to manoeuvre; the passageway was completely blocked by bodies. The unprecedented number of people was due to the family's upstanding in their church. Faith and family had kept them positive during this time and they were glad so many were there to support them.

Taking charge of the situation, the pastor switched off the television as the room became silent. One of the worship leaders began to sing softly, causing an avalanche effect as people picked up the tune and joined in. Eyes closed, they harmonised, stretching forth their hands unto the heavens in worship. Atmosphere set, hearts focused, the pastor began to pray.

'Eternal Father, Mighty God, we are here today to seek your guidance. The devil is at work again, trying to rob your son Junior of his future. We are here gathering so you can intervene. We pray that your presence will be felt at the trial, Father. We know nothing is impossible for you, oh God, and your ears are always open to our prayers. We believe in your miraculous power. Touch those who will make the decision, show them that Junior had no part to play in that horrendous crime.'

Mid-prayer, Jason decided to leave the room. He pushed his way through the crowd, causing a commotion. Samuel, realising it was Jason, sighed and returned his focus to the prayer.

'We pray, Lord,' continued the pastor, 'that justice shall be done and Junior will be set free. We pray that Junior will be set free in Jesus' name.'

'Amen!' everyone in the house shouted, clapping and praising God.

Samuel and Jamie found Mrs Okoli and had to queue up in order to say their goodbyes. As they exited the house, they saw Jason pacing on the sidewalk, looking disgruntled, barking and swearing into his phone. Disgusted, Samuel refused to acknowledge him and walked off. Jason ignored Jamie, so Jamie rushed to catch up with Samuel who was away ahead.

Eventually, Jason ended his conversation and caught up with them both. Samuel was irritated.

'What's wrong with you, Jason?' said Samuel. 'You have no respect.'

'What the fuck you talking about?'

'So, you don't think walking out in the middle of the prayer is disrespectful?'

'I had to take the call,' said Jason. 'Besides, you lot know I am not really into that whole God thing.'

'Well, fair enough,' replied Samuel. 'But, come on man, just show a little bit of respect. No one is telling you to give your life to Christ.'

Disinterest plastered on Jason's face, Samuel became annoyed. Observing the potential argument, Jamie stepped in, careful not to take sides.

'Look,' he said, 'at the end of the day, the most important thing is for us to be there for Junior and his family at this time. All this bickering is not helping.'

Jason brought his voice down. 'Look, all I am saying is that we are all going through some shit, maybe nothing compared to what Junior is going through, but that does not mean I should stop living my life too. I guess walking out of the room was not the best thing to do and I will apologise to Junior's mum when I see her.'

'That's what I am talking about,' said Jamie. 'Samuel, what about you?'

As they continued walking, Samuel was trying to avoid the dog waste that was littered all over the pavement. He had a disgruntled look on his face.

'We are cool,' he said. 'I don't have a problem. Let's just leave it.'

Jamie responded. 'Good! Well, what was the problem, Jason? Why were you shouting over the phone?'

'Some stupid girl was pissing me off.'

Samuel looked at Jason in disgust, unable to process that a female of no importance was the explanation for his behaviour.

'She was basically saying that I can't stay at her house anymore,' continued Jason.

'I thought you were staying at the hostel?' said Samuel.

'I am, but that place is too dirty and cold. It's fucked up. So I started chilling at this girl's yard. The plan was to stay with her till I sorted out something else.'

Unable to take any more of Jason's nonsense, Samuel made his excuses and left.

'Okay, I am gone,' he said. 'See you lot at the trial. Let's hope it goes well for Junior.' He then turned and walked away, leaving Jason and Jamie alone.

Junior awoke early, expectant and nervous. The day had finally come. Trial day. His thoughts on overdrive, he tried to remain positive as he approached his fate at Southwark Crown Court. It was unnerving, that someone else who didn't know him was about to make a decision that could change his whole life. There was little he could do except wait.

Slightly sweaty, he took a deep breath as he entered the courthouse. He had been briefed on the trial procedures, but it didn't make it any less intimidating. His mind wandered back to the day of the murder, recalling the incident, retracing his steps, changing his decisions that would have avoided him being in this position. It was useless. It was already done.

Shuddering in realisation, he looked around the courtroom, a chill passing up his spine. The room was soulless; the walls murmured the misery of a life imprisonment, the wooden floors uttered kidnapped steps of freedom. He felt overwhelmed by the finality of the room as his eyes caught the familiar faces of his friends and family. Jason was missing.

He noticed a woman in her mid-40s surrounded by family, inconsolable. Her sobs bounced off the ceiling and landed in his lap. He looked at them empathetically and received daggers of hate in return. Burnt by the response, he looked away, realising they attributed their pain to him. Affected by this judgement, he was barely attentive to the Jury as they were being sworn in.

Junior whispered to himself. 'This is it, stay calm and control yourself.' He knew his character would be called into question and the prosecution would attack him in an attempt to vilify him.

Taking a deep breath, he reminded himself he needed to control his emotions. Looking at his co-defendants, it was evident they were not taking the trial seriously. They looked smug, preoccupied and uninterested; none of them had bothered to wear a suit, like Junior. He sat upright, regained his composure and listened to the trial proceedings.

Disheartened, Junior was overcome as the first day of the trial ended. Not for himself, though; his thoughts were consumed by the victim, who had been introduced to the Jury. No longer an abstract entity, Junior felt connected to the young man, drawn in by the emotional plea of the prosecution. Having heard the intimate details of the victim's life, Junior could not deny their similarities. This could have happened to him, or even one of his friends. He was humbled by the information, reflecting that no-one deserved to die in such a manner.

The void that had been left within the family could never be filled. Resentment towards Face, Mo and Runner had increased and Junior could not contain his anger. It wasn't just his life that had been affected by their actions, but a boy's life was ended and his family had changed forever.

That night, sleep refused to comfort Junior and he wrestled with his decision to withhold the truth from the court. *Was it too late to reveal everything?* he pondered. Surely it could help his innocence, but what would be the outcome of snitching? Thinking about the way the boys had turned to murder without a second thought, he knew his family would not be safe. The issue continued to plague him as he tossed and turned till daybreak.

The trial continued, each day more difficult than the last as statements and damning accusations were made. Junior was stereotyped as being a gang member, tarnished with a violent brush; there was no mention of his achievements or his positive family background. He hated that he couldn't defend himself against their lies, but had to swallow it.

The faces of the jurors burnt in his memory as they seemed to have condemned him already. Every day his mother came and it was a bittersweet part of the day; being so close, but so far from her, knowing she was going home at the end of the day and not being able to follow her.

Days added up to weeks and the witness testimonies became a crucial part of the trial. Two separate individuals testified under oath about the incident. One said he saw Junior talking to the others just before they all attacked the victim. Junior gritted his teeth, incensed at the inaccuracy of the man's testimony.

Due to the lack of CCTV evidence, the case was based upon eye witness accounts. A middle-aged, professional man had testified Junior was at the scene and involved in the attack; this was serious. The other witness, a woman, could only corroborate part of the man's testimony. She explained that she had seen all four boys running away from the victim, who had been badly beaten. Managing to remember perfectly what all the defendants were wearing, she uttered her testimony confidently and concisely.

The defendants also had their chance to give evidence. Junior watched as Face, Mo and Runner were called to the stand, half wishing they would confess and absolve him from the crime. Cocky and confident, they all echoed each other – protesting their innocence, arguing they did not kill 'that guy'. In an ironic twist, the actual murderers claimed they were at the scene but not involved. Face ranted about institutional racism, police corruption and discriminatory attitudes.

Amongst them, no remorse appeared; they even managed to refer to the victim by the wrong name. Callous and uncaring, their presentation caused the victim's family to object loudly, shouting obscenities at all the suspects. Gaining control, the Judge managed to calm the family down, reminding them any other disruptions would require them to be removed and held in contempt.

Lost in thought, Junior almost didn't hear his name being called as a witness. Contemplating each potential decision, he paused, unsure of what to do. Knowing changing his story to the complete truth could go in his favour, he wanted to give himself the best chance. However, despite this, the effect on his family would be devastating and they had been through enough already. The decision was simple.

Maintaining his strategy, Junior accounted the day in question, careful to reiterate he was only passing by when he met the co-defendants; that he walked away soon after and did not see anything else. The prosecution put pressure on Junior, attempting to poke holes in his account.

'Junior,' said the barrister, 'if you did not partake in the attack, then could you please tell us who did? Because I find it hard to believe that you heard and did nothing.' Sweat patterns on Junior's forehead indicated his nervous system was overflowing under the spotlight.

'It happened like I said it did,' he responded. 'I spoke to them and walked away. I did not see who attacked the boy.' Junior fought to keep his composure, remaining respectful at all times. The questions kept coming.

'If you did nothing wrong, then why did you run away from the scene with the other defendants?'

Junior hesitated, unsure of how to answer. Remembering what his lawyers had told him, he kept calm and took his time. Gathering his thoughts, he replied in a confident tone.

'Growing up around where I did,' he began, 'you are surrounded by violence most of the time. I have learnt the hard way – when people run, you run too, then ask questions later. So, when I saw Face and the rest running towards me and saw the boy on the floor, I thought someone was after them. Which meant they were after me as well, because we are all from the same area. No one will ask you if you are involved in this lifestyle. So I did what most who grew up around my area would do, which is run.'

'No more questions, Your Honour,' said the prosecution. Junior breathed a sigh of relief.

Defence lawyers then proceeded to cross-examine Junior. Understanding the damage that had been done, they sought to reframe the evidence around Junior. Focusing on the positives, they took the jurors through a journey of Junior's upbringing – his ambitions, education and life. Junior was convincing; detailing his aims and career aspirations, he was portrayed as educated, respectful and genuine. Completely different to his co-defendants.

As the questions came to a close, Junior was confident he had done his best to show he was not affiliated with the lifestyle or the mind-set of the others. Closing statements were made and the Judge prepared the Jury for their deliberations. They were quickly rushed into a private room by two Jury bailiffs; they were unable to speak to anyone until they had reached a decision.

Anxiously waiting for the decision were Junior's family, alongside his friends. Samuel and Ngozi had not missed a single day of the trial; now that it was so close to the end, they were hoping for the best. Junior had noticed them every day and was thankful for their support and love. Especially Ngozi. Not a lot of girls would have been able to withstand their boyfriend being accused of murder. He was sure she had received backlash for it, too.

Jamie came whenever he could get away from work, his mum too. Malachi had also been instrumental in his lawyer representation and generally supporting and encouraging him throughout. Junior recognised that he was surrounded by people that loved, cared and believed in him. He was saddened that Jason had not bothered to come after the first week and wondered what was happening with him. All they could all do now was wait for the verdict.

The wait seemed to take forever, longer than his whole time on remand; every second dragged as he awaited the outcome. Twenty-four hours. A whole day of discussions before the Jury were recalled to give their verdict. As Junior stood in the dock, the weight of the burden that had fixated itself onto his shoulders since the day he was arrested became heavier. He took a deep breath.

'Have you reached a verdict on which you are all agreed?' asked the clerk.

The foreman stood up. 'Yes, we have.'

The clerk responded. 'How say you?'

Violently shaking in anticipation, Junior could not regain his composure; fear struck every bone in his body. His co-defendants had also been affected by the cold chill in the air; their faces were noticeably serious for the first time since the trial had begun. Clinging to her children, Junior's mother's eyes were clenched shut.

'We, the Jury, find James Reynolds guilty of murder.'

'Yes!' a voice shouted from the public gallery. Face, hearing the guilty verdict, knew the game was up.

'We, the Jury, find Martin Oke guilty of murder.' Runner dropped his head down; the arrogant smile that had been plastered on his face for the last three weeks disappeared.

'We, the Jury, find Mo Ahdeem guilty of murder.' There was no emotion from Mo; he knew what was coming.

Junior's name was next. He was still holding his breath. He opened his eyes and looked directly at the foreman.

'We, the Jury, find Junior Okoli guilty of murder.'

His heart stopped. Choked by emotion, he closed his eyes, consumed by darkness. Hope had been strangled by fate and had died a painful, sudden death through the sentence. Nine words. Only nine. They had changed his life, his future. In the eyes of the law, he was a murderer.

Shocked into silence, Junior couldn't even bear to look at his mother. Crumpled in a heap on the courtroom floor, the weight of the verdict had left her unable to stand and she had fainted. Junior's family gathered around her, swallowing their own emotions so as to be of assistance. Disbelief on every face, except the victim's family, whose joyous celebrations were felt around the room. Justice. Victory. Conviction.

Samuel was fighting to control his anger at the decision. His large hands covered most of his face as he stood up to leave the courtroom.

'In light of this majority verdict by the Jury,' continued the clerk, 'the defendants will return on another date for sentencing.'

Junior could not stand when he was being escorted out of the courtroom. His knees weak. Victoria, his lawyer, looked at him apologetically; she gave him a hug before he was escorted out. Face, whose white skin was looking even paler than normal, looked at Junior and nodded at him.

'Mad respect fam, you ain't no snitch.'

That night was the longest in Junior's life. Unable to sleep, his mind replayed the nightmare that was his life. Outside, his family and friends were refusing to accept the verdict; seeking answers, they went to Victoria for the next steps.

'We can appeal the decision of this conviction,' she said. 'When Junior is sentenced, we will have twenty-eight days to put in our appeal. We need to wait for the sentencing first. While we wait, my team and I will work on what our best chances of an appeal would be.'

Three weeks passed before the defendants were back in front of the Judge. He addressed all four defendants; his voice was deep and commanding.

'You have all been found guilty of murder of Christopher Mpanga, with all the evidence given and which conclusively proved that you were all complicit in the murder. This was a crime based on gang and geographic violence. A young man's life was taken simply because he was not from your area. Life is something of value, which you had no right to take away. A family will now have to go on without their loved one.'

'This crime was serious; brutal force used was not enough for you, as one of you decided to also stab him. The lack of remorse some of you have shown is simply disgusting. Having said that, James Reynolds you are sentenced to life in prison to serve a minimum of twenty-one years. Martin Oke, you are sentenced to life in prison to serve a minimum of twenty-one years. Mo Ahdeem, you are sentenced to life in prison to serve a minimum of nineteen years. Junior Okoli, you are sentenced to life in prison to serve a minimum of fifteen years.'

The Judge hit the gavel and, in that moment, Junior's whole body shivered. He was now in a state of shock, unable to control his emotions for the first time since the trial had started.

'Fifteen years!' he shouted in desperation. 'I didn't do anything. Please, you have to believe me.' His shouting turned to sobs, his tears flowing.

Samuel and Jamie tried to console Mrs Okoli as they tried to hold themselves together. Jason was nowhere to be seen.

'Please, please, I did not do anything,' shouted Junior. 'This is not right.' He sobbed as he was led away from the court.

CHAPTER SIX

A body silhouette indented the mattress where Samuel was slumped. Confined to the basic necessities of survival, personal interaction was minimal. Refusing to succumb to the pressures of social etiquette, he hibernated for weeks in the crevices of his mental capacities. Cave man mode.

Blocking out interruptions, his ears were full only of his inner voice conversing to himself, unable to accept the outcome of the court hearing. Questions on repeat, disbelief rampant, stuck in a CD scratch of repetition.

Curtains firmly closed, denying the blazing sun access into the rectangular space. He had no interest in the pleasantries of school kids playing tag, the laughter of joyful souls basked in sunlight, the dog walkers and pensioners going about their daily exercise. The light was attempting to force its way around the curtain barricades, peeking over and under; Samuel closed his eyes.

The bedroom door swung open as his aunt walked in. She shook her head as she realised Samuel had not moved from the bed since she had left for work that morning. This was depressing, and she could not let him continue in this rut.

'Samuel! Samuel!' she shouted. Samuel slowly raised his head.

'Yes, Aunty?'

'You have been moping about in here for the last week,' said Felicity. 'You need to get yourself together. I know you are still down about what happened to Junior, but what you are doing is not healthy.'

Samuel sighed. 'What do you want me to do? I'm off from uni till October. There is literally nothing for me to do here.'

'Well, my dear, you need to find something to do, because you will not remain idle for the next three months.'

Knowing that this would not be the end of his aunt's appeal unless he physically moved, Samuel slowly prised himself from his sanctuary and into the bathroom. Dousing his body in cold water, his muscles awoke to the scent of Lynx shower gel. Adorning himself with his favourite jeans and a plain white tee, he grabbed his headphones and left.

With no real destination in mind, he allowed his mind to wander in step to the artist's lyrics as his steps followed suit. Despite the joy pouring out of those populating the streets, Samuel was unaffected. Sorrowful and moody, his playlist mourned along with his heart's condition.

Almost subconsciously, Samuel realised he had walked to Junior's house. He entered, blown over by the welcome he received. He felt somewhat useful here, engaged with Matthew and Gloria, filling the shoes of their brother. Occupying them with games and conversation, he gave their mum a much needed break.

The toil of the case and the burden of her missing son was affecting Mrs Okoli's ability to function; she looked worn, her cheeks stained with the trail of salty routes of her tears. She had taken compassionate leave from work, yet felt unsupported as her husband buried his emotions in extra shifts, refusing to discuss the main issue. Loss hung silently on the walls of every room, the house struggling to remain happy and vibrant.

Samuel spent the evening with Junior's family, knowing his friend would be pleased at his efforts to keep everyone positive. As he left, he felt refreshed in his spirit, aware he had brought some comfort to the family. He was determined to be there for them; they were his extended family.

Walking back through the park to his aunt's, he took a moment to gather his thoughts. Sitting on the bench surrounded by excited school children, he noticed their white shirts had been scribbled on by their peers. 'Good luck William' one read in bright red capitals on the back. 'Keep in touch' read another on the sleeve of a younger girl.

Samuel smiled, remembering his own transition from primary to secondary school; the expectation, the excitement, the glee with which they had scratched their names and their words all over their friends' shirts. *Those were the days*, he thought, *when we were all carefree and happy.*

Samuel watched them for a few minutes more, enjoying their play, wishing he could turn the clock back. On his way out of the park, he caught sight of a large group of young people loitering around in an estate opposite. He recognised his younger cousin in the midst of them, acting a fool as they all laughed. They were the resident foot soldiers – young people desperate to impress their elders, willing to follow orders in order to gain respect, protection, status.

Shaking his head at his cousin's friendship group, Samuel made a mental note to address the subject with him on another occasion.

Finally home, he started to tidy up. Focused on the task, he almost didn't hear his phone ring. Looking down and seeing an unknown number, he picked it up hesitantly.

'Hello...?'

'Hello.'

'Yo Junior! Is that you?'

'Yeah, I don't have much time on the phone, though.'

Samuel smiled, instantly full of cheer. He walked out of the kitchen and plonked himself on the sofa, giving Junior his full attention. He was anxious to hear from him but knew the clock was ticking.

'How you feeling, man?' said Samuel. 'Are you still in Feltham?'

'I'm alright,' replied Junior. 'Hanging in there still. No, they moved me two days after sentencing. I'm stuck in Chelmsford now. Gotta get used to a whole different system and screws. It's all a bit much, sometimes it feels like a dream.'

'Jay, believe me when I say this is actually fucked up. I still can't believe you got convicted. It's madness. Can't imagine how you're coping, fam. We're all on your side, though. We're trying everything we can to get you out and back where you belong. Victoria said we can appeal...'

'Yeah, she told me,' Junior cut in. There was a pause. 'I can't deal with this, Samuel, seriously. Remand was one thing, and I was counting down the days praying I would be out. I saw you all in Court and I had convinced myself I would be leaving with you. And now this?! Fifteen years! Fifteen fucking years! For some shit I didn't do. How the fuck is that possible?' Junior fell silent.

'The prosecution made you look guilty, bruv,' replied Samuel. 'Plus, them witnesses chatting shit about how they saw you involved. It's them lot as well, all pretending they had nothing to do with it. Fucked you over big time.'

'I do not even want to talk about it,' said Junior. 'I keep being told I need to adjust, but I don't think I can do that in here. This place is not for me at all.'

'I hear that.'

Junior was now rushing to get his words out. 'Look, I don't have much time. What happened to Jason? I hardly saw him in court.' Samuel responded with a tone of annoyance.

'Jason has been on his own thing for a while now. No one has heard from him for quite some time.'

'Well, I guess everyone is going through their own shit,' replied Junior.

'Fam, what can he be going through that's worse than where you are now?' asked Samuel angrily. 'He fucked up. No contact, nothing. Didn't even call to see what happened to you.' Samuel was standing up now, pacing up and down the living room. Junior could hear the aggression in his voice.

'Samuel, calm down, it's nothing. Don't assume anything. Just wait till he tells you what happened. Anyway, about this appeal,' said Junior, changing the subject. 'They said they are not sure how long it will take. The most important thing is to find a strong case we can make an appeal for.' Focused on the appeal, Samuel dropped the subject of Jason.

'Let's hope they can do it,' he replied.

'Yeah, I appreciate all your support,' said Junior. 'I need to go. I will write to you with my new details and I'll send out a visiting order as soon as I am allowed to. Tell Jamie, and Jason when you see him, to get in contact. Take it easy, bro.'

'Will do. Bless.'

After hanging up the phone, Samuel remained frozen, contemplating on the conversation, trying to imagine what it would be like to be in Junior's position. Shaking off the negativity, he turned his attention to the appeal process, which was more important right now. He needed to do everything in his power to help his brother.

A few hours later, Samuel was walking towards the centre of town to meet Jamie and Malachi. He noticed there were more flats boarded up; squatters had been taking over. *Local pests*, he muttered to himself as he passed Jobcentre attendees and betting shop addicts. Money was a commodity; the desire of many, the grasp of few. Shocked by a new addition of badly scrawled vandalism on a wall, Samuel stopped mid-step. 'Free Face! Free Mo! Free Runner!'

Anger pulsated through his veins as he was met with the ignorance of local bandits. How dare they protest for the freedom of these murderers while Junior was rotting alongside them. Innocent indeed! Their audaciousness was fuel to Samuel's emotions and he gritted his teeth as he continued his journey.

The youth club was packed; summer holidays had meant the young people had turned up in full force, desperate to fill their days with residential trip opportunities. These trips were the most competitive; jet skiing, canoeing, tunnelling and archery were a favourite amongst the group. A swarm of young people buzzed around Patricia, hounding her for a slot on the list. Their chatter was combined with the ping pong ball darting across the table, the putting of pool balls and the music pumping through the speakers.

Samuel's nose flared in response to the tantalising scent of jerk chicken on the barbeque. It was definitely the summer holidays. He squeezed his way through the commotion to the room where Jamie and Malachi were waiting; there was no sign of Jason. Samuel touched fists with Jamie and then shook Malachi's hand.

'It's crazy out there,' said Samuel. 'I don't think I have seen this place so busy.'

'Yeah, it is,' Jamie agreed.

'I don't think we were that bad when we signed up to go on trips.'

'Not at all mate, they are literally hounding Patricia.'

'She is used to it,' replied Samuel. 'She has been doing this for years. I have too much respect for her. It is a shame places like this in Hackney never get the positive press. All we get is the stereotypical bullshit day in day out. We are surrounded by negativity, but that is only made worse by the media.'

'Bad news is what keeps people interested,' interjected Malachi. 'It has always been like that. If I brought a reporter to do a story on all the positive work that is being done in this youth project, they would only take it up if they had a negative angle to spin with it. Like, how many young people were in a gang that are now doing well in school?'

'All they know is gang this and gang that,' added Samuel. 'Not all of us are in a fucking gang. Sorry to swear, but it pisses me off.'

'But mate,' said Jamie, 'on the flip side, a lot of work still needs to be done. Some of these younger boys are more erratic and dangerous because they are now fighting over stupid things. Many are selling white on the bikes, while they are in school.'

'Definitely. A lot of work is needed,' Samuel agreed. 'By the way, Junior called me today.'

'How is he doing?' asked Malachi.

'Not great. He is trying to stay strong, but I know him too well. It is killing him inside. He said he could barely do nine months, and the thought of doing fifteen years is like a bad dream.'

'Mate,' said Jamie, 'it's not right. I was talking to my mum about it the other day. She was shocked at the outcome. Makes no sense. This time last year we were all here talking about the future. Talking about ambitions and striving for success while breaking down any obstacles together.'

Malachi moved his seat closer to where Samuel and Jamie were sitting. They were now sitting in a circle around a small foot table.

'What happened to Junior is unfortunate,' he said quietly. 'He was truly at the wrong place at the wrong time. In the short time I have known him, he has always kept his head high. So it is important that we are all there for him at this time. This is, without a doubt, the toughest test he has had to take in his life.'

Jamie started coughing uncontrollably.

'Are you okay?' asked Samuel.

'I think so,' replied Jamie. 'It's all that cigarette smoke from the restaurant. Ever since I started working there I have been coughing. They really need to ban smoking in public places. Sorry, carry on Malachi.'

Malachi picked up his pen and paper. 'What I wanted to do today is brainstorm the best way for us to help Junior while he is in prison. Is he still in Feltham?'

'No, they moved him to Chelmsford,' Samuel replied.

'So,' said Jamie, 'on top of everything he has had to go through, they move him to another prison.'

Samuel then brought out a folded piece of paper from his back pocket. 'I did some research on joint enterprise, which is what they used to group Junior together with Face and his boys. Basically, there are lots of people in prison who have similar cases. I have spoken to my lecturer and he said it is an old doctrine, over three hundred years old, but it is now mainly used for gang and youth violence.' Samuel turned the piece of paper around so that the others could read it.

Putting their heads together, they sat working intensely around the table for hours; bouncing ideas around the room, problem solving and strategising. They barely noticed the youth club noise subside as the young people made their way home. Samuel spoke up.

'So, just to round up on the things we have come up with. I suggested that we start a campaign to raise awareness on Junior's case. Malachi suggested that, based on the research I found on joint enterprise and how unfair we think it is, we should also campaign against that as well.'

'Yes,' said Malachi. 'That way, we can raise awareness on cases just like Junior's.'

Samuel continued. 'Jamie suggested that we approach local communities, including the youth project, to help fund the campaign. I also think, as part of the campaign, we need to make our own public enquiry for witnesses who might have seen what happened that day. Someone who can back up Junior's testimony that he had no part in the attack.'

Given the summary and direction of the campaign, they all agreed on the roles they would play and the assigned tasks they would be responsible for completing. Making arrangements for their next meeting, they parted ways. Samuel felt empowered; his mood had lifted as he now had a purpose and a plan of how to help Junior.

It was a Saturday evening and Jason was alone, wandering around the streets. A couple in love approached him, asking for directions to his parents' restaurant. They were on the right road, a few yards on the left, he explained to them. They thanked him, smiled and left, arm in arm.

Jason's mind was filled with regret as he watched them eagerly enter the restaurant. They were strangers, about to be welcomed by his family, on the inside, while he was left out in the cold. Curiosity burnt within him and he peered through the window of the restaurant, catching a glimpse of his mother in full flow – greeting customers, taking orders, working hard, a smile firmly fixed on her face.

Seeing his mother's face impacted his heart. He missed her dreadfully; he longed to walk into the restaurant and embrace her. It had been a whole year since they had last been in contact. His decisions plagued him and he contemplated apologising right then and there; to reconcile with his family and give up all the struggles he was facing.

As his mind toyed with the idea of repentance, Jason saw his dad looking in his direction; he quickly moved from the window and hurried down the street, his heart pounding through his chest. No way. The sight of his dad turned his grief and longing to anger and frustration; no way would he apologise. His dad threw him out on the streets like an unwanted pet; he hadn't bothered to find out if he was okay. *Forget them*, he thought as he approached his parents' house.

Fumbling in his jeans for his old door keys, Jason half expected the locks to have been changed and braced himself for disappointment. As the lock turned clockwise in his grasp, he chuckled and entered boldly. Snooping around his old house, he flung open doors and drawers, grabbing a handful of biscuits from the cupboard and drinking the orange juice from the carton in a rebellious attempt to punish his father.

Not much had changed; his room, unlived in and uncared for, was exactly as he had left it – except for his dad's vinyl collection, which was now occupying space on the floor. Nostalgia knocked him over as he fully realised all he had given up for pride. Gaining his balance, he shrugged off his regret and strutted into his parents' bedroom. He was on a mission.

Money, that's what he needed, not memories. He knew two places where his dad kept cash – one was the safe tucked discreetly inside his mother's wardrobe. He didn't know the combination and there was no time for trial and error.

Stealthily, Jason pulled open the bottom drawer of his dad's chest and scrambled frantically under the neat, organised rows of socks. Feeling a wad of paper, he pulled the treasure out; crisp, folded twenty pound notes secured with an elastic band. Smiling, he snapped back the band and counted the notes, taking his time and enjoying the moment. Four hundred and twenty pounds. Jackpot. He left the house, a new spring in his step.

Feeling confident, the money filling a much needed void in his jeans pocket, Jason decided it was time to show his face to his friends and explain his absence. As he stroked the money, hands firmly in his pocket, the fluorescent sign of William Hill seduced him and, without hesitation, he entered, chest puffed up.

Casting his eye around the shop, he recognised the faces of the resident gamblers. There was an air of defeat in the room as desperation and regret greeted him in silent looks of acknowledgement. Making his way to the machine situated in the furthest corner, Jason was determined not to leave without a wealth of riches; money flowing out of every available space. He was not like these local losers; he had luck on his side. Or so he thought.

Roulette was the game of choice. He fed her his father's hard-earned cash; note after note, begging her to release her pearls for him. He caressed the machine, willed her to pity him as her hunger continued and he submitted to her flashing lights. She was not satisfied.

After three hundred pounds had been handed to her, Jason became incensed. His left foot struck the side of machine with a force of fury, yet he still tried his luck. Inserting another note, he decided to play smarter, spreading his one pound bets. As she reacted to his touch, spinning, he turned his back on her; unable to look. She mocked him and he could no longer fight her power.

Jason left, refusing to look at the others; sore loser. He passed a number of shops on the high street and noticed a number of them had posters on their windows. As he stopped, he realised they were about Junior. 'Justice for Junior' was the slogan, with a picture of his friend and information on how to get involved.

Before arriving at Jamie's house, Jason decided he would check to make sure he was in. Reaching for his phone, he dialled.

'Hello…'

'Jason, fuck me, mate! Where the hell have you been?'

Samuel was with Jamie. 'Is that Jason?' he whispered.

Jamie looked at Samuel while he covered the phone with his hand.

'Yeah, it is.'

'I am around the corner from you,' continued Jason. 'I was going to pass by.'

'No problem,' said Jamie. 'I'm with Samuel. There's so much we need to talk about. Hurry up, though, I have speed training soon.'

'Cool, no problem. I'll be there soon.'

Ten minutes later, Jason arrived at Jamie's block. Jumping into the urine-scented lift, he arrived, beaming at the door. Jamie embraced Jason in a man hug, obviously happy to see him. Samuel, however, barely managed to touch fists with Jason; he was unable to even make eye contact. The rage inside him was boiling over.

'So Jason, where have you been?' said Jamie. 'We were worried, especially when you disappeared during Junior's trial.'

Jason leant against the wall, taking a moment to answer the question. Looking at the ceiling, he replied.

'So much has happened. Long story short, my hostel was robbed. All the money and decent clothes that I had were gone. So I went to Watford to stay with a girl for a while. I ended up staying there because I had no money to come back.'

Samuel rudely interrupted him. 'Are you being serious right now? How can you stand there and give that bullshit excuse? Don't phones work in Watford?'

'Samuel, what the fuck is your problem?' shouted Jason. 'He asked me what happened and I am telling you. I was going through some other shit.'

Samuel shook his head. 'Fair enough, you were going through some shit of your own. But come on, man, you could at least have shown some support towards Junior.'

'What happened to Junior is messed up,' said Jason. 'How did they decide he was guilty?'

Samuel looked at him. 'Well, if you were there you would know, init. You prick.'

Jason walked over to Samuel, looking him dead in the eye.

'Oi! Jason!' shouted Samuel. 'Move out of my face! SERIOUSLY! Jason! MOVE OUT OF MY FACE!'

Jason did not move. Jamie walked in between them.

'Look, you both need to calm down,' he said. 'What's done is done. We are all family, man, let's just move on.' Samuel walked away from the situation and sat down on the sofa. Noticing the gesture, Jamie continued.

'Yes, it was bad at court. They made Junior look like he was part of the NN1 family and that he was involved in the murder.'

'How long did he get?'

'He got a life sentence and has to serve fifteen years.'

'Fifteen years?' replied Jason. 'Now that's fucked up.'

'The lawyers say we can appeal,' replied Samuel, having calmed down. 'They are currently working on that. What we decided to do is to start a campaign to raise awareness on Junior's case. I am sure you saw the posters in most of the shop on the main road?'

'Yeah, I noticed that still.'

'Good, well we need all the help we can get. Are you going to stick around to help?'

'Yeah, man. I'm involved.'

Over the next forty-five minutes, Jamie and Samuel explained their plan of action to Jason. Jamie did most of the talking, aware of the growing tension between his friends. Issues still hadn't been resolved and, at many points during the discussion, tempers flared. Jamie, acting as mediator, would calm them down, smoothing it over momentarily. However, it didn't take much before they were again at each other's throats.

Finally deciding enough was enough, they left the flat. Jason accompanied Jamie to his training session, while Samuel made his way home.

During the following week, Samuel ploughed through the campaign, dedicating every available moment to its success. His aunt Felicity had noticed a change in him; no longer wasting away in bed, he was determined and focused. His passion and hard work did not go unnoticed. Arranging meetings with local businesses, he managed to gain support and funding from a number of sponsors. Posters and flyers with their message were widely publicised and the local community became aware of the campaign for Junior.

With that set, the new goal was to find fresh evidence or witnesses that could help with Junior's appeal. On top of that, Samuel was anxious to spread his newfound knowledge about joint enterprise to other young people; to warn them of the consequences. Although local publicity was a good first step, Samuel wanted the campaign to go viral in the media spotlight.

Soon he was back in Victoria's office at Tower Bridge to get an update on the appeals process. Sitting in reception, he watched as Victoria approached him. He noticed she was putting on weight around her waist, but knew better than to comment.

'Happy Birthday, Samuel.' Samuel looked surprised.

'How do you know it is my birthday?'

'I spoke to Malachi yesterday and he mentioned it,' replied Victoria. 'So, do you have anything planned for today?'

'Nothing special,' he said. 'Just going to chill with my friend. We might go and play pool.'

'That sounds good. Nice and simple.'

She walked Samuel through to her office and they both sat down. Samuel noticed a number of greetings cards with 'Congratulations' on them. Putting the dots together, he realised the weight he noticed around her midriff was for a good reason.

'Congratulations,' he said. Victoria looked at Samuel confused until she realised he had read the cards.

'Aww, thank you,' she smiled. 'But don't worry,' she assured him, 'this baby will not distract me from helping Junior.'

'When is the baby due?' Samuel asked as he tried to adjust the seat.

'February.'

'Well, I hope it all works out for you.'

'Thank you,' Victoria replied as she searched through the piles of files on her desk. Empty-handed, she tutted and walked to the other side of the room and looked inside her bag. Victorious, she pulled out a file.

'In regards to Junior's appeal,' she said, 'I have been working with the barrister to make sure we find something of substance which would hold up in an appeal hearing. We are happy with what we have so far. I will speak to Junior this week before we submit it.'

'How long will all this take before they let us know if it is approved to go to the hearing stage?' asked Samuel.

'The time frame varies from case to case,' replied Victoria. 'If the case is a bit more complex, then it will take longer.' She took out some digestive biscuits and some custard that was in her mini fridge.

'Sorry,' she laughed, noticing Samuel's bemused expression. 'You will have to excuse me, I get these cravings every now and then. Would you like some?'

'No thanks,' replied Samuel. 'I have been campaigning against joint enterprise as well as for Junior's case. The more I find out about it, the more it annoys me. What do you think is the best way for me to generate more attention on the subject?'

Busy munching on her biscuits, Victoria covered her mouth with her hand.

'I applaud your determination,' she said. 'You really are a good friend, Samuel. In regards to joint enterprise, the best thing you can do is raise awareness amongst your peers. Let them know of the dire consequences that await them if they are amongst people who are capable of committing a serious crime. If they are, then they too are liable for someone else's actions. It could be as little as encouraging someone while another is getting beaten or stabbed. In worst-case scenarios, like for Junior, it was about him just standing there. This is the most important thing; once you have done that, we can take it to the politicians. Write, make posters, make videos, have a march. Just make sure you keep going and always have content and information for people.'

Appreciating Victoria for her time, Samuel left, his mind full of new ideas to raise awareness. His journey home was populated with the constant vibrations of his mobile phone; friends calling to wish him happy birthday. A few girls even sang to him down the phone. Feeling loved and happy, he entered his aunt's house.

Announcing his arrival, he wandered into the living room, expecting to see his aunt. Instead, he was struck dumb. Fury erupted from his soul as his dad's face greeted him. Venom spewed from his lips as his mind attempted to process what was happening.

'What the hell is he doing here?' Samuel spat in disgust. His voice shook the walls. 'You know what? He can stay, I'll leave.' Retracing his steps, Samuel backed out of the room and walked straight out of the front door, slamming it behind him. Seconds later, his aunt chased after him; however, by the time she got to the door he was nowhere to be seen.

Enraged, Samuel needed to vent. Grabbing his phone, he called Jamie.

'Jamie, you at home?'

'Yeah, I'm home,' he replied. 'Samuel, you okay? You sound pissed off.'

'I'll tell you when I get there.'

'Cool.'

Heart pounding, Samuel soon arrived at Jamie's flat. Minding his manners, he went into the kitchen to say hello to Mrs Heale. Bent over the stove, her bones were showing through her plain uniform, her face tired and stressed. Life was chaotic; two jobs, barely enough sleep and still not enough money to pay the rent. Exhausted from work, she still had to upkeep her home between shifts. Looking up, she managed a smile for Samuel.

'Hello, Samuel. How are you, sweetheart?'

'I'm fine, thanks.'

'Happy birthday, by the way. Are you the last one to turn nineteen?'

Samuel smiled. 'No, Jamie's first. Then Junior, then me, and then Jason in December.'

'It is a real shame about Junior,' she said. 'He spent his last birthday in prison and now possibly the next fifteen years.'

'Well, we are trying our best to make sure that is not the case,' Samuel replied.

Jamie shouted from upstairs. 'Samuel, I'm in the bedroom.'

'Speak to you later, Mrs H,' said Samuel. 'Jay, I'm coming.'

Jamie was in the middle of tidying up his room. The stench from the pile of dirty socks, boxers and sweaty training gear scattered on the floor was overwhelming; it almost catapulted Samuel back into the corridor.

'You need to crack open a window, man,' said Samuel, covering his nose.'

'I know, help me do it then,' replied Jamie. 'Don't just stand there.'

Samuel made his way past all the junk on the floor to get to the window. It was a tight squeeze. Jamie had inherited the box room and had filled every inch with his possessions, including boxing gear and equipment.

'So, what happened?' he asked.

'Can you believe I went home and I saw my dad there,' replied Samuel. 'I was so pissed off to see him. I just walked out.'

'I know you don't get on with your dad,' replied Jamie, 'but it seems like an over-reaction to me, mate. Unless there is more to the story I don't know about.'

'It's his fault my mum is dead,' said Samuel. 'Since then, I have just hated him.'

'I know all that, but it doesn't make any sense. Your mum was knocked over. How is that his fault?'

Samuel took a deep breath. He kicked away some of the shoes that were scattered all over the room and sat down on the floor. Jamie looked at him.

'Mate, it's okay if you do not want to talk about it.'

'No, it's fine,' replied Samuel. 'It's just I haven't really told anyone what happened apart from Junior.'

Jamie put down the black plastic bag full of rubbish and sat down opposite Samuel.

'When I was twelve,' began Samuel, 'my mum and dad argued a lot. I could hear them shouting all the time. Most of the time I tried to drown out the noise with my Walkman; some days were worse than others. The day my mum died, I remember the fighting was extreme. I went and poked my head around the living room. I saw my dad hit my mum for the first time. She was crying. She picked up her handbag and ran past me. I was angry at my dad for hitting her, but that anger turned into hate when we got the call saying she had ran into the road and was hit by a car. She died in hospital. Ever since that day, I blamed my dad for what he did to her. When I had the chance to move out, I took it.'

There was an awkward silence when Samuel finished talking. Jamie did not know what to say. He stared down at his hands while he gathered his thoughts.

'Mate, I am sorry to hear that,' he said at last. 'I had no idea. I can see why you are pissed off. If I was in your shoes I would be pissed off as well.' Jamie felt sorry for Samuel; he knew what it was like to lose a parent. He still had his mum, whereas Samuel had no one apart from his aunt.

'It has been just over a year since my dad died,' said Jamie. 'I miss him every day. At random times, I think about him and tears flow down my face.'

'But you were lucky to have such a positive relationship with your dad,' replied Samuel.

'I guess I was, but I miss him so much.'

'My dad might as well be dead,' said Samuel bitterly. 'He means nothing to me.'

'Don't say that,' replied Jamie. 'He is still your dad. You should be grateful that he is still around. Have you ever stopped to think about what he wants? At least he is trying. He is always trying to get in contact with you; last year he called, wrote you a letter. This year he came to see you. Maybe you should hear him out.'

Samuel was not responsive to Jamie's comment. He got back up from his seated position on the floor to continue clearing out Jamie's room. He quickly changed the subject.

'So how is Emma?'

'She is fine,' replied Jamie. 'Always busy, though. Having said that, so am I. I can't wait till the day I leave this stupid job.'

'Keep at it man. You are making a difference, helping your mum out.'

'I guess so. So, birthday boy, what girl are you spending your evening with?'

They both started laughing. Samuel rubbed his hands over his head.

'Jay, to tell you the truth, I am tired of all these loose chicks. The chase was fun, but I am looking for a chick like Emma. A serious girl.' Jamie gave him a surprised look, then started laughing again.

'I have been telling you and Jason this for years,' he said. 'All that having multiple girls will eventually get boring. Look at you now.'

'You clown,' replied Samuel. 'I am not looking for anyone. If it happens it happens. All I know is I am not paying any of these side chicks any attention.'

After helping Jamie clean his room, Samuel felt calmer and eventually made his way home. Thankfully, his dad had left; only his aunt was present. As he entered, his aunt called him into the living room.

'Samuel, I'm glad you're back. I just want you to know I had no idea he was going to show up. He said that he just wanted to speak to you.'

'I have made it clear I want nothing to do with him,' said Samuel. 'He tried last year and he's back again. I don't need him. I am doing just fine without him.'

'Samuel,' replied his aunt, 'we had this discussion before and I don't want to repeat myself. But there are things that you need to know. Only a conversation with your dad can bring those things to light.'

'What could he possibly have to say to me?'

'Well, you will never know unless you talk to him. Anyway, that's enough of that. I do not want the rest of your birthday to be about this issue.'

Samuel smiled and gave his aunt a hug. The kitchen was full of food – fried rice, plantain, barbeque chicken, salad and drinks. All in celebration of his birthday. He looked at the spread, eager to tuck in, licking his lips at the prospect. His aunt looked at him and smiled.

'Samuel, everyone will be back shortly and then we can eat. I need you to speak to Andre; he has been keeping some bad company. When I talk to him he thinks all I am doing is nagging. He needs to be careful with who he hangs around with. Besides, he is starting college in September and does not need any negative influences.'

'No problem,' replied Samuel. 'I have been meaning to speak to him about that. I have seen him a few times with some people he has no reason to be with. Don't worry, I will talk to him.'

A few moments later, the whole family were back home. Fuelled into immediate action, Ebony rushed to set the table. Upstairs, Mr Brown was soaking away his troubles in a steaming hot shower. Before rushing upstairs, he had spent a few minutes conversing with Samuel and wishing him a happy birthday. Their interactions were pleasant and genuine since Samuel had moved out to go to university. Samuel had always known his presence in the home had affected their relationship. This was part of the reason he wanted to be independent.

While everyone was preoccupied, Samuel decided to tackle the concept of peer influence with his younger cousin, Andre. They had always had a good bond and Samuel was worried that Andre was being misled. He wanted to instil morals and values into him while he had the chance; once he was back at university, he wouldn't always be available to monitor him. As Samuel walked into the bedroom, Andre was removing his football gear.

'How was the match?'

'We won, as usual,' Andre gloated.

'That's good, did you score?'

'Yeah, I banged in one from twenty-five yards and assisted two goals.'

'Keep it up, man,' replied Samuel. 'It's a shame your team is not as good as my lot.'

Andre started laughing. He could not stop himself.

'Allow chatting shit man,' he said. 'You guys cannot keep up with us.' Andre chuckled even more. 'You've got jokes, Sam.'

'All jokes aside, I wanted to talk to you about something important,' said Samuel. 'I have been seeing you chilling with them boys on New North Road. You do know what them guys are about, right?'

Andre put his head down, not wanting to make eye contact with Samuel.

'All they do is sell drugs for the older lot,' continued Samuel. 'The guys my age, you saw what happened to some of them, and they managed to drag Junior down with them. You are smarter than that.'

Andre interrupted him mid-flow. 'I don't do none of the things they do. I just chill with them sometimes. Buss jokes, nothing serious.'

'You say it is nothing serious,' replied Samuel, 'but when people see you with them they will assume you are part of them. Even worse, if something happens and the police come, do you think they care why you are there? They will arrest you all. Junior is the best example and he was not even hanging around with them. Andre, all I am saying is be smart and be careful.'

'Okay,' Andre muttered under his breath.

'Now we have sorted that,' said Samuel, 'let's go and eat because I am starving like Marvin.'

The rest of the evening was spent around the family table as they celebrated, ate, laughed, ate some more, and reminisced till they were bursting at the seams and content. Samuel enjoyed his birthday; looking around the table, he appreciated his support network, the love he felt, and realised he was home.

The following week, Samuel had a session with Malachi, Jason and Jamie. Malachi was glad they were all present. After he did his usual inspirational talk and activities, they moved on to talk about the campaign and appeal for Junior. Samuel updated them and told them that Junior's lawyers had submitted the appeal to the High Court.

'The campaign is now picking up traction,' he said. 'More people have heard about the case and want to be involved. People are getting to know what joint enterprise is about. The majority are against it and are now making their voices heard. I have also been writing different newsletters and an information pack that we can start sending out. Malachi, I will run them by you so you can check them.'

'Yes, no problem.' Malachi nodded his head in acknowledgement.

'I also wanted to add that I want to set up a public meeting and debate to talk about the issues we have with Junior's case and joint enterprise,' continued Samuel. 'Hopefully, we can get that arranged and set a date.'

After setting targets and actions to be completed before the next session, they departed.

Two weeks later, they had scheduled another strategy session. Jason had been absent from the previous week and, as such, his tasks remained incomplete. Despite his willingness and apparent desire to be involved, Jason had not made any attempt to contact the group and explain his absence.

Jamie, the resident peace-maker, made excuses for him, assuring everyone something important must have cropped up. Samuel felt strongly that Jason's lack of commitment was evidence of his self-centred nature. Taking on Jason's incomplete tasks, Samuel attempted to shrug off his displeasure at Jason's behaviour.

Walking towards the youth club, Samuel caught sight of Jason talking on his mobile. The repressed emotions thundered his walk into a sprint in Jason's direction.

'Where the hell were you last week?' Samuel shouted.

'Who are you fucking shouting at? You need to calm down,' Jason replied arrogantly, returning to his phone conversation.

'I am talking to you. Get off the phone.' Annoyed, Jason hung up his call and looked at Samuel, who was still ranting.

'If you don't want to be involved or help out, then don't come and act as if you do,' said Samuel.

'Like I said before,' replied Jason, 'I am going through my own drama.'

'Drama? It's always about you, innit?' replied Samuel. 'Ain't ever got time to help no one else. Fine, deal with your shit, but don't come here acting like you care, because clearly you don't.'

'Samuel, you need to stop talking like this before I get mad.' Tempers were flaring up. Jason had his fist clenched, looking directly into Samuel's eyes.

'Bruv, get mad then, you fucking prick,' shouted Samuel. 'Think I give a shit about you getting mad? Truth hurts. You're fucking selfish. How many times has Junior been there for you in the past? He's locked up and you can't even find time to come to court, won't give up two hours to help him get justice. What kind of a friend are you?'

'Call me a prick again and see what happens to you,' barked Jason.

'Ha! Ultimatums, yeah? You think I'm scared of you? Listen to me, you spoilt prick.' Samuel was staring into Jason's eyes, pointing his finger at him.

'Your drama is your own fucking fault,' he continued. 'Your situation is self-inflicted. What do you know about real hardship, you unappreciative fucker? You come from wealth and money; your family took good care of you. When you were prancing around in brand new kicks every week and flaunting name brand garms, you were enjoying life. Then you flopped yourself, let your ego get the better of you, caused aggro with your dad because he wanted you to get an education.

'These times some of us have real issues with their dads. Jamie lost his, mine's a waste, but you ditched yours to prove a fucking point. The point is, you can't make it on your own. You haven't got a fucking clue about real life. You live in a bubble, thinking the world revolves around you and can't understand when people don't give a shit. Go home to daddy and let him take care of you. Stop pretending your life is some kind of tragedy. The sight of you makes me sick, you good for nothing, selfish *prick!*'

Jason couldn't retaliate because, as much as he was filled with rage, Samuel's words had stabbed truth into his veins and he was fuming. Faced with his own reality, he refused to acknowledge his flaws and instead projected his disgust at himself onto Samuel.

Clenched fist poised, he worked up enough fury to land an uppercut to Samuel's chin, knocking him backwards. Samuel rose with determination and launched himself head first into Jason's midsection, unbalancing him, causing him to fly to the floor. Sensing his advantage, Samuel sat on Jason, throwing weighty punches to both sides of his face, drawing blood.

Using his core strength, Jason overthrew Samuel and wrestled him till he had pinned him down. He then proceeded to return the treatment as he screamed into Samuel's face.

'So, Mr Uni, you think you can chat shit about me like you know me. Don't fucking act like you're above me, you fucking dick. I don't need your fucking approval to live my life. Ain't got shit to do with you. Junior's my boy and I will holla him myself. Carry on playing the hero, that's your thing, but don't ever chat shit about me. Fuck off!'

At that point, Jamie came around the corner and ran towards them when he saw that they were at blows. He managed to drag them apart.

'What the fuck happened?' Jamie shouted.

'Nothing,' Jason claimed.

'Samuel?'

'I told you already about this prick,' said Samuel. 'We got into a fight, that's all.'

'Are you still talking?' said Jason.

Samuel slowly got to his feet, holding his ribs. Jason was clutching his head and trying to stop the blood from dripping down. Jamie was shocked that it had come to this. Both Samuel and Jason walked off in separate directions, not saying another word.

Jamie went back to the youth club and told Malachi what had happened. There was no session that day. Jamie decided to do the outreach on his own.

CHAPTER SEVEN

8pm. Lock-up, the most detested time within the prison. Begrudgingly, the inmates would make their way to their assigned cold closets. It was often a time for the officers to perform random raids; this evening, it was the cell on the left to Junior's. He and Sanchez could hear the commotion through their walls and fell silent as they tried to make out the conversation.

'Let go of me,' a voice shouted.

'You know you should not have a phone in here.'

The authoritative tone echoed through the prison wing, followed by unidentified bumps. The prisoner was probably being restrained forcefully. Curiosity captivated Junior and he peered through the small, thick glass in the middle of his steel door: outside, a young man's wrists were shackled as his writhing body was dragged mercilessly through the wing. A large audience to the incident began chanting obscenities at the officers in support of their inmate; cups clanged against the metal doors and a roar erupted from all corners.

Junior, silently witnessing the event, shook his head, disinterested. Sitting back on his bunk, he attempted to turn his attention to his book, but his mind was elsewhere and he was unable to concentrate.

'Junior! Junior!' Sanchez called.

Preoccupied with his thoughts, Junior was unresponsive to the calls. Sanchez, annoyed at being ignored, jumped down from the top bunk and called Junior's name again. Eventually, Junior looked up at him.

'Are you okay?' Sanchez asked, noticing the distant look on Junior's face.

'Yeah, I'm cool,' replied Junior. 'I was just thinking about my family.'

'I hear that, bro. I sometimes get lost in my own thoughts as well. For you, it must be different, based on what you told me and how you ended up in here. I cannot even begin to imagine what must go through your mind.'

Barely hearing the end of the sentence, Junior's mind began to wander again. Images of his family filled his inner eye and he smiled at the memory. Split second lapses were commonplace for him; every passing day it became more difficult to block them out. Conversations were harder to focus on as he preferred escaping in his thoughts than dealing with the reality of his circumstance.

'The thing is, I cannot begin to accept it,' he replied. 'If I did, I think I would lose my mind.'

'For me it is easy,' said Sanchez. 'I knew there were risks to what I was doing. When I got caught, I was pissed off. But I did the crime, so no one to blame but myself. Now look at me, stuck in this shit hole for eight years.'

Junior looked confused. 'I don't get it,' he said. 'This is not your first time in prison. Why continue to live a lifestyle that will only get you back here? It makes no sense to me.'

Sanchez stood up and walked over to the side of the cell where the toilet was. Sanchez eased himself as he started to explain.

'For me, it started from school. Growing up in Tottenham was no joke. My school was a piece of shit. The teachers didn't care about us getting good results. I even had a teacher who would say

"I do not care what you do, either way I get paid". Can you believe that?'

'I had a teacher like that when I was in school,' said Junior. 'Only in it for the money and couldn't care less whether we succeeded or not.'

Sanchez smirked. 'So you know exactly what I'm talking about. Anyway, I was not the most intelligent person in school. Sometimes I needed extra help, but when I didn't get that help and the class began moving forward, it got to the point where I didn't want to look like I was dumb, so I started disrupting. Eventually I was suspended, and then permanently kicked out of school. Put in a centre full of other so-called "bad" kids.'

'I know what you mean,' agreed Junior.

'I just stopped going there full stop,' continued Sanchez, 'and started moving with some of the older guys from the area. Before I knew it, I was going on robberies, just small things at first, but gradually it became armed robbery. Security money vans, you name it we robbed it. I got caught the first time. I did a year at Feltham, and when I came out I promised myself I would not go back to all that fucked-up shit. There was not enough support for me, I had to declare my conviction if I wanted to work, so no one gave me a chance. I needed money and didn't care how I got it. Eventually I went back to what I knew. That first job I was on is what got me this long stretch now – armed robbery and false imprisonment.'

Junior looked shocked. 'It's crazy how life can be,' he said. 'What you mentioned in regards to school life is similar to how mine was, but I was one of the kids who did okay in school. But the area we lived in did not portray success for people like us. My friends and I took a different path from you. It's funny how we are both in here now.'

'You just have to stay strong, man,' said Sanchez. 'Just hope that somehow, someday, you get to leave this place.' He got up from where he was sitting on the floor and started doing some push-ups. 'Maybe you should start writing some things down,' he continued. 'You read a lot, maybe it's time you got back to what you love doing.'

After enough push-ups to tire himself out, Sanchez jumped on to his bunk and went to sleep.

Awake, eyes fixed upwards, book still in his hands, Junior contemplated their conversation. Walking over to the table, he located a note pad and pen. Flipping open the pad, he looked down at the blank lines, unable to start. Time passed. An hour later, the ink still had not kissed the perfectly uniformed lined paper. Frustrated with his inability to write, Junior grabbed a picture of his siblings. In that exact moment something struck him, fuelling inspiration. He began to write.

16/09/2006

Today marks two months since I was convicted for murder. Murder! My hands are shaking just having to write that word. This can't be real. How can I be here for that? My life has significantly changed. I was on my way to university, to start my pathway to success. I should be writing notes for lectures, yet I'm writing my thoughts to keep me sane in this prison cell. My recollection of the trial has been painful; standing as a suspect in a dock for a horrific crime; watching the distress on the mother's face; believing I took her son's life. Projected pain. I felt it. Yet the real murderers were cocky as shit throughout, mocking the justice system, taunting the family with the trial. Unsympathetic losers. And I got roped in to that collective on the basis of some second-rate eye witness testimonies and that notion of joint enterprise. My lawyers did their best to counteract the case against me and I had hope. That the Jury would see I was not cut from the same cloth as those dickheads, even though we were raised on the same streets.

One by one their names were called and pronounced guilty. Mine was last. I couldn't catch my breath, clinging to hope, awaiting my release. Yet that didn't happen. Guilty. My knees gave way, heart disintegrated by a justice system that had wrongly convicted me. Let down. Labelled. Stereotyped. Guilty by association. I saw my mother break down as I was ripped away from her. Twenty-one days remained before I would hear my fate. Every day dragged, every night fuelled with insomnia. Haunted, that my decision to withhold the truth had brought me to this place.

Sentencing. Words changed my life; the next fifteen years cemented in a graveyard of forgotten souls. Each word hammered the final nail in my coffin. Buried alive, my screams and shouts unheard. Hopelessness bound me as I was transported to my new home. Freedom was a fantasy. Not only was I back in prison, but I was moved to a different location, unsettling me completely. Thrown back into a den of lions, I was subjected to repetitive violation; stripped and searched; mistreated. Armed with the experience of remand, I attempted to adjust quickly; Chelmsford held both young and adult offenders, a massive shift. Induction over, they moved me to B-wing with a guy in his 30s whose frequent toilet visits left the cell stinking. I had to be moved. Constant cold, lifeless internal structure, rows and rows of cells. In some ways, all prisons are alike.

Keeping connected to the outside world is therapeutic for me; I regularly communicate with my family and friends. It hurts sometimes, knowing all I have to hold on to is the sound of their voice, the physical touch no longer part of my life. My little brother and sister completely out of my reach. I'm grateful for Samuel, though, like really! He has thrown himself in the mix to help me and watch over my family and words are not enough. I have love for all my friends; they know I'm innocent and their effort on the outside to free me warms my heart. Now I've just got to be patient; one of the hardest things to do is wait. The appeal has been processed; counting the days till the outcome; something to look forward to.

Not everyone in here is innocent, though; some people are open enough to admit their guilt and talk about their offences. Like Sanchez, my cellmate. Our conversations have opened my eyes to the risks people are willing to take for riches, status, power. Vicious crimes for the love of money, for the *love of women, for the love of power. Murder, abuse, robbery, drug dealing; most of them are connected by their belief that they were untouchable. Until they found themselves here. In this rat hole. And here I am, punished along with them; unjustly. There are still times I wish I had just snitched and been rewarded with my freedom. Too late for regrets now. What's done is done. Well that's enough for now; I'm sure I'll be picking up the pen again soon.*

Rubbing the dent in his finger from where the pen had been resting, Junior sat back contentedly. Massaging his wrist, he realised it had been a while since he had written so much. The ink flowed words from his veins, and he enjoyed this personal type of expression. There was no judgement in a blank page; he could write the truth. His truth. Undiluted. His words were his soul and they were not for general consumption.

He took his notebook, carefully placed it within his hardback book and hid it amongst his clothes, under the bed. Exhausted, he crashed on his mattress and quickly fell into a deep sleep.

The following day, after finishing his work in the laundry room, Junior couldn't wait for his one-hour social time. The work had been tough that day and he was tired. All the long hours added pennies to his wages, but it was worth it to spend the credit on luxury items. Longing to speak to Ngozi, he anxiously dialled her number from memory; excited, hoping she would answer.

'Hello.'

'Junior, is that you?'

'Yeah, babe, it's me.'

Ngozi stopped what she was doing; she treasured the moments she got to spend with Junior, even though they were few and far between. She sat, giving him her full attention, picturing his face, desperate to see him, to hold him, to comfort him.

'I've missed you so much, J,' she said. 'It sucks that I can't call you; I miss our morning texts. How are you? I was wondering when you would call me again.'

'Yeah, I miss you too, Ngozi,' replied Junior. 'All I want to do is hold you. Don't worry about me, I'm good. You know me, just dealing with each day as it comes; readjusting to being in a different prison.'

'I know that you hold all your feelings inside, trying to be strong for everyone else,' said Ngozi. 'I want you to know I'm here, babe. You can talk to me.'

Junior put his hand on his forehead, rubbing it side to side. He took a deep breath and calmed himself down.

'I am trying not to think too much about it,' he said. 'Let's not dwell on me, every day's the same. I called to find out about you. Make me smile. Tell me what's going on with you.'

Ngozi realised that Junior did not want to talk about his situation and so changed the subject to more positive things.

'Okay,' she replied, 'but you know I find it hard to talk about myself all the time. To be honest, I've just been sorting myself out, getting ready for uni.'

'Uni, yeah? Which one did you decide on?'

'Well, it was hard to pick between London School of Economics and Warwick. Warwick is far away and my mum convinced me to stay in London, so I'm going to LSE.'

'I told you your mum would have none of it,' said Junior. Ngozi smiled. 'Babe, I am so proud of you. I know you will do great once you get there.'

'I hope so,' she said unconvincingly.

'What's wrong?' asked Junior. 'You don't sound like you are looking forward to it.'

There was an awkward silence between both of them. Ngozi was hesitant to speak, but Junior kept probing her. He was concerned.

'Talk to me,' he urged.

'It's just not fair,' she whispered softly. 'I am going to uni and moving on with my life, while you sit in there.' Ngozi was holding back the tears, unsuccessfully. 'Even now you are more worried about me than your own situation.'

Junior could hear her silent sobs, and felt helpless to comfort her. He wished he could embrace her, but all he had were words.

'Please stop crying,' he said. 'You going to uni is an amazing thing and I don't want it to be dampened by what I'm going through. One of the reasons I don't call you as often is I want you to focus on being successful. Don't try and carry the weight of my burdens. I'll be okay. I just need to know you're going to be okay, too. We still have the appeal process.'

Although it was his lips that were moving, Junior didn't feel like the author of the speech. In all his bravado and strength, inside he was still struggling with uncertainty and doubt. Ngozi regained her composure, wiping the tears from her cheeks. They changed the conversation to the appeal and the hope for the future.

'I spoke to Samuel the other day,' said Ngozi. 'I know there is a growing amount of support for your case. We are all working hard, especially Samuel.'

'I appreciate all the support from the outside,' replied Junior. 'It is what is keeping me going. I have to go now; I do not have much credit available. I will speak to you soon.'

'Bye babe,' answered Ngozi. 'Make sure you call me soon.'

There was rare sunshine for what was a late September. The summer glaze had truly began to disappear. On this particular Saturday, the sun was out and it improved the general mood of the prison. Even the prison officers were more agreeable than they would be on a normal day. Most of the inmates decided to spend their social time outside.

Junior went outside to get some fresh air. There was not much to see, as the only thing in sight was the high wall with its barbed wires. The mid-autumn sun hitting his face reminded him of his summer days playing football in the park with his friends. Most of the inmates wore grey, worn-out jumpers and tracksuit bottoms. They used their jumpers to make football posts. Junior did not mind playing football at all.

As he was warming himself up, he saw from a distance Mo and Runner. He was shocked to see them both; the last time was at the sentencing. His stomach cramped. They were the reason for his incarceration, yet here they were, smiling and approaching him as if they were old friends. He suddenly felt sick.

'Yo cuz, what's happening?' Mo shouted.

'Nothing much,' Junior replied.

They both clenched their fists. Junior reluctantly touched fists with both of them, secretly wondering what they were doing in B wing.

'We never got a chance to speak to you,' Runner said. 'These men were worried that you would end up being a snitch.'

'Don't listen to this waste, man,' said Mo. 'I had my doubts, but it was mainly Face who thought you would sing in court.'

While they were speaking, Junior glanced around to see if they were being watched. Prison was full of animosity; enemies were located in every area, often packed in the same wings. It was territorial, just like the streets, but here there was nowhere to hide.

Mo and Runner were notorious as members of NN1; tattoos always on display, boasting to anyone who was watching. There was an essence of trouble between them and they carried their intentions in the scrunched-up expressions in their faces. Junior did not want to be associated with them; he had done his best to avoid wars and to ensure he was not inked with their brand. They had already placed him inside the jail; he didn't need any more bonuses.

'Well, I am here, innit,' Junior sneered. 'So we all have to do what we have to do.'

'Mad respect, fam,' barked Mo.

'Yeah, definitely,' added Runner. 'You are one of the man dem now.'

One of the man dem, Junior repeated in his head. Never. He would never be one of them. He became extremely uncomfortable.

'I have been in B wing since the sentencing,' he said. 'How come you guys are both here now?'

'We were all on remand in here, but in a different wing,' replied Runner. 'So when we got sentenced they moved Face to Belmarsh Prison. Mo and I were in C wing but things were heating up. We had too many fights with some south guys. So they moved us to B wing.'

'So what is it like in here, then?' Mo asked.

'It is okay,' replied Junior. 'I was in Feltham before when I was on remand. In here, I have just been doing my own thing, keeping myself to myself. There are guys in here who are on hype. Loads of fights, though, many because of bullshit.'

'I think a few other man from the area are in here as well,' said Mo. 'So if anything kicks off we all have to stick together, right?'

Unwilling to commit to this demand, Junior used the football match as an excuse to remove himself from the conversation. As he ran to join the team, he glanced back. Mo and Runner were already in full conversation with other guys from the area. Truly recruiting an NN1 army.

It didn't take long before Mo and Runner had cemented their reputations on the wing. Within a week, they were already causing divisions and tensions between groups. Noticing their motives, Junior did his best to avoid the commotion, often with little success. Purposefully picking him out of the crowd, Mo and Runner continued to approach him regularly, engaging in conversation and generally hanging around him.

Changes came thick and fast and Junior could no longer walk around the wing in confidence; intimidation, stares and points were becoming more frequent and he did not like it. Another two boys from NN1 were also inside with them; violent offenders, they had both committed grievous bodily harm. They quickly became rampant, walking around like they owned the prison, bullying and threatening anyone who attempted to stand in their way.

It was no different this evening. Junior was still trying to stay low-key, avoiding large groups of people. Although this plan seemed like a good one, it backfired as he found himself alone in the social rooms. Feeling suddenly vulnerable, he got himself together, rushing to get back to his cell before lock-up.

As he was exiting, three large shadows blocked his light, towering over him. Two of them appeared to be in their mid-20s, athletic in build; the other one looked to be around the same age as Junior, and slimmer. They had now fully surrounded him, trapping him. Fear gripped him; Junior knew something bad was about to happen.

'So you're part of NN1, yeah?' the younger man yelled.

'What are you talking about?' Junior asked.

'We see you chilling with Mo and his goons.'

'Look, I am not involved in none of that, trust me.'

'Shut up! Did I give you permission to talk?'

Suddenly, Junior's cheek deflated. His neck twisted in a frantic whiplash movement to the right as a perfectly placed fist knocked him off guard. As expected, the other two jumped in; one kneed his calf muscle, while another repeatedly threw punches into his lower abdomen. One on one, Junior knew he could hold his own, but he was outnumbered.

Struggling to protect his face, Junior tried to fight back, landing a few punches. His determination only made them more infuriated and they increased their punishment, managing to get him in a vulnerable position on his back. Raising his arms to cover his head,

Junior winced in pain as his ribs collapsed under the pressure of their toe kicks.

Bent over like a foetus, Junior's body was in pieces; pain soared through his veins as they signalled surrender flags in his nervous system. Powerless, he gritted his teeth, refusing to give them the satisfaction of hearing him scream. Torturous minutes passed; the aggressors began to lose their energy.

'Pussy, tell them man we are coming for them too,' said one. 'Bunch of dickheads. You don't run us! We run you! Fuck your waste crew. Fuck New North Road. Go spread the message, you little bitch!!'

Like predators surrounding their prey, they continued to mock him, stamping their authority all over his cranium. He prayed silently for it to stop, hoping they would quickly realise their point had been made. Silently suffering, he focused his attention on other things, trying to forget the pain.

Without warning, the kicks stopped and his body was free from the attackers. Relief sprang through his body as he uncurled his spine to see what had saved him. Another inmate was bent over him; he had heard the commotion and investigated. Grabbing the boys off Junior, they had attempted to take him on as well; however, realising who it was, they fled instead.

'Are you okay?'

Using his core strength, Junior slowly tried to get onto his feet, spitting out puddles of blood in the process.

'I will be,' he replied in agony.

'Hmmm, I doubt it,' replied his saviour. 'You've taken quite a beating. Come, let me take you to the nurse.'

'Nah, please don't. I'm fine, trust me. They will ask me who did this to me. I can't tell them.'

'Listen, you need to be checked out. No arguments.'

Refusing to take no for an answer, Alim began leading Junior in the direction of the nurse. Although a decade older than

Junior, he was highly respected, dark like midnight, muscular and strong.

'Seriously, I'll be okay,' replied Junior. 'All I need is rest. Thanks, though. I really appreciate it. Don't know what would have happened if you hadn't showed up when you did.'

Seeing the intensity in his eyes, Alim backed down, offering to escort Junior back to his cell instead. Stumbling, Junior finally made it, greeted by a shocked Sanchez.

'Fam. What the hell happened?'

Unable to verbalise his emotions, Junior responded by clenching his fists and punching the wall in a furious rage. Causing more damage to his knuckles than the concrete wall, he collapsed on his bed, defeated, clutching his bruised ribs. While Sanchez tried to make conversation, he ignored the questions; instead, he pretended to fall asleep.

Later, he began to pour out his thoughts in his notebook, scribbling away to the sound of Sanchez's snores.

Having been targeted and severely attacked while defenceless, Junior woke up with a start, preferring to remain in the safety of the cell. This was the first time he had felt this way and he hated it. Sanchez noticed the change in Junior's persona; he was extremely quiet and withdrawn. He tried to convince Junior into talking to someone about the incident, but Junior was having none of it. Insisting he was absolutely fine and able to deal with it himself, he watched Sanchez leave his cell for work.

On the way out Sanchez bumped into Max, a prison officer who had taken a liking to Junior. Unlike the other officers, Max was approachable and wise; he always noticed changes in the prisoners, even the slightest ones. He had continued to keep an eye out for Junior because he noticed something different in him and he reminded him of his own son.

That morning, Max noticed that Junior hadn't come out of his cell. He was always on time for his duties, so Max decided to go and find him. Approaching the cell, he was shocked by Junior's battered and bruised appearance. He began to talk to Junior at length, probing information about what had caused his injuries. Junior knew Max's concerns were genuine, but still couldn't bring himself to reveal the finer details of the attack. Max persisted and eventually managed to get Junior to see the nurse.

The nurse checked him over, disinfected the cuts to his face, and bandaged his ribs and ankle. Junior thanked her and left. Seeing Sanchez in the social area, he limped over to him. In the middle of their conversation, Mo and Runner approached Junior, sending scowls in Sanchez's direction. Not looking for trouble, Sanchez walked away.

'Yo, Junior...' Mo paused, looking him up and down. 'What the fuck happened to you, cuz?'

'It's minor,' Junior replied, uncomfortable with the attention, his eyes darting around the room. 'I dealt with it.'

'What do you mean it's minor?' Runner shouted, getting worked up, pointing in Junior's face. 'Have you *seen* your face, fam?!'

'You need to tell us what happened,' Mo insisted. 'Right now.'

Beads of sweat formed on Junior's forehead as his mind ran through mathematical equations of the pros and cons of giving up this information. In the silent space, Mo and Runner exchanged looks of annoyance.

'Speak up, fam. We ain't got all day,' said Runner.

Across the room, Junior caught the eye of Alim, who was discreetly watching the encounter play out. Sighing, Junior's lips started moving.

'I think it was those guys from Green Lanes, two white guys and a black guy. One of them, the younger, he is always hype. Walking around like he is untouchable.'

Mo interrupted.

'Yeah, I know who you are talking about. Runner, remember those pricks we first saw when we came into the wing? We fucked up too many pricks from Green Lanes when we were on the road. So they must know about us then.'

'Those pussies!' Runner started to laugh.

Junior continued.

'So I was here on my own, they came in started hyping to me. Before I knew it, I was on the floor taking hits from all angles. They were shouting fuck NN1, fuck New North Road. That is basically it. Oh yeah, they said they are after you two next.'

Mo smirked in arrogance.

'Fuck NN1? Are they mad? They obviously don't know who they're dealing with. So, we are next, yeah? They think they can threaten us and we will be running scared. Fuck that. They won't even get the chance. Let us catch them. It'll be a wrap.'

'Look, Junior, don't worry about what happened,' said Runner. 'We have your back.' Mo and Runner both touched fists with Junior as they walked off, scheming and intimidating everyone in their path.

Junior sighed, thankful it was over, but secretly knowing this was just the beginning. He did not want to be associated with gangs or violence, but any revenge attack would be linked to him. It was inevitable.

Lost in his thoughts, Junior did not notice Alim walk over to him. Grateful for the distraction, Junior sat down. Alim introduced himself properly and Junior thanked him for his help. They sat for a while, talking. Junior took to Alim instantly; something about his perspective on life, wisdom and advice reminded him of Malachi. He needed that kind of friendship inside.

Over the next week, Alim and Junior's relationship blossomed. Junior felt comfortable enough to share with Alim his predicament and not feel judged. Many of their conversations centred on the appeal process and how to survive jail, including ways to improve yourself regardless of the situation you found yourself in. Alim was able to bond with Junior over books, believing in the power of education and the need to know one's history and ancestry. Junior was riveted by the subjects they discussed; very deep and meaning-ful in comparison to what other prisoners spent their time waffling about.

Eager for knowledge, Junior lapped up all the information he was given, keen to develop his own understanding. His spare time was spent mostly in the main social hall, face firmly planted within the pages of his favourite books. Today was no different; avoiding the competitiveness of table tennis, Junior's eyes were scanning book spines. He was joined by Alim.

'Hey Junior, how are you doing?'

'I'm cool, man,' Junior replied, looking up from the book shelf. 'Just looking for that book you were telling me about the other day.'

'Which one is that?'

'The philosophy and opinions of Marcus Garvey.'

'They won't have that in here,' said Alim. 'I have a copy of it in my cell. I can let you borrow it, as long as you keep it in mint condition.'

Junior smiled. 'Yeah, of course.'

'Cool,' replied Alim. 'Come grab it from me later so I don't forget. I saw you on the phone earlier – any news on the appeal?'

Junior looked down despondently. 'No, not yet. I was on the phone to my mum. I like to keep in contact with her or else she worries. I'm always asking about the appeal, but no. Nothing to report, unfortunately. I'm getting a bit impatient to be honest.'

'I'm not surprised,' replied Alim. 'I feel for you. After hearing your situation the other day, I really do hope things work out for you. You shouldn't be in a place like this. You have a future and a bright one at that.'

Junior sat back on the uneven wooden chairs – complements of the prisoners. The furniture was designed and made by other inmates; they were decently made, if you didn't mind finding a splinter in your arse every now and then. Desperate to find out more about Alim, he hesitated, wondering if this was a good time. Their friendship had grown and he had shared his story with Alim, but he was still anxious about asking. He had hoped Alim would volunteer the information, but that hadn't happened. Taking a deep breath, he plucked up the courage to ask. He looked over Alim's head, not making eye contact.

'Alim, I have been meaning to ask how you ended up in here.'

Alim smiled at Junior; it was a warm smile.

'I was wondering when you would ask me that, young brother.'

'Can never be too careful in here,' replied Junior, relieved. 'Some people are really private about their situations.'

'Well, get comfortable because my story is a long one.'

Junior laughed. 'It's not like I have anything better to so. I have nothing but time.'

They both laughed.

'I am in here for the same reason you are,' said Alim. 'But the only difference is that I am guilty. I took someone else's life.'

Junior was shocked. Alim did not seem the type of person who could kill someone. Having got to know him and see him as a role model, Junior assumed that Alim was also innocent and wrongly imprisoned.

'I can see the shock on your face, Junior. I can understand why, but don't be fooled. I was not always the way I am now. To tell you the truth, brother, I was just like those guys who were the cause of you being in here. I can honestly say I was worse than them. I made the biggest mistake of my life and now I have to live with it, not only till I get out of here but until I die.'

With that, Alim paused, stopping momentarily to gather his thoughts, considering his history, the events that made him who he was today. Unable to remain quiet any longer, Junior broke the silence.

'What exactly happened?'

Alim looked at Junior for a moment before replying.

'I was in a gang from when I was about fifteen. At first you wouldn't have called it a gang, just friends who lived in the same area hanging out. Then hanging out turned into robbery. Soon, we gave ourselves a title, a name that would be known which would terrify others. That's when I could classify us as a gang. Some people like to sugar coat that term. But if it smells like cheese and looks like cheese, it probably is. Soon after, we were having fights with guys from other areas, guys who looked just like us. Who were probably going through the same bullshit we were going through at home. Guys whose mothers were probably out working endless shifts as their sons fought and killed each other on the streets.'

Alim's voice had changed from being calm and collected to snapped and retorted. Fully engaged in the story, he became animated, throwing his hands out, his voice emphasising key areas. Junior listened intently, completely mesmerised by Alim's perspective on life. This was the first time he had opened up about his life; the life he no longer led.

'Over the years,' continued Alim, 'I became known in my area. I guess I was around twenty at this point. My family life was good; I had people who really cared about me. But for me, at that age, with all the money and respect I had, I felt like it was too late to go straight. I turned my back on education. My mum and dad were worried about me; they tried to talk to me about my decisions, but no amount of talking would change the course of my destiny.'

Alim reflected, eyes raised to the heavens, reminiscing on his past.

'For me it was a choice,' he continued. 'It was a lifestyle I enjoyed. The girls, money and respect; if anyone messed with either one of those things, then they would have to answer to me. I have been stabbed twice and shot at many times. People were after us and we were on the hunt to take out our enemies, too. My mum and dad disowned me, not wanting anything to do with me or my lifestyle. A week after my twenty-first birthday, I got arrested and charged with murder. I am guilty. As sin. One night, three of us went to look for the people that shot at me. When we found them, I lost it and stabbed the boy ten times. No remorse. No compassion. I watched him die. Eventually, I took the blame for the murder and two of my boys were found not guilty.'

Junior gasped, bringing his hand up to his open mouth. He was finding it difficult to link the story with the man that sat before him. At that moment, Alim rolled up the sleeves of his grey jumper, revealing permanent ink decorating his bulging forearms.

'Junior, look at these tattoos. They are from when I used to rep my area. The loyalty I showed then was misplaced. It has been eight years since I was convicted and the love, money and respect I had have all gone. I am completely alone. My biggest mistake was being easily influenced. I chose to be around people who had a negative impact on my life.

'Now, I can honestly say that, when I see these younger hoodlums come in and out of here shouting out the name of their areas, like they have a stake on the land, it makes me sick. To think I was part of that! I try my best to talk to the younger ones who come in here for small sentences, so hopefully their eyes would open. It took me a long time to educate myself and to find peace. I have thirty years to pay for the life I stole. I do not go through a day without thinking about the life I took, his family and the void that can never be replaced. All for what!'

Tears were now rolling down Alim's face. He was overcome by emotion. He used the arm of his jumper to wipe away his tears.

'All for what?' he spoke in between sobs. 'To rep the area that showed me no love or loyalty when I was caged up. I have to live with my decisions. I just hope that your destiny does not have to be in here as well. Stay away from those guys; they are the reason you are in here. They will drag you down further, even in here.'

'I hear what you are saying,' said Junior. 'Can I ask you something?'

'Yeah, go ahead.'

'When you killed that guy, what was your attitude then? Was there remorse?'

'To be totally honest,' replied Alim, 'I was arrogant, happy that we killed one of them. My redemption only took place while I was in here, through reading and learning.'

Junior stood up and shook his hand.

'I appreciate you telling me all this,' he said. 'It gives me a different perspective on how things can be where we grew up.'

'No problem, brother.'

Junior and Alim parted ways and headed to their respective cells for lock-up.

Days passed, weeks passed, the weather changed. Winter arrived, Christmas came and went but there were no festivities. Every day was the same; yet, somehow, this particular evening felt worse. The ice pinched the prisoners, their meagre clothing no match for the selfish frost. A pure blanket of beautiful snowflakes caressed the football pitch, slowly transforming into deadly ice.

The mood in the prison was miserable, the nights bitter. Complaints about the temperature fell on deaf ears as there were no extra provisions given. Struggling to maintain body heat under their allocated blankets, the inmates tossed and turned in anger. Junior was not complaining; although he, too, had noticed the cold shadows massaging his spine, his mind was on his journal. Routine; at the sound of Sanchez's snores, he would uncover his book from its hiding place, peel open the pages and graffiti his thoughts on every line. Tonight was no different.

31/12/2006

Another day, another disappointment. I am still here. Four months in and nothing changes but the weather. Numbness has become my friend and blackness covers my once beating heart. I feel empty. It's the Christmas season, a time of joy, family, good food, presents and laughter. Yet I am surrounded by criminals, bland excuses for nourishment and no present but my pain. Thinking about my mum's jollof rice, stew and supermalt makes my mouth water. What I wouldn't give for some home cooking right now!

This journal has become my outlet, my saviour, my friend. I would get mocked for this; constantly writing my thoughts like some dear diary teenage girl wimp, but literally my sanity is found in the pages of these books. Hopefully, one day, I can look back on this experience and find peace in my journey; for now, I'm just praying for that day to come. It's not that I don't have people to talk to; trust me, Alim and Sanchez have made my days easier to deal with. But no-one wants to sound like a whingeing bitch all the time. So it's better for me to write. Right?

Life has been more difficult since Mo and Runner graced the wing with their presence. Constantly up to no good, their actions cause a reaction, and I'm the one getting burnt. Flying solo, living under the radar and remaining low-key is now a myth. My face is etched on the revenge list of many an inmate; and fighting me has become the norm. I've been in brawls, scraps, full-on fights because of these two and I don't even have NN1 as a badge on my arm. Yet, again I fall victim to their exploits; guilty by association and I'm fucking tired of it. Forever watching my back, looking over my shoulder, grimacing in the faces of everyone who looks at me funny. This is not who I am. But this is who they have made me.

I couldn't take it anymore; especially when one conflict had me in isolation for a whole week! Mental stability is rare, voices whisper maddening statements in your ears and I found myself talking to myself. Driving me to insanity. Literally. I had to stop it. I had to finish it once and for all. When I got out, Mo was scheming about stabbing one of the rival gang members and I lost it. I told Mo and Runner I was done, cutting all ties with them and would no longer be part of their madness. Fallen soldier; they were vex, told me they wouldn't have my back anymore, but I'm glad. Since then, I've been cool and the threats and fights have subsided. I hope it stays that way.

Tomorrow marks the start of a new year; usually, I would be out celebrating with the boys, but I'm just watching the moon, pondering on the joy of others. It's frustrating, being here, life passing me by. I can't even speak to family and friends because they just remind me of all the things I'm missing out on. I get emotional; and, once my soul is unlocked, I find it hard to lock it up again, often crying myself to sleep. But forget that. New Year, New beginnings. Hopefully my year of freedom. Jamie is coming to see me in a few days and I can't wait. Happy New Year to me.

CHAPTER EIGHT

Disco lights, drunken behaviour, strangers kissing, sweaty bodies pressed together in celebratory movements to the rhythm of new chapters. The old passing away; regrets forgotten in the bottom of wine glasses; shots fired; tequila. A new year meant time for celebration and the town was alive with the sound of fresh starts. In anticipation of clean slates, broken relationships were killed before midnight, promises to shake off the old were made, unused gym memberships renewed and resolutions made.

Away from the noise, Jamie sat in the warm cocoon of his living room. He had no desire to spend the new year in the presence of intoxicated revellers, pretending this was his idea of a good night out. Drawing the curtains on the outside, Jamie submerged himself in the complicated melodies of his favourite soft rock instrumentals, reflecting on his life.

He awoke on 2nd January to the sound of 'Happy Birthday' sung by his mum in a joyous whisper. Peeling open his eyes, he looked upon a scrumptious cupcake stabbed in the centre by a flaming candle. Jamie smiled, blowing it out.

He momentarily closed his eyes and was transported back to younger years, when birthday wishes were believed in. Internally, he said a prayer; grasping onto hope; desperate for change. He wished for better days; that the financial burden that hovered over their flat, darkening each day, would vanish. That his mum's face would be free from worry.

His mother watched him tenderly, reminiscing on his fifth birthday, when he had been dressed as a boxer, his small body swamped in the oversized shorts they had customised with his name. His dad had been so proud; the whole community had come round to share the birthday cake she had almost burnt in the rush.

Mrs Heale sighed, wishing she could spend the day with her son. There never seemed to be enough time these days. Desperate for quality time, but struggling to make ends meet, she glanced at her watch and realised she was running late.

'So, what do you have planned for today then?' she asked.

'I am going to visit Junior in a few hours,' replied Jamie. 'Then I'm working later on tonight.'

'Is it just you going to visit Junior?'

'Yeah, Samuel is busy with some campaign stuff and couldn't make it. As for Jason, he doesn't seem interested.'

'What Samuel is doing for Junior is really inspiring,' said his mum.

'Yeah, he is dedicated to making sure Junior doesn't spend fifteen years in prison for something he did not do.'

'Well, I'm off to work. Make sure you wrap up well, Jamie. It's freezing out there.'

'Yes, Mum.'

'I love you.'

'I love you too, Mum.'

His mum gave him a hug before she made her way out. Jamie sat on his bed for a while; he looked through some old pictures of when he'd just turned thirteen. One of the photos was of him, Samuel, Jason and Junior, each holding a big piece of chocolate cake. His dad was in the background serving the burgers; the picture represented a time when life was good and there were no worries.

Jamie continued looking at images of the past, feeling nostalgic and wishing things could go back to how they used to be. Eventually, Jamie managed to get himself together and got ready for his long journey to Chelmsford prison. He was looking forward to seeing Junior; it had been a while since he'd last seen him and had a good meaningful conversation with him.

Although pleased to be visiting Junior, Jamie was apprehensive about the prison procedures. He hated the gruelling process; being treated like a criminal, touched, rubbed down, looked at accusingly. He would never get used to it.

Today, the surprise addition to his torment were the growling dogs sniffing around, searching for narcotics. Beads of perspiration formed on Jamie's forehead and he immediately became anxious. He was innocent; no drugs on his body, yet under investigation he began acting suspiciously. Wishing it was over.

After the thorough search was finalised, he along with forty other visitors were moved on through the prison. The constant stopping and starting was irritating; every gate had to be unlocked and then locked, the constant clanging of keys resounding through the hollow halls. Shuttled like cattle into the large hall, each visitor was allocated a table number and told to find it and sit down.

Jamie walked through the aisles until he found table 21, a small, cheap table with plastic chairs on either side. With each step, his jeans pockets jingled with the £20 in coins he had brought with him to treat Junior to food and snacks. Readjusting the coins that were weighing his pockets down, he eventually sat and looked around the room, observing all the other visitors. They were mostly mums, a few younger people, but not many.

He watched with interest as the inmates entered the hall, enjoying the reunion smiles and excited grins. It was almost like being at the arrivals area at an airport; families waiting for their loved ones, scanning the crowd for a familiar face, bursting with love.

Jamie stood up, searching for Junior, but he was nowhere to be seen. He felt an inward tug; he was worried something had happened and he wouldn't get to see his friend. Just as he began to mentally go through all the possible explanations, he saw Junior and relief cancelled out all previous concerns. He raised his hands to get Junior's attention and waited for him to make his way over.

Standing to the side of the chairs, they embraced in a silent man hug, only to be rudely interrupted by an over-zealous guard, who told them that touching must be kept to a minimum.

'It's been a long time,' said Jamie. 'How are you?'

'Before we get into that,' replied Junior, 'happy birthday, man! No longer a teenager.'

They both laughed and sat down.

'It is crazy,' said Jamie. 'I still can't believe I'm twenty.'

'Don't worry, I am right behind you,' said Junior. 'April is my turn. Hopefully, I'll be out of here by then.'

'Yes, hopefully mate,' replied Jamie, 'because this place is not for you. I can't even imagine what you are going through.'

Junior rubbed his left hand on his head, his hair uncombed and unkempt. There was a brief silence between the two.

'Jay, it is a struggle,' said Junior in a sombre tone. 'Every day, I ask myself how I ended up here. I feel like my prayers go unanswered. It's like I am talking to myself most of the time.' Jamie nodded in acknowledgement, barely making eye contact.

'How is it in here? Are you okay?' he asked.

'To tell you the truth, I can't stand it,' replied Junior. 'My biggest problem is just being free to do my own thing, always having to follow instructions. Being locked up is the worst part; having to stay in your cell for long periods of time. That is what gets to me the most. You know me, sometimes I just like to go for a walk and think. I can't do that here. Some of the people are cool. I tend to just keep myself to myself.'

Noticing a queue forming at the shop, Jamie drew out the coins from his pocket.

'Yo, Junior, do you want something to eat or drink?'

'Yes, definitely,' said Junior. 'You know I love my Fanta. Just get me a burger and some biscuits. The last time I had anything like that was a few months ago when my mum came to visit.'

'Cool, no problem,' replied Jamie. 'I will be right back.'

On his way back, Jamie struggled to balance the two burgers, large Coke and Fanta in his hands. Weaving between the aisles, he paused awkwardly mid-step, waiting for a young boy playing to give way to him. The prisoner nearby instantaneously grabbed the young boy into a bear hug and apologised to Jamie. Recognising the tender embrace and look in the prisoner's eyes, Jamie knew he was the boy's father. His mind wandered to his own dad and the privilege of having him around in his childhood. Prison was robbing that boy of time with his dad, while stealing the key proud moments from the man.

'Here you go, Junior,' he said. 'Tuck in and make sure you finish it.'

Jamie carefully placed the items onto the small table. The smell of the fresh burgers infused Junior's nose with excitement and, without a second's hesitation, he rewarded his taste buds with a huge bite. The grin on his face was undeniable and Jamie realised that small pleasures made a massive difference when you were locked up.

'Aren't you eating anything?' asked Junior.

'No, do your thing, bro,' replied Jamie.

'Are you sure? Because you know how I am with food.'

'I know!' Jamie laughed. 'That's why I bought you two.'

'I miss my mum's cooking so much,' continued Junior. 'I just wished, when she visited last time, they would let her bring me some fried rice and some plantain.'

They both laughed. Junior was well into the second burger now.

'So, how is your boxing going?'

Jamie sighed, his facial expression defeated at the mention of boxing.

'It's not going how I expected, to be honest mate,' he replied. 'I'm not feeling in shape and as sharp as I use to be. Finding time to train and focus is much harder due to work.'

'You know how the saying goes,' said Junior. 'We have to go through struggle to get to our success. Just keep at it.'

'I will,' said Jamie. 'I have a big fight next week. Hopefully, when I win that, I will be back on track again.'

The burgers Jamie had bought for Junior were now gone. He'd wasted no time in eating them.

'Guess what?' Junior asked, sipping his Fanta.

'What?'

'Mo and Runner are both in this prison.'

'Seriously?' Jamie looked worried. 'Like, have they bothered you?'

'Yes, ever since they were transferred here things have not been easy. Seeing them every day in the wing just reminds me why I'm here and who put me in here. I even got into some madness because of them. Some guys thought I was part of that NN1 rubbish.'

'Mate,' replied Jamie, shaking his head, 'you are a stronger man than me. I don't know how you are coping.'

'It's all over with now, anyway,' said Junior. 'I'm just keeping a low profile and doing what I need to do, no more no less.'

The prison officers were walking around and looking at every interaction with a prisoner to make sure no one was passing on anything illegal. Their presence was very intimidating. Jamie looked at the large, white clock that was placed in the centre of the hall, right by the canteen.

'It's almost time for me to go,' he said. 'Before I do, I wanted to tell you about what is going on between Samuel and Jason.'

Junior had a worried look on his face. He was trying to anticipate what Jamie was about to tell him.

'They have been falling out ever since your trial,' explained Jamie. 'A few months ago, shit got serious, mate. They had this big fight outside the youth club. They haven't spoken to each other since.'

Junior was not entirely shocked by the news; he knew something was up with Jason, especially since he had not seen him during his trial. Plus, Jason had not made any attempts to contact him during the time he'd been in prison.

'Do you know why they had the fight?' he asked.

'Not entirely sure, mate. Samuel has just been pissed off with him for not being there to help with your campaign.'

Junior sighed. Resting his head in his hand, he was thinking about what to say to try and make the situation better.

'Jamie, you have always been the middle man from when we were young. Any little arguments, you would fix it. Nothing has changed except the seriousness of the issue and our age. Try and make peace between them both.'

In that moment, a deep voice shouted.

'Time is up. Prisoners stand up and wait on the orange sign on the floor behind you.'

Junior stood up and shook Jamie's hand.

'Remember what I said,' he said. 'Oh, and when you see Jason, tell him to get in touch with me. Give him my prison details.'

'Will do, mate,' replied Jamie. 'Take it easy, bro.'

The two parted ways. The visitors were made to wait as the prison officers escorted all the prisoners back to their wing. Eventually, they were escorted out of the building.

Eyes glazed, Jamie sat on the train, thinking back on his visit with Junior. He realised that, as much as he was disappointed with the way things were happening in his own life, at least he had his freedom. In comparison to Junior, he had nothing to complain about; the trip had definitely changed his perspective. Zoning out to the consistent rhythm of the train, Jamie's thoughts delved into various aspects of his life. He was determined to put in the effort in all areas: finances, relationships, aspirations. There were opportunities to improve, especially with his upcoming fight. He knew he needed to get his head in the game. It was his birthday; a perfect time to start afresh.

Once home, there was little time to relax; he had a shift that evening. Not the greatest way to celebrate, but needs must. He wanted to hang with Samuel and Jason, but they were still in conflict and wanted to individually spend time with him. Refusing to allow their issues to cloud his day, Jamie rejected both offers. Instead, he went over to Emma's house after work; he just wanted to be with her.

He was not expecting the fanfare that greeted him – a beautifully cooked meal, birthday banners with his name on, balloons, candles and music. It was perfect. He was overwhelmed by the effort Emma had put in to make his day special. He pulled Emma close, hugged her tightly and kissed her passionately. Everything was perfect.

Aimless footsteps clonked along the Hoxton pavements; it was a cold, winter Saturday and Jason had nothing to do. He pulled his jacket around his neck as the bitter breeze nipped the back of his head. Although he was staying at a new hostel, it was still boring, looking at the same four walls over and over again. He wanted his own place, but the council waiting list could take forever. Single male, no dependants and no real reason to leave home, his priority ranking was very low. All he could do was wait.

Fresh air was necessary and, as he was closer to his old neighbourhood, he felt comfortable walking the streets. The familiar streets caused him to reflect on old times and he began thinking about his mum. He missed her dreadfully, but the thought of his dad had prevented him from making contact. Checking the time, Jason reckoned his mum would be at her favourite salon getting primped. His mum was a stickler for routine and, unless something drastic had changed, she would keep her schedule. It would be quite a walk, but Jason's urge to see his mum outweighed the 40-minute journey.

As he approached the corner, he hoped she would be there; his legs were tired and he didn't want it to be a waste. Expectantly, he peered through the window, scanning the leather chairs, looking through the steam. She was there. He almost missed her; she looked so different. Chubbiness had dissolved, leaving behind a slim and slender shape, while her hair had changed from the long, luscious locks to a shorter, stylish cut with a sweeping side fringe. The drastic change threw him; he almost didn't go in. Courage redirected his feet and he walked in anxiously, his huge frame blocking out all the natural light as he entered.

'Susan, look who it is!' cried out one of the hairdressers. The woman had the name tag 'Pinkie'. This was obviously referring to her love for the colour pink, as shown in her shocking pink hair and various pink accessories.

Looking up from her magazine, Mrs Burrell's eyes widened in tremendous surprise as she recognised her only son. She got up so quickly her bag flew across the room and her magazine dropped. Jaw open, she rushed to embrace her son, half expecting him not to be real.

'Oh, Jason...' she repeated as her arms tightened around him.

A year had passed since she had last seen Jason and many nights had passed with sleep rejecting her pleas; worrying, frantic about where he was, who he was with, how he was surviving. Her marriage had suffered as arguments centred on their son and his behaviour.

Clutching on to her baby, she wanted to live in this moment. However, Jason noticed the other customers' bewildered expressions and asked his mum to step outside.

'It's cold outside,' Pinkie exclaimed, offering them the back room instead. They accepted and both entered. Jason closed the door behind them.

'Jason, it is so good to see you,' his mum whispered, tears welling up in her eyes. 'I have missed you.'

'I have missed you too, Mum.'

'So, what have you been doing with yourself this whole time?' Mrs Burrell asked. 'You've had me worried. I don't go a day without thinking about you.'

'I'm sorry that you had to worry, Mum,' replied Jason. 'But it reached a point that I had to make my own decisions.'

'You should have just come back home, I'm sure we would have worked something out with your dad.' Jason's mum could not help but look at him and hold him as if he was still a toddler.

'I was angry at the time,' he replied. 'And going back home was not an option for me, to be honest.'

The room they were in was small and cramped; Jason had to bend his head so as not to hit his head on the low ceiling. They decided to leave the shop to get something to eat.

They walked along an affluent street in Angel Islington looking for a small café. They eventually found one that was half empty. It was on the side of the main road, red bricked walls inside and out. Jason was glad to be in his mother's company again; he had missed their conversations. He ordered a hot chocolate with a muffin.

'I see you still love hot chocolate, sweetheart,' said his mum.

'Yes, I do,' he laughed. 'I don't understand how you lot drink coffee. It's so nasty.'

'I guess I'm just used to it.'

'So, how are things at the restaurant?' Jason asked.

'Business is going really well,' replied his mum. 'Your father and I are thinking of opening another restaurant in West London. Imagine Burrell's Kitchen all over London one day. We have been looking at different locations. It will be a good fit if we can find the right location.'

'That sounds good, Mum. I hope it all works out for you.'

'I am more worried about you,' she replied. 'Some time ago, money went missing from the house. There was no sign of a break-in and the culprit knew exactly where the money was kept. You wouldn't happen to know anything about that? Would you, Jason?'

Jason had never liked lying to his mum, but admitting that he took the money would reveal that he was not coping with the pressures of trying to make it on his own. Jason put his head down and was unable to look directly at her.

'Yes, Mum, it was me.'

She shook her head in disappointment.

'Jason, why would you do that? If you needed money you should have just asked.'

'I could not look like a failure in front of Dad,' he replied. 'Plus, I was in a really bad place that time and I needed the money.'

Jason's voice was sincere and apologetic. His mum grabbed his hands and gave him another hug.

'I am so sorry, Mum.'

'It's okay,' replied his mum. 'You need to come home. It is your father who you should be apologising to.'

Jason was annoyed by the mention of an apology to the man who had kicked him out of the family house.

'No, I will not come home,' he said. 'Not until I prove him wrong.'

Hours passed, hot chocolate was replenished and the conversation flourished. It was evident they had both missed their relationship and there was much to say. His mum's constant attempts to persuade him to move back home fell on deaf ears and Jason quickly changed the subject.

Focusing on his endeavours, he walked his mum through the past twelve months, choking up as he recalled the difficulties he had faced and the loneliness he'd felt. Soaked in the emotional upheaval of her son's life, there were moments when Susan was brought to tears as she realised what he had been through; it pained her that he had not made contact sooner, but was overjoyed that he was back in her life.

The subject of Junior arose and Jason's eyes fell to the floor; he was ashamed that he had nothing to report. Having been so self-centred, he had ignored his friend's plight.

Time was slipping away and Jason's mum had to get her hair done. As they left the café, she paused at a cash machine and withdrew £200 and gave it to him. Jason hugged her and they parted ways.

With cash in his pocket, Jason walked with a spring in his step, his hands rubbing against the Queen's head in delight. En route to his hostel, the betting shop screamed his name in seductive tones and he entered, knowing his luck was in. Roulette swallowed his £100 whole and burped out absolutely nothing. Lost. Undeterred, he reloaded the machine, feeding his greed. Another £90 in.

Frustration set in, but Jason was desperate. His last £10 locked on to his favourite numbers – 2, 3, 6, 7, the birthdays of his and his three closest friends. Unable to look, his eyes connected with the dim light above in the hope that his numbers would land. The roulette machine, however, had no favourite numbers. For Jason, this was his last hope.

He spread his bets, £2 on each number and £2 on zero. The same ritual adhered to again, he hit the button then turned away as the animation on the screen began to spin the ball. He heard as it landed and spun around to see it on 7. Thumping the air in triumph, he was happy he hadn't lost all the money. Being £72 up, he contemplated on whether to risk it all. Commonsense finally clicking in, he cashed out. He had won on Junior's birthday; he took it as a sign. He needed to talk to him.

Meanwhile, only a few minutes away down the street, Samuel was being dropped home by his driving instructor. Now a fully-fledged driver, he had passed his test with only two minors. He was ecstatic! Thanking his driving instructor, he bounded out the car and called Jamie. Preparing for his next fight, Jamie only had a few moments to spare, but he was as excited as Samuel about the news.

Bursting into the house, Samuel was chanting and singing at the top of his lungs, shouting out that he had passed. His younger cousin joined in, adjusting the words to the song.

'Our new cab driver has passed, he has passed his test. YES, he has passed his test!'

Samuel stopped, gave his cousin a dirty look and laughed with him as he put him in a headlock.

'Sing that again, and see what I do to you.'

'Samuel, come here please,' his aunt called from the living room. Samuel went into the bedroom to put his certificate in his folder. He then went straight down to the living room to talk to his aunt. Mrs Brown was taking out her hair from the twists.

'Congratulations on passing your test,' she said. 'We need another driver in the house!'

'Thanks, Aunty,' replied Samuel. 'I tried my best. Hopefully I can get a car soon.'

'Humph,' she murmured loudly. 'Car this, car that, you need to focus on more important things. What is the progress with your application for next year? You see, if you didn't defer, we would be talking about you going into your final year.'

'Aunty, please, we have talked about this,' said Samuel. 'I do not regret the choice I made. Uni is not going anywhere, but I need to do this now. Look at all the awareness we have achieved for Junior while I have been here. To answer your question, I have applied and I have retained my place for September. So you have nothing to worry about.'

'Good,' replied his aunt. 'I just hope you know what you are doing.'

The following day was the day of the big public meeting which Samuel and Malachi had organised. Samuel woke up in good spirits. After a quick breakfast, he made his way to the Elevate youth project for some last-minute preparation for the meeting later on that evening.

Samuel had all the access and resources he needed because he was now working for the youth project on a temporary contract. When Samuel had decided he would defer university for a year, Malachi was able to get him some voluntary and paid work at the youth project.

Samuel enjoyed his new role at the youth project; he was getting valuable experience as a mentor for the younger children around the area. His focus was to enlighten them about the dangers of peer pressure. He was a natural orator; he was very convincing when he spoke and got people's attention when he did.

That evening, the stage was set. Samuel was hoping people would turn up, despite the wet and windy weather that had been the theme for the last few days. The chairs in the local community hall were neatly arranged in rows, but empty. However, while Samuel got himself together, the place began filling up and, by 7pm, the hall was full. All the seats were occupied, causing a small crowd of people to stand at the back.

Colourful T-shirts in support of Junior were decorated across the hall. Samuel picked out Jamie amongst the crowd. Junior's mum and dad sat in the reserved section in the front row, receiving a warm welcome from all around them. They were overwhelmed by the support the community was giving to their son.

Samuel took to the stage to address the crowd; he was smartly dressed in a shirt with a jumper over it and some denim jeans. Since his recent appointment and responsibilities with the youth project, Samuel had taken it upon himself to change the way he dressed, often putting away his beloved Nike Air Force Ones for boat shoes. It was all part of the new attitude Samuel had been developing under the guidance of Malachi, who was still a mentor for him, Jamie and Junior.

'First and foremost,' he began, 'I would like to thank everyone for taking the time to come out today. I am sure it would have been easier to stay at home in the warmth, but you decided to come here and show support for the cause. Thank you all very much.'

The crowd clapped for Samuel.

'Just before I get into it,' he continued, 'just some important information. There are four fire exits, two in front here, one on my left, another is behind the stage here on the right. The other two are at the back. Toilets are also at the back.'

People looked around as he was talking, taking note of the exits.

'As you are all aware by now, this is a public meeting to promote our agenda against joint enterprise and to raise awareness of Junior's case, who is serving a life sentence of a minimum of fifteen years based on that notion of joint enterprise for something he did not do. Those that know Junior know that what he has had to go through is not right. There are more than two hundred young people who are in a similar situation because of joint enterprise. Some of the things we want to achieve as a result of this meeting are some ideas on how we can move forward, how to get our message across to the people who can make a change.

'In regards to Junior's case, we are still going through the appeal stage. What we want to do is to have a bigger push for new witnesses. Spurious witness testimonies and half-truths put Junior in prison. We need to find someone who saw the whole incident and can back up Junior's story. As you can all see, we have posters and thousands of flyers to distribute in an appeal for witnesses.

'I will stop there and hand over to Malachi, who will chair the meeting. Thank you all for being here again.' The crowd were simultaneous in their applause for Samuel, who handed the microphone over to Malachi.

Two hours later, the meeting had come to a close. It had been very successful. The aims of the meeting had been accomplished, as now they had set goals on how to proceed with the campaigns. Many people took flyers appealing for witnesses to help exonerate Junior.

Victoria, Junior's lawyer, made a short appearance to update them on Junior's appeal case. She was now heavily pregnant and was expecting her baby in a month's time. She told them that they were still waiting to hear whether they had enough information to progress to the next stage of the appeal process, which would be to get a court hearing for the appeal.

Junior's mum and dad came over to thank Samuel and Malachi for all their hard work in trying to help Junior. Mrs Okoli was in a state and looked broken; the pain of not having her son at home could be seen in the stress lines on her face. Events like this gave her hope and something to hang on to. The support received from so many people was something she had never expected.

As the crowds departed, Samuel, Malachi and Jamie began clearing up the hall. They only had thirty minutes before they had to return the keys.

'Samuel, that was a great event,' said Jamie. 'You've done really well, mate.'

'Thanks, man,' Samuel replied. 'It wasn't easy, but we got there in the end. So, are you ready for your fight tomorrow?'

'I think so. My preparation has not been what it used to be. We'll see.'

'You don't sound too confident,' Samuel stated.

'I am... where should I put these chairs?' said Jamie.

'Just over there by the door,' Samuel replied.

'Jason said he is coming to the fight tomorrow,' added Jamie.

Samuel's face changed at the mention of Jason's name. They hadn't seen each other since the fight a few months previously and Jamie was worried that something would happen when they next met up.

'Look, I have nothing to say about Jason,' said Samuel. 'Let him do what he needs to do and I will do the same.'

Malachi overheard the conversation as he came from behind the stage where he was putting the tables away.

'Samuel, maybe it is time you make peace with Jason,' he said. 'This situation is not healthy.'

'To be honest, I have nothing to say to him,' repeated Samuel. 'Personally, I do not think I have done anything wrong. He knows where to find me when he is ready to apologise.'

The three continued to clean up the hall and were able to make the 11pm deadline to hand the keys over.

York Hall in Bethnal Green was bursting with dramatic energy and great expectation; from all over London, boxing fans had travelled to watch the big fight. Full to the brim, the hall was ablaze with people eager for it to begin. Amongst the sea of faces, Samuel and Emma sat ringside, chatting about Jamie's demeanour.

Emma had noticed that he was not as confident today; despite his unbeaten record, she hoped the day would bring back his joy and passion for the sport with a tremendous win. Samuel was also anxious for Jamie to win; his job had sucked out his soul and he was a shadow of the man he was. Winning would bring back the Jamie he knew – tough, courageous and ambitious with one hell of an uppercut.

Warming up in the ring, Jamie's thoughts were all over the place. Sizing up his opponent, his legs felt heavy beneath him, his stamina nowhere near his regular standard. The first round started.

Jamie was an experienced boxer, his talents in the ring were noted by all, yet his movements were not as swift or his reactions as quick. His opponent had studied Jamie's fighting techniques and was eager to prove himself to the opposing crowd; jabbing and throwing combinations of deadly blows, he quickly gained the upper hand.

Hands over his face, Jamie was playing defence, struggling to match the blows of his opponent. This was an unusual space for him; he was unfamiliar with the taste of blood in his mouth, the dizziness and slow reactions. Blow after blow came and Jamie was faltering fast. Shouting support at the top of his lungs, Samuel was on his feet. He had seen all of Jamie's fights and never seen him in this position so early on.

He turned to speak to Emma and saw Jason, who had just entered the hall. Frost cemented the air between them as they made eye contact. Emma attempted to cut the awkwardness; she made a point of acknowledging Jason and greeting him. Cutting his eye, Samuel returned his attention to the fight while Jason found another seat.

The fight was not going well for Jamie; with one round left, his anatomy was in agony from the beating he had endured. Legs weak, body fatigued, lungs gasping for air; he tried to break through the pain, forcing himself to fight back, gaining strength from the shouts he heard surrounding him. It was too late. The bell signalled defeat and his opponent jumped in the air, certain of victory.

Inside, Jamie's heart crumbled. He could not bring himself to make eye contact with his trainer, as the look of disappointment would destroy him. The official results confirmed his worst fear; he had lost. Graciously congratulating his nemesis, he darted into the changing rooms. As he drenched himself with regret in the shower, his mind was plagued with distressing thoughts. *You're a loser, Jamie. Give it up. You haven't got it in you. So much for making Dad proud.*

He cursed himself, dawdling before finally exiting the changing rooms. Emma threw her arms around him, hugging him tightly.

'Aww babe, don't worry. You're still a champion to me,' she said, planting a kiss on his cheek. Jamie did not react; his face blank and expressionless.

'Unlucky, Jamie,' said Samuel. 'Maybe next time.'

Shrugging his shoulders in ambivalence, Jamie sighed, his eyes planted on the floor.

'I doubt there will be a next time to be honest, mate,' he replied despondently.

'Seriously?' Jason asked.

'Yeah, to be honest I don't really wanna talk about it. I'm not in the mood. I'm going to rest at Emma's. You two have your own issues and I can't deal with your tensions. Later.'

Grabbing his gym bag and tossing it onto his shoulder, Jamie and Emma walked off together. Left alone, Samuel and Jason couldn't bear to look at each other. Without saying anything, they both walked off in opposite directions.

Routine set in and Samuel continued working at the youth project with Malachi. Everyone was doing their own thing and so he delved into his tasks, too. This particular evening had been extremely draining and Samuel couldn't wait to get home and rest. Reaching home, he barely had the strength to take off his coat. Kicking off his trainers and dashing his bag in the hallway, he clambered upstairs.

His cousin, Andre, had been waiting for him to get back, anxious to beat him at his favourite PlayStation game – Pro Evolution Soccer. Samuel was knackered, but he couldn't turn down a challenge from Andre, especially when he was goading him on. His fatigue meant he couldn't concentrate and he repeatedly lost matches, much to the joy and enjoyment of Andre. Frustrations mounted as they started to play their sixth game. From downstairs, Samuel heard his aunt calling him. *Saved by the bell*, he thought to himself.

'You have been practising non-stop,' he said to Andre. 'You are lucky, because I don't play as much anymore.'

'Yeah, yeah,' replied Andre. 'Excuses, excuses.'

Andre laughed at Samuel as he walked out of the room. He heard his Aunt Felicity calling him again and rushed down into the living room. His aunt was surrounded by books; she was marking. As Samuel entered she paused, putting her pen down, shuffling around on the sofa.

'Yes, Aunty? You called me.'

'Have a seat, Samuel.'

Deep inside, Samuel sighed, nervous as to what this was about. He was already slightly frustrated and knackered; he hoped it wouldn't take long. His bed was calling him. Sitting upright, a serious expression on her face, his aunt looked directly at Samuel.

'Samuel, you know how close I was with your mother,' she began. 'Losing the only sister I had was the most painful thing I have had to go through.' Samuel became subdued, thinking about his mum always made him upset. His aunt continued. 'One thing we both learnt growing up was the importance of family. We have all made mistakes, I have, your mum too. The reason I am telling you all this is because you need to have a relationship with your dad again.'

Flaring up with anger at the mention of his father, Samuel's face screwed into a fierce expression.

'Samuel, do not give me that look,' said his aunt. 'You better respect yourself and respect me when I am talking to you.' Her authoritative tone shook Samuel and his face softened.

'Your dad has been trying to reach out to you for years,' she continued. 'He is genuinely concerned about you and wants to be part of your life. He calls me now and again to find out what you are up to. It should not be like that. All I am saying is you should just talk to him. Find out what he wants to say; from there, you can make your own mind up on whatever he tells you.'

Samuel kept quiet, not knowing what to say.

'This is not what your mum would have wanted,' said Felicity. 'She would want peace within the family. Please, Samuel,' she begged.

Samuel looked up at his aunt and saw the passion in her face. He immediately found his words.

'Okay, I will arrange to meet him and speak to him,' he replied reluctantly.

'That is really good to hear. I am sorry I shouted at you earlier.'

'It's okay,' said Samuel. 'I guess I needed to hear it like that.'

Samuel then said goodnight to his aunt and went up to his room. Although still tired, he was not able to sleep. He had deep feelings of resentment towards his father and could not imagine starting a relationship with him. Things had changed since his mum had passed away and it would take a lot of effort to change his opinion of his dad.

As he reflected, his aunt was downstairs on the phone to his dad giving him the good news that Samuel had agreed to meet him. This news meant a lot to his father, who was overjoyed that he had an opportunity to rebuild his relationship with his son. They made arrangements for the meeting to take place.

Two sunrises later, Samuel was dragging his feet along the emotive route to his old house. Only a ten minute walk from his Aunt's house. His footsteps set a pace of days passed, each step fuelled with memories of his former life. With grave difficulty and part reluctance, he trod; he was aware that, in a few short minutes, he would be face to face with his father. Clouded by conflicting thoughts, he wondered what they would discuss; it had been a long time since he'd had a conversation with his dad on amicable terms.

He felt cheated; his aunt had roped him into this. He would rather be anywhere else than outside Number 35, the yellow bricked bungalow he used to call home. He inhaled history, scanning over the house with familiar eyes. Like a long-lost friend, it had changed somewhat – new windows, fresh paint, yet so much was the same.

Hesitating by the gate, he shuffled his feet, heart pumping. Was it too late to turn back? He sighed deeply. Long minutes of awkwardness morphed into courage as he paced confidently to the door and banged it twice, then stepped back slightly.

'I'm coming,' a voice called from inside the house.

Inside, Mr Wise was also anxious; although he had wanted this moment desperately for years, he was unsure how to react now the time had finally arrived. Sweaty palms, nervous stomach meshed with an unconfident expression, he walked slowly into the hallway.

Opening the front door, the silence magnified as they examined each other. His son resembled him; he could see himself in the strapping lad that stood awkwardly in front of him. Greetings were extinct; not even a handshake between them. His dad broke the silence.

'Come in, son.'

Brushing past his dad, Samuel stepped into the hallway and headed straight to the living room. Although the layout was the same, the interior decor was miles apart from what he remembered. Clean lines, leather furniture, cream walls; there was an emptiness to it, hollow and cold. The colours of family life had disappeared; gone were the lilac palette his mum had loved. This was his dad's bachelor pad.

Slightly disgusted, Samuel took a seat. *At least the pictures made the cut*, he thought as he nostalgically recollected the stories hidden in each frame. His eyes found the photographs of his mother and he choked, suddenly overcome with emotion. Hiding his tears, he looked up as his dad entered the room, orange juice in hand.

'Here you go, son.'

'Thank you.'

His dad sat in the armchair opposite him; the air was still tense and Samuel was increasingly uneasy. His aunt's words echoed in his head and he decided he had to at least try to get through this.

'So, how have things been with you?' Mr Wise asked.

'I have been fine,' Samuel replied. 'Just working and trying to live my life right.' His voice was vacant, devoid of depth.

'That is good to hear,' said his dad. 'I try to keep up to date with what you have been doing for Junior's case. How are things going on that front?'

Samuel looked irritated and could no longer hide his frustrations. He slammed the glass of orange juice on the side table next to him.

'Look! Can we just bypass the small talk and get on with what it is you have to say to me? To be honest, I am not here to talk about my life. I am only here because Aunty Felicity persuaded me to come here.'

Surprised by the outburst, his dad realised he was on edge. Not willing to ruin the opportunity, Mr Wise humbled himself.

'Okay, fine, we don't have to do the small talk, as you put it, son. The reason I have been trying to reach out to you is because I want us to be a family again. It hurts me knowing that our family is so broken. I have been very successful with my business, but none of that means anything to me knowing that my family is not how I want it to be.'

'Family?' replied Samuel. 'Hah! Like you know anything about that. What did you get... a revelation? Because last time I checked, it was your fault we all ended up like this. All I remember of you is being aggressive to mum. Your actions, your words, your inability to be a good man pushed her to the edge. She couldn't take it anymore. That night you screamed at her till she left. Your words pushed her out the door, into the path of that oncoming car! You might as well have killed her yourself. She died running away from you.'

Samuel could barely catch his breath as he tried to calm himself down. He could not stop the tears from rolling down his face. This was the first time he had confronted his father directly about the death of his mum. The pent-up anger and animosity could be felt in every word.

'Samuel, please try and calm down so we can talk,' said his father.

'This *is* me talking!' shouted Samuel. 'Isn't that what you wanted?'

'Look, there is more to what happened between your mum and I...'

'Like what?'

Mr Wise stood still, contemplating what to say to Samuel. The awkward silence continued as Samuel's frustrations began to grow again.

'You see what I am saying?' he shouted. 'You have no valid point. You said you wanted to talk and you stand there in silence. What more of the story should I know, then? You see, just as I thought, nothing. This was a big waste of my time.'

Anger erupted in Samuel's belly and he stood up, inflamed with emotion. Veins popping out of his neck, hand clenched, the sight of his father infuriated him. He couldn't bear to look at him for one more second. The arguments between them resonated with his memories of childhood and he felt trapped in that space. He shouldn't have come.

Enraged, he stormed out of the house, refusing to turn back to his dad's pleads. Boiling, he stomped home, disappointed at himself for not controlling his emotions, but more angry over the fact that his dad had refused to open up. Flinging open the front door, the storm on his face was undeniable.

'Samuel, what happened?' asked his aunt.

'I told you! I told you that it would be a waste of time!' he shouted. 'ARGH! I went there and he tried to come at me with all that small talk bullshit...'

Samuel's aunt interrupted him in mid-flow.

'Samuel,' she replied sharply. 'I know you are upset, but control yourself when you are speaking to me.'

'I am sorry, Aunty.'

Samuel knew he'd messed up and was very apologetic about his choice of words. He normally never used language like that around his aunt, but on this occasion the anger and frustration inside him took over.

'Samuel, continue with what you were saying, please.'

'I opened up to him,' Samuel replied. 'I told him how I felt. I told him I blamed him for my mum's death. He told me there was more to the story, but when I asked him to tell me he stood there in silence. I gave him another opportunity to tell me but he didn't, so I left.'

'I had a feeling he would not be able to tell you,' said Felicity. 'Your dad has always been soft.'

'You know what it is? Tell me what, Aunty. It seems like everyone knows something that I don't.'

'Samuel, it is not my place to say,' she replied. 'I am sorry, but it is something you and your father need to talk about.'

With that, the conversation ended. Samuel retreated to his room, still full of anger that secrets were being kept from him, not just by his dad, but also his aunt.

A feeling of anxiety filled the room; amidst the chatter and laughter there was great expectation. The living room at Junior's house was full with family members, as well as Samuel and Jamie. Today was the day; the day they had prayed about, campaigned for, sweated, protested and fought about. The decision of the appeal was due and they were gathered together to receive it as a unit.

Biding their time, waiting for the phone call, Samuel and Jamie were entertaining Junior's siblings. His mother was acting as the hostess, making sure everyone was topped up with drinks and snacks. As she catered to her guests, the door knocked; expecting it to be one of Junior's friends, she half opened the door before realising it was Victoria. This was completely unexpected; especially as she was almost due to give birth. Everyone assumed she would just call.

As Victoria waddled into the living room, Samuel sprang up to offer her his seat. She graciously accepted, sitting down with a tired sigh. After accepting a drink and making herself comfortable, she addressed everyone.

'It has been a long few months, and we have worked extremely hard. I know that many people in this room have made sacrifices to help Junior's case. I, too, have put my heart and soul into the process, desperate for good news.'

Eager faces around her, Victoria's face dropped.

'I wish I had better news, but I am sorry to say that Junior's appeal has been rejected.'

Silence. Confused looks. Disbelief. More silence. Victoria looked to Junior's mother to see her reaction. Tearing her hair out in grief, Mrs Okoli's anguished shouts echoed throughout the house. Everyone felt her despair. Falling to her knees, she raised her eyes to the ceiling.

'God, please, why have you forsaken us?' she shouted. 'You know Junior is innocent.'

She continued to cry to the heavens. Samuel and Jamie were both in shock; they believed that, after all they had been through, this would be the break that would help get Junior's conviction quashed.

'So what happened exactly?' Samuel asked Victoria.

'The panel that make the decision came back and said there was not enough grounds to take it to the next stage of an appeal,' she replied. 'This would have been our opportunity to present our appeal to a Judge.'

Samuel had both hands over his face, trying to digest the news.

'So, is there anything we can do now?'

'Nothing,' said Victoria, 'unless there is conclusive evidence which can help add more weight to another appeal process. I am so sorry it has come to this.'

'This is just not right,' exclaimed Jamie. 'Junior does not deserve to spend fifteen years in prison.'

'Does Junior know that his appeal has been rejected?' asked Samuel.

'No, not yet,' replied Victoria. 'I will be going to tell him in person when I leave here.'

'Hearing more bad news will just tear him up inside,' Samuel said.

Victoria then made her excuses and headed to the prison to break the bad news to Junior. Samuel and Jamie stayed for a while, trying to console Junior's mum. They could not understand how this had all happened. Samuel felt defeated; all his hard work over the last few months, trying to make sure that something positive would come from the appeal, all seemed for nothing. Samuel no longer knew what he could do to help Junior.

CHAPTER NINE

Footsteps signalled the end of a depressing conversation, cut short by disappointment. Disconnected from the bearer of bad news, Junior's heart was resting in his shoes. Broken by words. Again. Stick and stones might break his bones, but these words were destroying him.

There was no correct way to deliver the message. The sentences tormented him; whispering evil 'I told you so' taunts.

Without looking back, he exited the visiting room, leaving Victoria dumbfounded; not even a goodbye between them. As his feet pounded the cement, his brokenness converted into rage; eyes blood red, throat dry, face scrunched. He ignored familiar faces, his shoulders bearing the burden. This was his home now. It was final. He would never escape the misery of this undeserved cage; trapped with these blasted animals for eternity.

The walk to his cell was dismal; his heart clouded by the gloom of reality. He didn't belong here. *Let me out! Let me out!* His actions screamed words his mouth couldn't speak as his fists pulverised the concrete walls. Pain stabbed his hands, reminding him he was alive and he continued to self-harm. Attacking the wall with fierce determination, he painted it with the blood from his knuckles, the ink of his soul. Fists in a flurry, mind in a cage, he barely acknowledged the prison guard who rushed to interrupt his ferocious attack.

Blood boiling, temperature sky-rocketing, there was no peace for Junior. Exhausted, his knees crumbled, arguing with the Creator, debating with the King of Kings, shouting at God in frustration.

'Why me? Why have you forsaken me?'

Junior's Christian faith was tested. His years of Sunday attendances at Church, hearing testimonies, believing in an all-powerful God who looked after His people, who answered prayers, had led to this moment. He remembered Paul and Silas in Acts who had been falsely imprisoned, who had prayed and God had freed them. Why, then, had God faltered at the first hurdle? Why had *his* prayers not been answered? Junior struggled to understand; struggled to sleep. Sleep was his only escape from the constant nightmare he was living.

Distance became the norm; daily hibernation. Junior hid from social interaction, fled from meaningless small talk, removed himself from situations he couldn't deal with. Not even Alim could get through the intense security system Junior had placed around himself. He didn't want to be disturbed; his barriers were up.

Alim persisted in trying to draw Junior out of his shell, but Junior would not relent. Junior politely told Alim, as well as everyone else that knocked on the door of his life, that he needed time and space to process the next fifteen years of his life. The truth made him quiver; disbelief set in and Junior retreated to his haven in silence.

This continued day after day. Junior became a shadow of his former self, barely participating in life. His emotions varied, mood swings frequent, especially when he saw Mo and Runner. Their faces represented prison, death, punishment. They were the cause of his suffering, yet they walked around freely, creating havoc. He wanted to smash their smug faces into the doors they'd locked him in, but knew it was a recipe for chaos. Since the day he had confronted them, they had left him out of the gang hype and, with his future set, he had no desire to re-engage.

All Junior knew was his appeal had been rejected; he hadn't bothered to finish the conversation with Victoria and hear any more details. The not knowing plagued him, however, until he found himself at the phone, dialling her number. Apologising for his behaviour, he queried what had happened. Victoria was glad he had got in contact, especially after his reaction at her last visit.

She explained to him that, despite their best efforts, they did not have a strong enough reason or case to make an appeal as there was no new evidence. Allowing himself to acknowledge the truth, Junior accepted that this was the outcome. Victoria was very patient and understanding throughout; she said she was very disappointed at the result herself. She empathised with his position and wished she had better news to deliver; but she had done all she could, often spending nights going over paperwork on a pro-bono basis.

After the conversation, Junior began to think more clearly and his mind wandered back to his previous hopeful position. This was the time he would spend scribbling his thoughts in his journal. He reached for it, flicking to the last few entries. Reading his words was difficult; the page was alive with his dreams, detailing what he would do when finally released from prison. The optimism glowed on every line and Junior vividly recalled his intentions and hopes. Those pages became wet and blurry with the tears that flowed from Junior's cheeks; he cried silently as each page was a vision of his freedom drifting further away into the distance.

He reached the next blank page and marked it open with his pen resting in the centrefold. Contemplative, he sat solemnly, seeking inspiration for another entry. Minutes passed and the page lay empty; Junior was unable to muster any words. He lay in bed, trying to pray, yet he felt he had exhausted all words. Plus, it felt like a one-sided conversation; up till now, he had received no response. After a while, he fell asleep.

Visiting hour. The hall was bursting with outsiders; a welcome change from the drab melancholic grey. Dressed in rainbow colours, their clothes and smiles brightened up the bland room. Amongst the crowd, Malachi and Samuel sat waiting for Junior. This was the first visit Junior had agreed to since learning of his appeal and they were anxious to see how he was coping. It had been a surprise to them when he had accepted their visit; they had all noticed a decline in the amount of contact they had with Junior.

Samuel saw him first, strolling towards them in his uniform grey tracksuit. His eyes were vacant, mustering up a smile for his friends, although his heart was heavy. Malachi and Samuel rose to greet him; minimal hugs and handshakes.

'How are you feeling, Junior?' Malachi asked.

'I am good,' Junior said unconvincingly. 'Just maintaining. That's all I can do in this place.' His eyes were downcast.

'That appeal rejection was a blow to us all,' said Samuel. 'I can't even begin to imagine what you must be going through, bro.'

'It is what it is,' replied Junior. 'I have to live and deal with it.'

'If you only knew how many people were supporting your campaigning,' said Samuel. 'The amount of work we have done to raise awareness. Malachi, tell him.'

'Samuel is right,' replied Malachi. 'The support we have generated is immense. Even though the appeal was rejected, our main body of work has not relied on the outcome of the appeal. We are focusing our energy on finding new evidence to back up your claim and putting that stupid joint enterprise notion under the microscope.'

The words were floating around Junior's ears; his attention was elsewhere. Although he appreciated their support, he felt irritated and uneasy. How could they possibly understand how he was feeling? He looked at the time.

'To be honest with you, I appreciate everything you guys have done, but this is it. There is no point trying to bullshit ourselves.'

There was an uncomfortable silence between them all. Malachi looked over at the canteen area. He offered to buy Junior some snacks, but Junior refused. Malachi used that opportunity to break the silence.

'Junior, I know it has been a tough journey for you, but you need to keep the faith and have hope—'

Junior slammed his fist on the table.

'Please, don't mention faith and hope to me!' he hissed. 'Those fucking words have no meaning to me anymore! When I was young, I was told to always have faith and believe in God. That no matter what the situation, he will always help. Look at where I am now. My faith has got me nowhere. When you talk about hope, look at it this way. I had hope I would not be charged. I had hope I would get bail instead of remand. I had hope I would receive a not guilty verdict. All that hope means nothing. I had hope I would be out of here with this appeal, but no, I am still here!'

Samuel was in total agreement with his friend. He shook his head from side to side with both hands on his forehead.

'I understand where you are coming from, fam,' he said. 'If I was in your position, I am sure I would feel the same way.'

Junior sighed. 'The honest truth is that there is no more hope for me,' he replied. 'I am starting to come to terms with what happened and all this talk of hope will only put my mind in a bad place. Samuel, you just need to get on with your life, bro. Get back to uni and get that degree. Malachi, I appreciate your love and wisdom, but I cannot deal with all these visits. It will only make it harder for me to cope. I will just keep wondering what it would be like to be out there. So please, no more visitors' requests. When I am ready, I will reach out. We can keep in contact by writing letters.'

Samuel stared at him for a moment. 'Junior, you know me well enough, we are like brothers. Just know that I am here for you and I will not give up on you, no matter what you say.'

With that said and done, they concentrated on enjoying the rest of the visit. Slipping into their old ways, they momentarily forgot their surroundings and reverted back to banter and jokes. It had been a long time since Junior had heard himself laugh. He knew there were inmates who didn't get any visits and he truly appreciated their love and support.

Despite Junior's despondency, Samuel and Malachi's visit had had a major impact on him; they had broken through his defences and reached out to him. He now felt back in tune socially and understood that social interaction was important for survival. Making an effort to reconnect, Junior began talking to Sanchez and Alim again; he wasn't happy, but knew this change was for the better.

He attempted to be more sociable, but there were episodes when he would relapse into cave-man mode, drifting away into isolation and self-consumption. These times were temporary and his friends would allow him his space, knowing he would return when he was ready. Although he was surviving in prison, Junior felt like he was merely existing and real life was a myth. By separating himself from reminders of his former life, he began to cope with his long sentence.

At the phone, Junior dialled Ngozi. She had been bugging him to send her a visiting order for the past week and he had been ignoring her. Time to face the music. The phone rang out; no answer. Junior decided to try the number again. Just before it was about to go to the voice message again, she picked up.

'Hello? Junior, is that you?' she shouted in excitement.

'Yeah, it's me.'

'How have you been?'

'I have been good, just learning to move forward. How are you?'

'I am fine,' she replied. 'Just same old, work and uni life. It's not easy.'

'I am glad you are doing well, though,' said Junior. 'Keep it up.'

'I will, babe,' said Ngozi. 'I'm glad you called. I wanted to ask you about the visiting order. I really want to come and see you.'

There was a brief moment of silence on the line.

'Babe, are you still there?' said Ngozi.

'Yes, I am,' replied Junior. 'Ngozi, the main reason I called you is to tell you that we need to put an end to things. It just doesn't make any sense. I am going to be locked away for a long time. You need to move on.'

There was another moment of silence.

'What?' she whispered, deflated. She didn't not know what to say.

'Are you still there?' Junior asked.

'Yes, I am,' Ngozi replied quietly. 'I never ever thought you would be in here for so long. I believed and hoped that you would get off. I still do!'

'There goes that word again,' barked Junior. 'Hope. There is no hope or justice for me. This is it and nothing can be done to change that.' He paused, calming his voice. 'Look, I am sorry for shouting, but it is hard for me to accept all that is going on.'

Junior could now hear her sobs. She cried into the phone, knowing that their relationship was coming to an end.

'I just don't want you to give up,' she sobbed. 'But at the same time, I can understand why you feel like that.'

'Look,' said Junior, 'I do not have long left on the phone, but feel free to write me if you want. I promise I will reply. I truly hope you succeed in everything you want, Ngozi, even though most of the things we wanted to do were together. Even though we will not get that chance, make sure you stay focused and achieve it. Take care of yourself.'

'Bye, Junior,' she sniffed.

'Bye.'

The line went dead. Ngozi sat, dismayed; she loved Junior and didn't want this to be the end. How could she continue life knowing he was stuck in that dump? She had envisioned their celebrations when he walked out acquitted, but now she had nothing but the memories of their time together. Grieving inside, she looked at the picture of them both on her desk and sobbed.

Junior, meanwhile, stood there for a while, contemplating what he had just done. Deep down, he knew it was for the right reasons; he didn't want to hold her back. He loved her enough to let her go, even though his heart was broken. But he had to move on. The image of her face, constantly in his head, was all he had left; all the photographs he had destroyed.

He then suddenly picked up the phone and dialled his house number to speak to his family. Hiding his real emotions, he tried to stay positive and strong for his mum, knowing his pain would only increase her devastation. He urged his younger siblings to write to him as much as possible; he also checked they were behaving and not giving his parents any unnecessary grief. They promised they would write soon and they ended the call.

On the outside, liberated and free, Jason was hot-stepping to meet his mother. It was Saturday afternoon and he was hopeful his mum would be as generous as she had been on their last visit. He had already made a mental note of the nearest betting shop to the restaurant. The thought of the thrill made him salivate, his fingers fidgeting for the cold buttons of the roulette machine. He loved the sounds, the lights and the risk. Mostly, he loved the potential to be rich.

He walked past labourers, office workers, cashiers, bus drivers — people that made his life easier — yet he couldn't imagine walking an hour in their shoes. Why get your hands dirty sweating at work when you could make more than a month's pay in a well-timed bet? Forgetting the large probability of losing, Jason clung to his fantasy of increased wealth. It had been a while since he'd had enough money to make a serious win, but today would be different. Mum wouldn't let him down.

Reaching the Chinese restaurant in good time, he looked around, but his mum was nowhere to be seen. Sitting on a nearby bench, he glanced at the time, wondering where she could be. Always punctual, this was not like her at all. With each passing moment his mind created negative situations and he was worried. Maybe his dad had found out and stopped his mum from coming? Maybe she'd been in an accident? Maybe she forgot and made other plans? No. If she didn't come, it would be his dad's fault.

Jason's heart spewed hatred as he thought about his dad, blaming him for all his misfortunes. Never able to take responsibility for his actions, Jason projected his hopelessness onto his father. *He* was the cause of Jason's pain and suffering, his lack and poverty.

1:20pm. Fashionably dressed, hair coiffed to perfection, Mrs Burrell walked up the escalators in mature style. She noticed her son and walked towards him. Relieved, Jason stood up and hugged his mum.

'Sorry for making you wait, son,' she said. 'I got here on time, but finding a place to park was a nightmare. Took me twenty bloody minutes to find somewhere.'

'It's okay, Mum,' replied Jason. 'I was beginning to think that maybe you had told Dad we were meeting and he'd told you not to come.'

'Oh Jason, you always have been paranoid.'

They walked into the restaurant. It was a classy venue; one of the waiters, who was smartly dressed and extremely polite, escorted them to a table for two. Around the room, oriental art and sculptures complemented the soft Chinese instrumental music. There was an all-you-can-eat buffet, and Jason and his mother helped themselves to the vast selection of steaming food at the table. They spent the afternoon laughing and joking, with Jason going up for plate after plate, each one piled dangerously high.

'I see you still love Chinese food, Jason,' said his mum.

Between mouthfuls Jason nodded, 'Yes, I do.'

Shaking her head at her greedy son, she laughed. 'I'm glad you are well fed. I want to talk to you about something important.'

'What is it, Mum?' Jason looked up anxiously.

'What do you do for money apart from signing on every week?' she asked.

'Nothing at the moment,' replied Jason. 'I have been looking for work, but can't find anything at the moment.'

His mum always seemed to know when he was lying, but on this occasion he got the feeling she really believed him. Jason was not actively looking for work and was worried his mum would see through his lies.

'Well, I have secured an interview for you,' his mum continued. 'It is a warehouse job. You will be lifting boxes and itemising shipments that come in, as well as sorting van deliveries, for various chain stores.'

'That sounds good, Mum,' said Jason, feigning interest. 'Where and when is the interview?'

'The interview is next Friday. I will text you the address and who you need to speak to. This is just to get you on your feet while you think about what you want to do in the future.'

'Thanks, Mum.'

As they were leaving, Mrs Burrell gave him another £200, entrusting him to buy a good suit and shoes for the interview. Walking back to her car, she was glad that Jason was back in her life, but wondered how long she could keep it a secret. His father wouldn't approve, especially as she was spoiling him again.

But she was Jason's mother; they had a special bond and she cared for him. She couldn't watch him go without. Her husband, on the other hand, operated in the tough child-rearing he had learnt from his Caribbean heritage. She decided she would keep it from him, to avoid the arguments and to prevent Jason leaving her again.

Money securely folded in his pocket, the smile on Jason's face was huge. He knew his mum wouldn't fail him. £200! Forget the interview. Jason was about to work some magic on the roulette machines. He blew it. Again. With a little change left to spend on some girls, he left the shop. Walking towards his hostel, he bumped into Malachi.

'Jason, how have you been?' said Malachi.

'I am alright, you know,' Jason replied.

'Long time. What have you been up to lately?'

'Nothing much. I am just working on a few things.'

'That's good,' said Malachi. 'I have not seen you in the Young Ambitious Minds sessions in a while. You should come to the next one. Plus, I think it is about time you and Samuel settled your differences.'

'Forget all that,' replied Jason bluntly. 'That's not for me. As for Samuel, he is a dickhead. End of story.'

'Look, I really do think you can benefit from coming back to the sessions,' said Malachi. 'I have a few more contacts that could help you in whatever area you would like to get into.'

Jason shouted, suddenly irritated. 'Like I said, I am not fucking interested.'

Storming off, Jason left Malachi standing in bewilderment. Jason was now in a mood, money gone and the encounter with Malachi had rubbed him up the wrong way. What did he know, anyway? He was tired of people telling him what to do, acting like he didn't know how to make his own decisions. Company, that's what he wanted. The company of sexy girls willing to take off their knickers for him. He'd had two of those already today, but he wanted more. Not up for spending the night alone in the hostel, Jason reached for his phone, scrolling through the selection of numbers. Before he could decide on a target, his phone began to ring. An unfamiliar number lit up the screen.

'Hello?' he said wondering who it could be.

'It's me, bro.'

Jason was stunned by the voice he heard on the phone. He knew exactly who it was and he hesitated because he did not know what to say.

'Jason? Jason, are you there? It's me, Junior.'

Jason forced himself to answer. 'Yeah, I'm here, family. What's going on?'

'You tell me... I haven't heard from you in over a year,' said Junior. 'Throughout my trial, nothing. I end up in jail, nothing... What's going on?'

Jason stuttered. 'Cuz, I won't even lie to you. I have been going through some shit. I know it's nothing compared to what you are dealing with, but I just did not know how to handle it. As time went by, and I still didn't get in touch, it made it harder for me to do so. I won't lie, I know I have fucked up. I know I haven't been there or been much of a friend...'

'Jason, it is cool,' said Junior. 'I am not even mad at you, cuz. I just wanted to call you and find out what you are doing. Make sure you are still alive.'

'I am here, man,' replied Jason. 'Things are still fucked, but I just have to keep moving forward.'

'So tell me more. How is the family?'

'My mum is cool, not sure about my dad. We don't talk. I am on my own out here trying to make it. But I should be asking you how you're doing.'

'I am sure you heard about my appeal case,' said Junior.

'Yeah, I did.'

'Well, ever since that got rejected, I have been trying to readjust with a new mindset.'

'You're a stronger man than me, Junior. I seriously mean that.'

'Once you are in a situation like this, you have no choice but to deal with it,' replied Junior. 'That is what I am doing. Listen, my credit on this line is limited. Get my prison details off Samuel.' Junior began to laugh. 'Oh yeah, I forgot. You two are not talking! Side note – you both need to sort that out. Get the address off Jamie, yeah?'

'Yeah, I will, fam,' replied Jason.

'Take it easy, bro,' finished Junior. 'You know I got love for all my brothers, regardless. Bless.'

When Junior hung up the phone, Jason felt numb. He was shocked at how calm and collected Junior sounded. He thought he would be angry at him for not being there for him. He was bewildered by Junior's graciousness.

He was suddenly no longer interested in calling the girl he was planning on seeing. He walked to his hostel, thinking about Junior and that phone call. Jason thought about how selfish he had been. Even though he was facing a 15-year sentence, Junior was still the one to reach out to him. Jason felt low and embarrassed at himself. Deep down inside, he wanted Junior to blast him; at least that reaction would have made sense to him. That night, Jason stayed in, thinking about Junior, his own life and his parents.

Shouting erupted throughout the house, loud, malicious arguing. Upstairs, a disagreement was in full swing. Sitting in the living room, Samuel was surprised by the intensity of the screams. Entertaining Junior's siblings with card tricks, he tried to draw their attention away from their parents' row. Samuel was often at the house, feeling useful as a substitute older brother.

'What kind of father does not show his son support? Look at your life,' Mrs Okoli shouted.

'Woman! Respect yourself and mind how you are talking to me if you know what it good for you,' shouted back Mr Okoli.

'Who are you calling woman? I am telling the truth. Examine yourself. When your son was here, you did not show him love. All you did was abuse him. He was hard-working. Now he is in trouble, how many times have you gone to see him? Junior does not know how to talk to you. How can a boy not want to talk to his father? Some of these useless boys on the estate do not have their fathers around. What is the essence of you being here if you are also absent in your son's life?'

Remembering their children and Samuel downstairs, they slammed the bedroom door shut. However, their words vibrated throughout the house.

'Listen to me very carefully,' shouted Junior's dad. 'I support this house the best way I can. I work hard so you can all eat.'

'Look at this foolish man!' replied Mrs Okoli. 'Are you the only man to work and provide for his family? What about the emotional support your children need? If you are not careful, Gloria and Matthew will not have any connection with you, either.'

Samuel heard the door open and slam shut immediately.

'Look at him!' shouted Mrs Okoli. 'Always running away from the problem.'

It was time to leave. Consumed by the breakdown in the relationships within the home, as well as Junior's incarceration, the tension was building. Samuel felt the change but was hopeless to address it. Hugging Junior's siblings and saying goodbye to Junior's mum, Samuel departed.

A few days later, Malachi was set to host his Young Ambitious Minds session with Jamie and Samuel. He was already at the youth project with Samuel; they were both planning a workshop they would be showing at the local schools in the coming weeks. They were waiting on Jamie to arrive before they started their session. The youth project was busy, with young people playing table tennis and pool; it was an open session, which meant there were no workshops or talks planned for that day.

Jamie arrived fifteen minutes late and went straight to the back of the youth project, where Samuel and Malachi were waiting.

'Sorry I'm late,' he said. 'I had to wait for the person who was supposed to be covering me at work. He was late and my manager said I couldn't leave till they came.'

'It's okay,' said Malachi.

'How was work, though?' Samuel asked.

'It is a shambles, mate,' replied Jamie. 'Too much bitching and backstabbing between staff. I can't deal with that type of shit. Don't get me started on my manager. I need to leave that place sooner rather than later.'

'I hear that,' said Samuel. 'Just do what you need to do for now.'

Malachi gathered three chairs together and placed them in a circle; Jamie and Samuel sat down, while Malachi went to grab some supplies. He came back in the room with his notepad, a bottle of water and some plastic cups.

'Okay,' he said. 'Since we are all here now, let's get started. It has been a while since we all sat down to have a session like this. We know we have been occupied with other important matters. I felt it was the right time to take a step back from all of that and come back together and talk.'

Jamie and Samuel nodded their heads in response to what Malachi was saying. Malachi continued.

'We all know what happened with Junior, but I want to focus this session on you guys and how you are feeling and progressing in your own endeavours. Jamie, would you like to start?'

Jamie cleared his throat before speaking. He paused for a while, looking down to the floor.

'Jamie, are you alright?' Samuel asked.

'Yeah, I'm cool,' Jamie replied. 'I was just thinking about something. For me, I am obviously sad and pissed off at the same time about the outcome of Junior's appeal. It just makes me think that the shit I am going through is a walk in the park compared to him.'

Jamie paused again; he was softly punching his right leg with his right hand.

'You know what?' he continued. 'I am just going to come out and say it. I'm giving up boxing. I have made up my mind. It is part of the reason I am in the situation I am in right now.'

Samuel and Malachi were shocked to hear those words come out of Jamie's mouth. They both looked at each other.

'How come?' asked Samuel. 'When did you decide to quit?'

'After my last fight, which I lost,' replied Jamie. 'I had to do a lot of thinking. Even if I'd won that fight, I think I would have come to the same decision. It all boiled down to what my dad told me. He said do not do anything half-hearted. Well, I've not had the chance in a long time to give my boxing a hundred per cent. I'm not training and I'm feeling out of shape because of the type of work that I do. The most important thing for me to do now is to find a new job that would lead into a career.'

'I am sorry you feel like that,' Malachi replied.

'What about your dream? The 2012 Olympics?' Samuel asked.

'That is exactly it,' responded Jamie bluntly. 'It is a dream. It's about time I woke up.'

'Have you ever thought about being a qualified gym instructor?' Malachi asked.

'No.'

'Maybe it is something you should look into,' suggested Malachi. 'I have a feeling you would love that type of work.'

Jamie sat there, deep in thought, thinking about a possible new career path. This was why Jamie liked being part of the Y.A.M. sessions; he felt like he could talk freely and be inspired to find new ideas.

'I will definitely look into that,' he said.

'Samuel. What about you?' continued Malachi. 'How are you dealing with things?'

Before Samuel could speak, one of the teenage boys from the club burst into the room.

'Malachi, do you have another table tennis ball? That fool Stefan stepped on this one.'

Malachi laughed. 'Hold on.' He went to the cupboard and took out a table tennis ball, then walked over to the boy to hand it over to him. 'This is the last one we have here. So if anything happens to it, that's it.'

'Thanks,' the boy replied as he ran off.

'Sorry, Samuel, you were saying?'

'Personally, I am fine,' replied Samuel. 'I am going back to uni in September. Working here with you has been great, but I have to get back. I just can't but think about Junior, to be honest. I feel like there is not much more I can do to help him. It just makes me think about our ambition pact, which has not gone the way we pictured at all. Junior is in prison, and Jason – well, fuck knows what is happening with him. Jamie has to give up something he loves. It's all a joke.' He sounded defeated.

Malachi looked at them both. 'The reason I told you guys about the ambition pact was because it would help guide you. Its sole purpose was for you to always keep each other on the right track. Ambitions and desire may change, but the real notion and idea behind it is that you always stick together and help each other, no matter what. You have both tried your hardest to help Junior in what we can call extenuating circumstances. The breakdown of your friendship with Jason and the unwillingness on both sides to not try and resolve things goes against that pact.'

Samuel looked down because he knew that Malachi was talking directly at him.

'I understand that,' he said. 'But there are certain lines you should not cross and he did that. I do not have time for people like that, to be honest.'

'You have every right to feel like that,' replied Malachi, 'but know that we are never complete the way we are. There is always room for us to grow as individuals. What I want us all to take from this session is the idea of persistence. To keep trying, regardless of what obstacles are in your way. Persistence is the word I am looking for. Jamie, I will have some information for you on getting qualified as a gym instructor. Samuel, stay positive with your campaigns and try and rebuild those bridges that have collapsed.'

With those words, the session ended and Samuel and Jamie left together.

'I still can't believe you quit boxing,' said Samuel.

'Yeah mate, it was a hard decision, but I had to,' replied Jamie. 'So, are you going to rebuild your bridge with Jason, then?'

'Nah, fuck that guy,' said Samuel. 'I respect Malachi and all that he says to us. But he just doesn't understand. I know you are still cool with him. But being the type of person I am, it's hard for me to deal with the shit he pulled.'

'The bottom line is, you are just both as stubborn as each other,' said Jamie. 'What I should do is lock you both in the same room till you kiss and make up.'

They both laughed at the suggestion.

'You have jokes,' said Samuel.

'Actually,' replied Jamie, catching his arm, 'on second thoughts, you both might end up killing each other.'

'You are probably right.'

The two friends talked and laughed till they parted ways and headed home for the night.

Sunday evening, Jason was walking towards his parents' restaurant. His mum had called and said his dad was away on business, so he felt confident about meeting her there. She knew he wouldn't step foot in the place with his dad in close proximity. It was straight pride. Jason was stubborn and wanted to prove his dad wrong; but, until he was in a better place, he couldn't face the 'I told you so' speech he knew he deserved.

Dressed in jeans and a hoodie, Jason stood out amongst the trendy guests in the restaurant. Fortunately, it wasn't a busy shift and his mum was eager to show him around; there were a lot of new developments.

'We only redecorated the main part of the restaurant,' she explained.

'It looks good, though,' said Jamie. 'Very different to how it was before.'

'Your dad and I thought it was about time we had a change. We painted some of the walls peach cream, and used light wood oak tiles for the other walls. It has helped with business, as customers find it more relaxing. Word of mouth started spreading and now it is always busy, except Sundays.'

'It's a good look.'

'So, how have you been, Jason?' his mum asked.

'I have been good. I spoke to Junior the other day.'

'How is he doing? That poor boy.'

'Surprisingly, he was fine when I spoke to him,' replied Jason. 'He just seems to be getting on with it.'

'Such a shame what happened to him,' said his mum. 'And what about your interview? How did it go? Did you get the job?'

Jason looked straight at his mum. He knew he could not lie to her this time. There was a slight hesitation.

'I didn't go to the interview. I do not think carrying boxes in some warehouse is what I need right now.'

Mrs Burrell walked around from behind the counter where she was standing, lips pursed, frowning in displeasure.

'Jason, what do you mean you didn't go?'

'I didn't go. I don't want that type of job.'

'Do you know how many favours I had to call to get you that interview?' she said angrily. 'And you could not even show up? So what exactly *are* you going to do with yourself for money?'

'I will sort myself out eventually, Mum. Relax.'

'So where is all the money I gave you?' his mum asked. 'Since you know how to sort yourself out. Hand it over.'

'I've spent it,' he sniggered.

His mother sat down on the nearest chair.

'Jason, I am so disappointed in you. Especially your attitude.'

'Mum, please don't start,' said Jason. 'You are beginning to sound like Dad.'

'Maybe your dad was right all along.'

'What is that supposed to mean?' he snarled.

'It means that I should have listened to your dad a long time ago,' she said. 'I've coddled you so much, now you can barely do anything for yourself. Take a look at yourself, Jason.'

Jason could not speak; he stood there in silence, listening to what his mum had to say. The only two customers, who were both at the other side of the restaurant, could hear what was going on between Jason and his mother and were looking over at them.

'I refuse to give you any more money,' Mrs Burrell continued. 'You need to learn to take responsibility for your own actions.'

'Whatever, Mum! I thought you cared!' Jason shouted as he stormed out of the restaurant. He was peeved; his one cash cow had stopped giving milk and his flash plans to spend the money were now up in flames. He had set his heart on spending the cash in the betting shop, but now had to walk past it. Murmuring and grumbling to himself, he felt hopeless again. Hopeless and alone.

With winter officially over, the first week of March brought the blossoming spring weather. Small doses of sunshine filtered through the skies and sun worshipers adorned themselves in beach clothes and shades.

Just as the season had changed, Samuel's role at the youth club was also blossoming with new ideas. Confident and qualified, Samuel was running workshops independently; he focused on supporting young people with behavioural problems in schools. Enjoying the opportunity to be creative, he was in his element and, combined with Junior's campaign and the joint enterprise awareness, he was working hard.

He had thrown himself into these projects to avoid being at home. The distance between him and his aunt was increasing and he was doing his best to avoid her. He knew the limits; he was still living under her roof so he would greet her as and when, but there was no dialogue between them.

One evening, when Samuel got home from work, he walked into the house and saw his aunt reading in the living room.

'Good evening,' he mumbled as he tried to quickly walk back out.

'Samuel, come here please.'

Samuel reluctantly walked back into the living room. His face was gloomy and he looked uninterested.

'Samuel, what is the matter with you?' said his aunt. 'For the last week or two your attitude has been off. You have been avoiding me, and when you do see me you do not talk at all.'

'It's nothing, Aunty.'

Samuel attempted to walk off again.

'Samuel!' she shouted.

'Yes?' he replied, raising his voice slightly.

'Have a seat.'

Samuel sat down on the sofa next to where his aunt was sitting. He looked at the television, but it was on mute. He refused to make eye contact.

'This is about your dad, isn't it?' his aunt said. 'You are upset because I didn't tell you the unfinished truth of what happened when you were younger. I promised your dad I would not tell you.

But, under the circumstances and everything you have been through these last few months, I will tell you. Then you can choose to do whatever you want with the information.'

Samuel sat up and looked directly at his aunt. He could see that she was nervous; she was tapping her feet repeatedly. Despite himself, Samuel was anxious to finally learn the truth and find out what his dad had been keeping from him all this time.

Sitting up straight on the sofa, and with a heavy sigh, she began talking in a hushed tone.

'It all started a few months before your mum died. When she and I were growing up, we were always very close. Even when we both got married, we were each other's maid of honour. We talked about everything; she was my best friend. At that time, after twenty years of marriage, things were not great between your mum and dad.'

Felicity stopped and looked at Samuel, grabbing his hands.

'Are you sure you want to hear this? It might upset you.'

'Just tell me, please,' Samuel cried impatiently. 'I will find out sooner or later.'

'Your mum started having an affair with another man she met on a work trip.'

'WHAT!' Samuel shouted.

'You said you wanted the truth,' said his aunt. 'I am giving it to you.'

Samuel calmed himself down and she continued.

'She started seeing this man on a regular basis. You see, I know my sister very well; there was nothing she could hide from me. I found out and confronted her. She had feelings for this man and was planning to leave your father.'

Head in his hands, Samuel remained silent. He could not believe what his aunt was telling him. The perfect image he had of his mum was being tarnished.

'Your dad started to suspect that she was cheating on him,' continued his aunt. 'He did not approach her until he had substantial evidence of her wrongdoings. So, the night he confronted her was that night you remember. They argued for hours and, in a moment of weakness, your dad lost control and hit your mum. In fear for her safety, she ran out the house and we both know what happened next.'

Samuel was in a state of confusion. He stood up, pacing around the whole room.

'So wait, let me get this straight,' he said. 'My mum. An affair. The night she died, it was because she was cheating! So why did my dad make you promise not to tell me?'

'He knew what type of relationship you had with your mum,' replied his aunt. 'He did not want this moment to happen and tarnish the memory you have of your mother. He was willing for you to hate him and blame him for her death. He still feels guilty and takes some of the blame for hitting her that night.'

'I can't believe what you're telling me.'

'I have no reason to lie to you, Samuel,' said Felicity. 'She was my sister. She loved you and your brother very much. But, just like everyone, she made a mistake.'

'I do not know what to say.'

'I know it is a lot to take in, but that is the truth. When you speak to your dad next, at least there will be no barrier between you two. If you both decide to become friends, then so be it. If not, at least everyone knows the truth.'

'I think I need to go for a walk.'

'Do what you need to do, Samuel. Just be careful.'

Flinging his coat over his shoulder, Samuel bounded out of the front door. With no destination in mind, he walked where his feet took him; following the evening breeze, lost in thought. The landscape was not pleasant or peaceful; boarded-up flats, couples arguing, babies screaming to the police siren soundtrack, shadows hosting drug-dealing exchanges.

Trapped in chaos, Samuel couldn't concentrate on his own thoughts; he needed to escape. His next option was Jamie's. Not an ideal setting, but at least it was free from younger siblings and annoying cousins. Dialling Jamie's number, he asked if he could stay over for the weekend. Jamie was more than happy to accommodate him.

Not a glimmer of hope could be felt inside the grim environment of Chelmsford prison. The calendar was useless to Junior now; time was a mere concept. His life was on repeat, like a scratched record. Day by day, routine prevailed; sleep, wake, work, study, eat, sleep. A slave to the system; unable to choose when or where he did his activities. Stripped of freedom, he took directions from slave masters on the plantation. He missed even the most trivial of activities, like running errands for his mum.

Repressing these thoughts in order to survive, Junior embedded himself in prison life. He relied heavily on Alim's company to get through each day. They had built a strong bond and would often share ideas and perspectives of the books they read, both anxious to increase their knowledge. During a social period in the prison, Junior and Alim were talking in the library.

'I just finished reading that book by Emefiena Ezeani,' said Junior. 'The one about the Nigerian Biafran war.'

'How did you find it?' asked Alim.

'It was a great read,' replied Junior. 'I knew about the civil war based on what my mum and dad told me, but that really opened my eyes.'

'That's what books do for you. It gives you a different perspective.'

'I hear that.'

'For me personally,' said Alim, 'I have read about so many struggles and revolutions, past and present. From people like Hugo Chavez to the civil rights movement.'

'I definitely need to read more,' sighed Junior.

'What about your writing?' asked Alim. 'You told me you stopped writing after your appeal got rejected.'

'To be honest, I lost the inspiration to write. I think I was fuelled on the fact that I believed I would be released.'

'Writing is a gift,' said Alim. 'You need to find new inspiration and start writing again. It will help you mentally to get words onto paper.'

'I guess you are right,' replied Junior. 'I will try and start again tonight.'

'That is what I want to hear,' said Alim smiling. 'You are going to be here for a long time. You won't be released till 2021. Who knows how much you could have written by then and how many people it could inspire.'

Junior did not respond. Instead, he stared at the wall.

'2021. Don't tell me that,' Junior mumbled.

The memories of when we was found guilty and told his sentence came flooding back. Alim's words had Junior thinking about the longevity of his stay in the prison. The thought of it made him feel numb inside. He picked up a few books that he was interested in and walked out without saying a word to Alim.

After a somewhat peaceful weekend at Jamie's, Samuel returned to his aunt's house. He thought that the weekend would provide him with the time to decide on his next steps; he had processed the information about his mum, but still didn't know how to move forward. There was still a distance between him and his dad and, even though he'd thought about calling him on umpteen occasions, he always stopped himself.

Samuel was in the kitchen that evening, cooking dinner for the whole family. His music was blasting out and he was singing along.

'Samuel! Samuel!' his aunt shouted.

'Yes, aunty?'

'Turn down that music, please. Besides, I think your phone is ringing.'

Samuel turned the music down and went up to his bedroom. There were five missed calls from Malachi. He was about to call him back when his mobile rang again. It was Malachi's number.

'Hello, is everything okay?' asked Samuel. 'I've got five missed calls.'

When he spoke, Malachi's voice was full of excitement. He could barely get the words out.

'I have some great news.'

'What is it?' Samuel replied anxiously.

'Somebody rang the youth centre today, saying there were witnesses to the murder. Their story backs up what Junior had been saying all along.'

'Seriously?' Samuel was blown over. Finally, something to be happy about. 'Please tell me you are being serious right now.'

'Serious?' replied Malachi. 'Of course I am serious! Come on, Samuel, would I joke about something like this?'

Samuel started punching the air in jubilation.

'Yes! Yes!' he shouted.

'I have taken their details,' continued Malachi. 'I also called Victoria. She said that, before we do anything or get too excited, she needs to speak to them. So I have arranged for all of us to meet them tomorrow at 6pm.'

'Awesome. Can't wait!'

That evening, Samuel could not help but think ahead. This could be the breakthrough Junior needed. It was a welcome distraction from his family issues. He called Jamie and told him the good news; Jamie was as excited as Samuel, but wouldn't be able to make the meeting. Samuel promised to keep him informed as soon as the meeting was over.

The following day at the meeting, Malachi, Samuel and Victoria were waiting for the couple to arrive.

Malachi looked at Victoria and smiled. 'You look good for someone who has just had a baby. How is the baby doing?'

'She is fine,' replied Victoria. 'This is probably the first time I have been without her. This case means so much to me, so I left her with my mum.'

'What is her name?' Samuel asked.

'Delphine.'

'That is a very nice name,' Samuel replied.

'Thank you.'

Just then, a man and a woman walked in. They looked around, obviously wondering if they were in the right place. Malachi went over to them to introduce himself. They were a middle-aged, white couple. They looked very much in love, holding hands like infatuated teenagers. Malachi introduced them to Samuel and Victoria as Mr and Mrs O'Neil. He then went and got refreshments from the youth project kitchen.

They couple sat down and were made to feel comfortable. The youth project was empty as it was a Saturday and it was mainly used during the weekdays. With all the introductions and small talk out of the way, the couple started to explain what happened the day of the murder.

'I remember it quite clearly, because it was the last day of us being in Hoxton,' Mr O'Neil began. 'We have grown-up children and they have all moved out, so we decided to sell our house and move to the countryside. We had finished packing and were only there to pick up bits and pieces. As we came out onto the balcony, I saw a boy in a grey hoody walking on his own. He stopped and looked behind him – that's when we saw three other young men who were attacking another man. We didn't read too much into it as it was not the first time I had seen young people fighting.'

His wife continued. 'We had no idea that that poor boy had been killed, because since that day we have not come back to the area. The only reason we are back is because we parted ways with the housing management company that was in charge of renting our house. So when we got in there to check the property, we saw all these flyers about witnesses to a murder. That is when we remembered what happened.'

'We truly appreciate you coming forward,' said Victoria. 'But just to clarify, can you confirm that you only saw three boys who were actually involved in the assault of the victim?'

Mr and Mrs O'Neil looked at each other. Mr O'Neil responded.

'That's correct. The boy with the grey hooded top had no involvement. He was walking away. Then, when the other three had finished beating the young man senseless, they ran towards the other boy who ran with them, but then he went in a totally different direction. We saw the whole thing. The boy who was beaten up got up holding his stomach and that was all we saw.'

'Yes, he got up,' said Victoria, 'but he did not make it very far. He collapsed thirty yards from there. He didn't know he was stabbed. An ambulance came and he eventually died in hospital.'

'It is so sad that these young men are willing to kill each other for no good reason,' said Mrs O'Neil.

'The next stage for me will be to begin a new appeal process on Junior's conviction,' continued Victoria. 'This time, you will both be our primary witnesses. Are you both happy to testify in court?'

'Yes,' the couple replied in unison.

'Thank you very much,' Samuel said.

Malachi showed them the way out. Samuel, meanwhile, could not hide his excitement; he was grinning from ear to ear. Victoria was also smiling.

'What we need to do now is to tell Junior's family,' said Victoria. 'I think it is important that we start the process first and see what the outcome is before we tell Junior. This time, I am sure the appeal process would get to the hearing stage, but only then do I think Junior should know. The last time, the disappointment in his eyes was heartbreaking. So, are we all agreed to keep it from him at the moment?'

Malachi and Samuel agreed. They then said their goodbyes and the meeting ended. Samuel called Jamie immediately and told him exactly what had happened. Jamie was shouting down the phone in excitement. Jamie and Samuel hadn't been this happy in a long time. It was the breakthrough they needed. Samuel was glad that he'd never given up on the campaign, even when the first appeal was rejected.

In the prison, it was social time for all the prisoners in B wing. Sanchez was excited at the fact that the weather was getting warmer, as more people were likely to be outside for the social, playing football. Alim had been looking for Junior but couldn't find him; spotting Sanchez, he walked over to him.

'Hey Sanchez, have you seen Junior?'

'Nah, I haven't, you know,' Sanchez replied. 'I assumed he was with you.'

'We were meant to meet in the library,' explained Alim, 'but he didn't show up. I wanted to give him this book. I just finished reading it and he wanted it.'

'Ah, well, I can give it to him if you want,' said Sanchez. 'No time to look for him. Social is over.'

'Yeah, would you? Keep it safe.'

Alim handed Sanchez the book as the inmates departed to their cells for lock-up.

Sanchez looked over the book as he walked to his cell. He knew Junior would be happy; he'd been going on about this book for ages. All he seemed to do these days was bury himself in the pages of some book or another. A form of escapism, he supposed. Sanchez didn't even need to read them; Junior always shared with him what he had learnt and they had some great discussions in that tiny cell. Approaching the cell, Sanchez dropped the book in shock, frozen to the spot.

'Fuck,' he shouted.

Strung by a roped bed sheet, Junior hung lifeless from the prison bars. His eyes were closed. Panicking, Sanchez rushed over, lifting Junior's body by his legs, praying he was alive.

'Help!' he shouted hysterically. 'Somebody help!'

Junior wasn't breathing. Sanchez couldn't let go, his eyes full of tears. Why wasn't anybody coming? Rocking on the floor, Junior in his arms, Sanchez was emotionally unstable. He looked around the cell, noticing the chair Junior had used to propel himself, on its side where he had kicked it away in his suicide.

'Help! For God's sake, will somebody help me!' he cried out.

Sanchez's throat was hoarse from screaming. Eventually, the prison guard arrived. Taking in the scene, he, too, became frantic; calling for backup, he tried to prise Sanchez from the body.

More guards arrived; being trained in first aid, they cut Junior down from the window and attempted to resuscitate him. One guard had opened Junior's airway, while another was giving him chest compressions. They worked in sync, but received no response. When the medical team arrived, they confirmed there was nothing else to be done and pronounced Junior dead. His body was removed from the cell by the medics.

Sanchez was inconsolable. He sat on Junior's bed, unable to settle, surrounded by Junior's journals and a stack of letters.

CHAPTER TEN

Sweaty bodies, bulging muscles and washboard abs: a catwalk of wannabe body-builders strutting in front of floor-to-ceiling mirrors. Posers flexed their pecs in extremely tight-fitting vests as the overweight walked on treadmills, embarrassed by the skinny marathon runners surrounding them. The smell of body odour mingled in a dramatic blend of protein shake.

Around the room could be heard grunts and groans from strained athletes, as well as the empowering sound of weights being thrown on the floor from great heights. In contrast, the 'jeans-wearing crew' struggled around the gym, looking out of place, holding up the machines, frustrating the locals.

In one corner by the free weights, Samuel was bench pressing with Jamie's instructions. Impressed by his natural strength, Jamie kept upping the weight for each set.

'I told you not to underestimate me,' panted Samuel.

'Well, I guess I was wrong,' replied Jamie. 'It's all that tough food you guys eat, mate. The yams and all that starchy food.'

'Exactly, so imagine what I'd be like if I trained?' said Samuel. 'I'm sure I could take you on.'

Jamie laughed as he loaded up more weights on the bench press.

'Now you're having a laugh, mate. It takes years to learn the techniques. Did you know my hands are considered to be a weapon? So be careful how you address me, Samuel.'

'I would happily take you on in the ring.'

'You wish, mate.' They both laughed.

'Jamie, on a serious note,' continued Samuel. 'You love boxing. I think you should keep at it.'

'I do love it,' he replied, 'but it was a part of my life. I am looking forward to the next phase. With the help of you and Malachi, I will be successful doing something else. Malachi got me this application form for an apprentice position as a qualified gym instructor.'

'That sounds good,' said Samuel. 'Malachi is a really cool guy, always looking out for us.'

'Yes, he is. So, when I get qualified I will quit my job at that stupid restaurant. The pay will be really good, as well. It will be something I like doing, anyway, so why not get paid for it? I might think about owning my own gym someday, but one step at a time.'

'I'm glad you have something else to focus on,' replied Samuel.

They switched over and Jamie took his position, ready to lift. The gym was his natural habitat and he loved the adrenalin rush he got from outdoing his previous goal. Arms pumped and ready, he started to bench press 80kg. Although Samuel was standing behind him, ready to help if needed, Jamie was not struggling at all. Finishing his first set, he decided to increase the weight. Inside, Samuel was discouraged; he had barely been able to lift 70kg, so watching Jamie was slightly irritating.

'Told you, fam,' laughed Jamie. 'I got this. Yams or no yams.'

'Mmm, keep talking, bro,' replied Samuel. 'You know, it's only 'cause I don't lift regularly. Gimme two weeks and I'll have you.'

'Yeah, yeah. All talk. Let's see the action first!'

After their arms workout was complete, Samuel and Jamie left the gym. The last two hours had been hectic for Samuel and he was looking forward to tucking into some good food at Jamie's house. On their journey back, they saw a notice calling for witnesses; someone had been stabbed and it was an appeal for information regarding the attempted murder.

'When will people learn that fighting with knives is a coward's way?' Jamie stated. He shook his head in disgust at the fact that someone else had been stabbed in the local area.

'I get the fact that people will not get along, but why use knives?' added Samuel. 'It makes no sense. If you fight with your fists, if you lose or get knocked out, at least you live to fight another day. The only thing that might be seriously damaged is your pride.'

'How many mothers need to cry before these fools wake up and realise?' said Jamie angrily. 'It makes me fucking sick thinking about it, mate.'

Their path was suddenly blocked by three large police officers. Sighing, Samuel and Jamie had no wish to create conflict or confrontation; this was a usual occurrence in their area and they had learnt how to deal with the interference.

Authoritatively, the oldest police officer confronted them, his uniform clearly identifying him as the senior member of his force. Stop and search. The Section 60 Act allowed this disruption to their journey; the police officer explained that, due to the recent stabbing in the area, they had increased their presence on the street. They were stopping and searching any suspicious individuals they felt may be carrying weapons.

Understanding the need for such procedures, Jamie and Samuel did not argue or become aggressive; instead, they allowed the police to carry out their necessary searches. It was annoying, especially as they knew they were not carrying weapons; however, they had learnt politeness made the experience more bearable.

Finding nothing, the officers thanked them for their co-operation and sent them on their way. The area was flooded with police; sirens, the soundtrack to their lives. This was due to the recent incident, but the boys knew the 'high alert' would be short-lived. By next week, the streets would be back to their normal state.

Jamie, still full of energy, sprinted up the stairs to his flat with Samuel huffing and puffing behind him. He burst into the flat, declaring himself the winner; out of breath and disinterested, Samuel followed seconds later. They entered the front room only to find Mrs Heale sitting dishevelled on the sofa. The lines on her forehead signalled intense worry, her cheeks damp with tears; mascara rivers dribbled down her face.

Noticing the pain on his mum's face, Jamie rushed over to the sofa. Sitting next to her, his arms embraced her. Samuel looked equally worried as he closed the front door.

'Mum, what's wrong?' said Jamie.

Unable to speak, she covered her face with her hands as the tears became torrential. Feeling uncomfortable, Samuel stepped out of the living room, assuming it must be a private family matter. However, Jamie's mum looked up and motioned to Samuel.

'Samuel,' she called to him. He turned to face her. 'Please come back and have a seat.' She pointed at the armchair. 'You need to hear this as well.'

Wiping the tears from her face with her jumper sleeve, she sat up straight and attempted to compose herself. Jamie held his mum's hand, anxious to know what had caused her to be this upset.

Moments passed and they sat in anticipation. Eventually, Mrs Heale began to speak.

'I'm not sure there is an easy way to say this, boys. It's such a horrific situation.'

She paused, unable to find the appropriate words. She looked at them both. Samuel was sitting on the edge of his seat, perplexed.

'Before you both came in,' she said, 'I had just come off the phone to Junior's mum. Something terrible has happened.'

'Junior? What's happened?' Samuel asked frantically. 'Is he okay?'

'Was there another fight? Is he hurt?' Jamie asked.

Shaking her head, Jamie's mum trembled under the weight of the news.

'He's... he's...' Her voice was breaking. 'Dead.'

Samuel jumped up and shouted.

'What!'

'Mum, what are you talking about?' said Jamie.

The commotion ensued as confusion reigned in the living room. Samuel and Jamie were talking over each other, both in complete shock.

'No!' Samuel was pacing up and down. 'This can't be happening.'

'He can't be dead,' said Jamie. 'I spoke to him the other day. It must be some other person.'

'Who did this to him?' Samuel shouted. 'What low-life bastard took the life of my best friend?!'

'Listen. Please.' Mrs Heale attempted to get their attention. They settled and she continued.

'I'm so sorry to have to tell you this. Mrs Okoli got a call in the early hours of the morning, telling her Junior died in prison last night.' She paused, wondering how they would take the rest of the news. 'He wasn't murdered.'

'What?!' said Samuel.

'He committed suicide in his cell.'

'Suicide? Junior? No way!' Jamie insisted.

Samuel echoed Jamie's sentiments.

'Dead by suicide? That's not my friend. He wouldn't do that.' Samuel covered his head with his hands, refusing to believe what he was hearing.

'Unfortunately, it is true,' Jamie's mum continued, understanding the pain they were going through. When she heard the news, she had crawled up on the sofa in distress. It was a lot to process.

'It must have been so hard for him, that he decided to end his own pain,' she added.

Jamie stood up and started pacing up and down the living room, unable to control his emotions. His eyes suddenly became watery, but the tears refused to flow.

'This can't be happening.'

Grief struck each heart and silence rested on each lip. In the quiet room, they pondered on the news, attempting to piece together the circumstances that had led to this point. Samuel and Jamie were dumbstruck. Each passing minute reminded them Junior was no longer with them. What could have caused him to kill himself? The lack of information was frustrating Samuel; he needed answers.

'Jamie, we need to go to Junior's house now and find out what really happened,' he said. 'Sitting here, not knowing what happened, is killing me.'

'Yes, let's go.'

'Bye, Mrs Heale,' said Samuel.

'Bye, Mum,' said Jamie. 'I love you.'

'I love you too,' she replied. 'Be careful out there, please.'

Footsteps the only sound between them, they journeyed in hushed silence. Believing and clinging onto the hope that, somehow, the news had been wrongly interpreted, they continued their mission to Junior's house. The urgency was evident in their pace and determined steps; purposeful and strong. Without speaking, they both quickened their pace to a light run, aware a sprint would only cause them to look suspicious to the ever increasing police presence.

Blood pumping, they arrived to a scene of horrible sentiment. Tears washed the front path as grieving neighbours overflowed their sorrow on the pavement slabs. Bodies tightly pressed together in mournful embraces, tissues littered the walkway. Samuel and Jamie needed no other confirmation. It was true. The front door, slightly ajar, beckoned them and they walked solemnly (heads bowed) past the crowds and into the house.

The sound of weeping engulfed the air, sounding the alarm of grief into the hallways, filling each corner with sadness. Wrenched of joy, emptied of peace, exiled from contentment, Junior's mum was a wreck, her soulful sobs sucking out the love that used to welcome visitors. There was only despair, distress and utter desperation. Soulful mourns echoed through the house as her body lay limp on the carpeted floor, her face buried in the lap of another woman. Across the room, Junior's dad sat in the corner, facing the wall, arms folded, head down, in another world, muttering to himself.

'They have killed my son. They have *killed* my son!' repeated Mrs Okoli.

Looking up momentarily, she saw her son's friends, broken. Rising to her feet in awkward movements, she embraced them tightly, soaking their cheeks with her tears.

Samuel felt her pain. He could barely stand straight, his legs weak beneath him. From his soul, aching rivers found their outlet in his tear ducts and his eyes overflowed in response. Usually strong, Jamie crumbled under the weight of emotion, unable to deal with the strain. Once released from the hug, he silently left the room.

Watching him leave, Samuel scanned the room for Matthew and Gloria. Unable to find them, he left the room and searched for them all over the house, eventually finding them in Junior's bedroom. Clinging tightly to her brother, her eyes closed, Gloria was rocking backwards and forwards. Matthew, trying to console her, looked worried. Relief swept over his face when he saw Samuel.

Samuel picked Gloria up and hugged her. Explaining the harsh realities of death to young children was difficult and Samuel was struggling to find the right words. Drawing from Gloria's favourite

Disney film, *The Lion King*, he tried to relate her to Simba, but promised her that everything would be okay.

She melted into his arms as she listened intently, trying to grasp what he was saying, knowing everything was in pieces. Her mum hadn't stopped crying and her dad acted like she didn't exist. All she had was Matthew, and Junior's hoodie, which she had on. She liked the comfort of it. Matthew, on the other hand, seemed to be in the first stage of grief: denial. He had not exhibited any emotion since hearing the news; the enormity of the situation had not yet been processed completely.

After spending some time with them both, Samuel went back downstairs; more people had piled into the house, offering condolences, coming to pay their respects. There was barely space to breathe. Samuel didn't believe that, although well-intended, this was helping the situation. Pushing through, he went outside to check on Jamie.

'How are you feeling, J?'

Jamie looked up.

'I actually feel physically sick,' he replied. 'Just keep thinking how can this be happening?'

'I know what you mean. I have so many questions and have no idea who to ask.'

Jamie was sitting on the step by the front door of Junior's house; he got up, bending over while he clutched his stomach.

'I keep feeling like I am going to throw up,' he said. 'But nothing comes out. After everything the family has had to go through, now this. It's all fucked-up mate, seriously.'

Samuel put his hands on Jamie's shoulders.

'I was just inside with Gloria. She can't stop crying. She has lost her big brother. She asked me why this has happened to Junior. I could not answer her. I couldn't find the words.'

'Why do you think Junior would kill himself?' asked Jamie.

'To be honest,' replied Samuel, 'all I can think about at the moment is the fact that he is gone. My mind has not even allowed me to think about him killing himself. It is all too painful.'

Samuel was trying his best to hold himself together. He tried to keep a straight face, but could not help the tears from falling down. The two friends sat outside together, thinking about what it must have been like for Junior and the horrors that he would have had to endure.

Hours passed and little by little, people filed out of the house. Samuel and Jamie were amongst the small gathering still present. Alongside close friends, family and church members, they congregated in the living room. Making a circle around Junior's mum and dad, a soft worship song erupted, heads bowed in reverence. Mood set, the pastor began to pray.

'Father God, we come before you on this terrible day to plead for your mercy on behalf of the Okoli family. Lord, they have lost a son and you, who gave your only son for our sins, know the hurt, pain and distress they feel. You hear our cry, Lord, and we ask for you to send your comforter to heal their broken hearts. Remember Junior in your mercies, God, he who took his own life. We ask for your forgiveness and for your love to cover his sin. We cannot come close to understanding his suffering; being put in prison like Joseph, for a crime he did not commit—'

Junior's mum, who was still wailing, interrupted the pastor.

'They have killed my son!' she shouted.

Reaching over to Mrs Okoli, the pastor clasped his hands over hers. His eyes still closed, he continued.

'Oh Lord, the distress of a woman whose child has been snatched from the nest. May these words comfort her; may your peace reside in her heart. Let your love outshine the darkness that has clouded her heart. In this trying time, she needs your strength; increase her faith and trust in you that she will draw close to your side. Not only her, Father, but all those affected by this terrible loss. We praise your holy name. In the mighty name of Jesus we pray. Amen.'

Following the prayer, the house emptied. Some of Junior's aunts stayed to prepare food and to take care of the house and the children. Mrs Okoli was in no position or emotional state to function normally. Overwhelmed by grief, her domestic duties were a shadow of her past. Noticing the shift in atmosphere, Samuel and Jamie prepared themselves to leave. Still desperate for information, they decided to ask Junior's father for more details. Mr Okoli seemed to be in a daze, oblivious to what was happening around him.

'Good evening,' Samuel greeted him.

Mr Okoli snapped out of his daydream.

'Hello Samuel, how are you?'

'Not great, sir,' Samuel replied. 'I'm very sorry for your loss. It has come as a huge shock for us. I can't imagine how you must be feeling. I just want to ask you, if I may, what information did they give you when they called to tell you the news about Junior?'

'It has shocked us to the core,' replied Mr Okoli. 'We received the call late last night. It was my wife who picked up the phone. I didn't know what had happened at first; she suddenly dropped the phone and started shouting. I picked up the phone and they told me Junior had killed himself. He had cut a bed sheet into a thin strip, which he'd used as a rope to hang himself.'

Mr Okoli's words were like a bullet to the hearts of Jamie and Samuel. They both felt uneasy hearing the details of the way in which Junior had taken his own life. Junior's dad continued.

'They said he had time to do this because he refused to go to his social break that evening; it was his cell mate that discovered his body. They tried to resuscitate him, but it was too late. They said they would investigate and find out if there were signs of Junior being suicidal. They told me that they normally keep a watchful eye on those who have been sentenced to life. Initial analysis shows that Junior did not seem like he was suicidal.'

'None of that matters now! He is dead,' Samuel shouted.

'We will get more information soon, before they release his body to us,' replied Mr Okoli.

Bidding him farewell, Samuel and Jamie left the house, both full of worry and anxiety.

Entering his house with a sigh, Samuel knew instinctively that something was wrong. The news must have spread. His cousins came to tell him how sorry they were to hear about Junior. Even Mr Brown, his uncle, gave his condolences. Although their relationship had always been strained, on this occasion they connected. Mr Brown shared intimate details of when he'd also lost a friend unexpectedly, empathising with Samuel's pain.

'I know the pain you are feeling right now, Samuel,' he said. 'The most important thing is to allow yourself to grieve. Do not hold your emotions in, otherwise they will consume you.'

Samuel nodded in agreement.

'It just doesn't feel real,' he replied. 'The worst part is that we were on such a high after we found the two people who could act as witnesses. After overcoming all these obstacles, hearing that he killed himself made me feel empty inside.'

Samuel's aunt came and sat next to Samuel. She held his hands as they talked. Calling out to her children, she asked them to bring Samuel something to drink. Samuel was grateful that he had people who genuinely cared for him, and for Junior as well. Everyone in the family had known Junior well; they were all affected by his sudden death. Junior was always with Samuel and they spent a lot of time at each other's houses.

'Andre, where is that water I asked you to bring?' his aunt shouted to a closed door. No reply came.

'I was sixteen when my best friend was killed,' Mr Brown recalled, looking directly at Samuel. 'At the time, I felt numb inside. I tried my best to appear strong on the outside, but inside I was a wreck. At first I was in shock, and then I was angry at the people who shot him; soon after, guilt set in, as I blamed myself for not being there to help him. Eventually, I was able to accept the situation and I wallowed in my despair. Do not be afraid to cry, Samuel.'

'It feels like that pain, which is sharp and penetrating my heart, will never go,' replied Samuel. 'Whenever I think about Junior, or I picture him in my head, it feels like my heart is racing and beating so fast that it physically hurts me. Does that pain ever go away?'

Mr Brown looked at his wife. He hesitated before he spoke.

'To be totally honest with you, Samuel, everyone deals with that pain differently. For me, it took a while before I felt any sense of normality again. With time the pain eases, but it never disappears. Even today, I often think what life would be like if he were still alive.'

Samuel got up from the sofa.

'I need some time to think,' he said. 'Thanks for talking to me.' He then walked out of the living room and went up to his bedroom.

Alone in his room, lights off, he lay, alone with his thoughts. He heard a knock on the front door.

'Who could possibly be knocking at this hour?' Samuel heard his aunt say.

'Good evening,' Malachi said respectfully as she opened the door. 'Sorry to bother you at this hour, but is Samuel home please?'

'Evening. Malachi, isn't it?' Mrs Brown struggled to remember. 'Yes, he is home, but he went to bed a while ago. I think he is asleep.'

Hearing Malachi's voice, Samuel jumped out of bed and rushed down to the front door. Giving him a knowing look, his aunt left them at the door, retreating back to the living room.

Seeing the distraught expression on Malachi's face, Samuel stepped forward and gave him a massive bear hug. Easing the front door closed behind them, Malachi and Samuel sat under the night sky. In silence, they looked upwards at the illuminating moon. After a few moments, Malachi broke the silence.

'As soon as I heard, I could not believe it. I was in Birmingham visiting a friend; I got back down here as soon as I could. I wanted to go to Junior's house, but by the time I got back it was late in the day.'

'Jamie and I were there earlier,' replied Samuel. 'So many people were there as well. You were right not to go there at this time. Junior's mum is in a terrible state. Only family members are there now.'

'It all feels so surreal,' said Malachi. 'It feels like just the other day we went to see him, and now he is dead.'

'I know, I have been saying the same thing all day.'

'I need something cold to drink,' said Malachi. 'Let's walk to the shop real quick.'

Samuel ran in the house to grab a pair of trainers, a jacket and his door keys. Closing the door quietly to avoid upsetting his aunt, they walked on.

'Suicide, though?' Samuel huffed.

'That's what I was thinking while I was on the M1 driving down,' said Malachi. 'The deeper I thought about it, the more I saw it made sense.'

'Make sense?' said Samuel angrily. 'None of this makes any sense! I find myself pissed off and angry at Junior for doing something so selfish. How could he take his own life, leaving his younger brother and sister behind?' He looked at Malachi. 'Does thinking like that make me a bad person?'

'No, it is completely normal to feel anger when it comes to suicide,' replied Malachi. 'What we need to understand is that we can never fully understand what he was going through. Don't forget, Junior had been through a lot in a short space of time. This was a young man who had his future set out. Then, in a flash, everything was taken away from him, including his freedom. Being sentenced to a minimum of fifteen years and being locked up twenty-three hours a day... You can see how it could have an adverse effect on a person who committed no crime, so imagine what it was doing to Junior.'

Approaching the shop, Malachi walked in as Samuel stayed outside.

'Do you want anything?' Malachi asked.

'Water, please,' said Samuel.

Malachi returned five minutes later and chucked Samuel the bottle of water. Samuel caught it mid-air, opened it and sipped.

'What you said has got me thinking,' Samuel said. 'Remember that time we went to see him after the appeal was over? That was the breaking point for me. Remember he went off when you mentioned the word hope?'

'I agree,' replied Malachi. 'I think he had given up then, and him telling us he wanted no more visits was his way of being emotionally detached.'

'I still can't believe I am talking about Junior in the past tense,' Samuel said as his voice softened and became croaky.

'I know what you mean,' Malachi replied as they approached Samuel's road. 'Let me leave you to get your rest. Besides, it's getting late. I will go and see Junior's family tomorrow. We'll catch up soon.'

'Yeah, definitely,' replied Samuel. 'Thanks for coming. See you later.'

Malachi turned back towards his home, while Samuel returned to the darkness of his bedroom. Restless, sleep disowned him and he was unable to find comfort. Desperate, Samuel felt inclined to talk to God.

Rising from the bed, he fell to his knees. This experience wasn't completely new; yet, Samuel hadn't prayed on his own since his mum had died. It took him a few moments to begin; he struggled to find the words yet, once he began, they flowed. He prayed for Junior's family, releasing the intensity of his emotions and handing them over to God.

Once he had finished, he lay back onto his bed. Minutes later, before he knew it, he had drifted off into a deep sleep.

Sunrise. Days continued; there was no pause of remembrance for the lost. Sunlight bursting through the cracks in his curtains, Jamie lay motionless on his bed. His thoughts paralysed him; while his body lay still, his mind was in constant motion. Death. Death. Death.

The rawness of the emotions resurrected from the tombs he had closed them in and the pain returned, as fresh as the first day. First his dad; that loss had utterly changed his life. His dad was his hero; not having his father's motivation, his support, his voice, had affected the decisions Jamie had made. Especially about boxing. He felt somewhat scared that, maybe, he was doing an injustice to his dad's memory by not being the champion boxer they had always trained him to be. Yet, he knew his dad would be proud of him for being there for his mum, working hard to keep them afloat. He would always be his father's son.

He sighed. At least his dad's passing had made some sense; Junior's death, on the other hand, was inconceivable. They were blood brothers; closer than family and had grown up together. Losing him was like losing a part of himself. Jamie wondered how much of himself would be left to pick up the pieces.

The early-bird of the house, Jamie's mum, was preparing for work. Walking into the kitchen, she noticed her son was not at his usual position – behind the toaster, frying pan in hand, rustling up a hearty breakfast. Now that she thought about it, she hadn't heard a peek out of him at all; and her son wasn't the quiet type. Slightly concerned, she knocked on his bedroom door. There was no response. She called his name and knocked again. Nothing. She opened the door and walked into the room.

'Jamie?'

Jamie was unresponsive; she walked over to his bedside and tapped him on the shoulder. As he rolled over to acknowledge his mum, he wiped the tears that were rolling down his face. His pillowcase was soaked with tears.

'Are you okay, Jamie?'

'I'll be alright, Mum. It just doesn't make any sense.'

'I know, Jamie,' she replied. 'We go through life questioning things and trying to understand the logic behind it. Sometimes, son, there just isn't any sense to it.'

'First Dad and now Junior. It makes me think, what is the point of all this?'

Mrs Heale was lost for words. She was struggling to think of a way to comfort her son, who was trying to comprehend the deaths of two people he held dear to him. After a moment of silence, as Jamie held his mum tight, she found the words she had been looking for.

'I know it is hard to take right now,' she began, 'but being around your other friends will help you all through the grieving process.'

Jamie shook his head.

'If only it was that simple...' Jamie stopped abruptly. He decided not to tell his mum about the breakdown of his friendship between Samuel and Jason. He was not in the mood to think about such petty things or to explain it to his mum.

'What were you going to say, hun?'

'Nothing.'

'Well, I need to head off to work, Jamie,' his mum said. 'Make sure you get up, have a shower and get something to eat.'

'Will do, Mum.'

'I love you.'

'Love you, too, Mum.'

As soon as she left, Jamie fell back into the exact same position his mum had found him in. Not wanting to move, his bed was the comfort he needed. As he closed his eyes, desperate to mould into the mattress, the annoying vibration of his phone interrupted him. He could feel it but couldn't locate the phone, so he became a detective, searching all over the bed. Eventually, he found it, caught between his mattress and the metal frame. Jason's name was flashing across the screen.

'Hello?'

'Yo, Jamie, what's up? I saw all your missed calls last night, but I didn't have my phone on me.'

Jamie hesitated. He sat up.

'Mate, I have some bad news.'

'Jay, what are you talking about?' said Jason. 'What kind of bad news?'

Jamie took a deep breath. His eyes were closed; he did not want to say the words out loud. Saying it would mean that it was real, and it was something he could not get to grips with.

'Erm... I don't really know how to say this.' He paused. 'Mate, Junior is dead, man. He died the other day in prison.'

There was a stunned silence.

'What do you mean, dead?' said Jason. 'Oi Jamie, stop fucking about.' He laughed.

'Mate, I'm being fucking serious,' shouted Jamie. 'Do I sound like I am joking? Why would I even joke about something like that? Junior fucking hung himself. He couldn't cope with all the bullshit he'd been going through.' He was angry at Jason, but equally angry at Junior for putting him in this position.

The tone snapped Jason into silence. Dumbfounded. Jamie heard his heavy breaths and knew he was still on the line.

'I was at his house yesterday with Samuel,' he continued. 'Most of his family were there. Everyone is in shock. His mum is heartbroken. I do not think she can cope with this type of pain. I just wanted to make sure you knew what happened, that's why I was calling you all last night.'

There was another moment of silence before Jason spoke, the full realisation of what Jamie had said began to sink in.

'I can't believe it,' he said at last. 'I spoke to him not too long ago. How can he be dead?'

'That is the same question I have been asking myself.'

'I need to go and see his family,' said Jason.

'Yeah, you should,' replied Jamie. 'I need to go, too. I have a few things I need to sort out for my mum.'

'Alright,' Jason responded in a low, toneless voice.

Jamie put the phone down and rolled back into the foetal position. He didn't move the whole day, except when he had to use the toilet. Refusing to eat, he lay, eyes on the ceiling, contemplating life. Alone.

Emma rang him, wanting to come over, but Jamie did not want company. Hours later, when his mum returned from her shift, she found Jamie still in bed, unwashed. She called out to him, but he was fast asleep. She was worried about the mental strength of her son, about whether he could cope with such pain at such a young age.

A few days later, Jason finally found the strength to do what he had been thinking about ever since Jamie called him to tell him about Junior's death. What would have been a straightforward visit was made complicated by Jason's absence and lack of involvement during Junior's time of need. There were various emotions running through Jason: he was saddened by the death of someone he considered a good friend; guilty of his lack of support when Junior needed him; angry that he would never see his friend again; anxious about how Junior's family would react.

Arriving at the home, Mrs Okoli greeted him at the door with a handful of soaked tissues and a massive hug. Overwhelmed by her response, Jason was humbled at the welcome he received. The house was full of family members, busily bustling around the Okolis, ensuring they were coping through the difficult time. They were also about to start organising the funeral arrangements.

Walking into the living room, Jason saw Samuel and Jamie sitting on the sofa. Feeling slightly awkward, he touched fist with Jamie and nodded at Samuel, who gave him a dirty look in response. Feeling the tension, Jamie was disgusted by their behaviour, especially given the circumstances. Aware of the cold shoulder he was receiving from Samuel, Jason left to find Gloria and Matthew. A few minutes later, he walked back into the living room and Samuel again responded negatively, kissing his teeth and giving him an evil stare. Jamie could not hold back his frustrations.

'Samuel, you need to let this shit with Jason go,' Jamie whispered. 'For Junior's sake at least.'

Samuel looked at Jamie for a moment. Then, standing up, he walked over to Jason and asked to talk to him outside. Noticing the arrangement, Jamie followed after him, concerned about the outcome of this talk, especially considering what had happened last time. He didn't want them bringing their drama to Junior's house and overshadowing the real issue.

'What is the problem?' Jason asked.

'Why did you bother coming here?' replied Samuel.

'Samuel, what kind of stupid question is that? Obviously, I am here to pay my respects to Junior's mum.'

Samuel clenched his fists together and positioned himself right in front of Jason. Jamie stood closer to them, ready to intervene if anything happened.

'So, when Junior was alive and going through all that bullshit, where were you?' said Samuel. 'Where were *you* when he was sentenced? Or when he was in prison? Now you want to come here and pay your fucking respects.'

Jason could not speak; he knew what Samuel was saying was right. He took a step back, but Samuel walked towards him. He then pushed Jason. Jason put his hands up, trying to block Samuel from pushing, showing no aggression. Submissive due to internal guilt; he found the willpower not to retaliate. Jamie stepped in between his two friends.

'Samuel, stop this,' he shouted. 'This is not the place or the time for you two to be at each other's necks.'

'Seriously though,' Samuel shouted back. 'Why is he here?' He turned to Jason. 'Like I told you before, you are a selfish prick. All you think about is yourself.'

Jason could barely look at Samuel. He stood there, taking the abuse. He felt like he deserved it. Unable to defend himself, all he wanted to do was to grieve for his friend. He replied softly and calmly, trying not to provoke a negative reaction.

'Look, I get why you are pissed off, but I spoke to Junior not too long before he died. I was surprised that he was not blasting me the way you are. In fact, he was calm and forgiving. Yes, I know I fucked up, but if the main person I offended was willing to let things go, why can't you?'

'Are you trying to take the piss?' Samuel asked sarcastically.

'You both need to stop this shit now,' shouted Jamie.

'You know what?' said Samuel. 'Jamie is right. You just do what you need to do and stay out of my way. I mean it. I'm not having you mess with me right now. Move.'

Samuel walked away and went back into Junior's house. Jamie and Jason stayed outside.

'Jamie, he is right, I did mess up big time,' said Jason. 'If I'd been there for Junior, maybe he would still be alive.'

'Mate, you can't blame yourself for his death,' replied Jamie. 'You made a mistake, that's it. We all need to move on from this. The most important thing now is to concentrate on Junior and his family. We need to focus on the good times we all had. Life is too short for all this dumbness. Look, my dad did not even make it to fifty. Junior would have been twenty next month.'

'Samuel is proper pissed off,' said Jason. 'I have never seen him like this. He proper hates me.'

'We are all dealing with this in our own way,' replied Jamie. 'Like he said, just don't get in his way.'

A date was set for the funeral; however, it was overshadowed by the constant ringing of journalists and reporters regarding the suicide. Samuel just wanted time to grieve. It had only been a week, yet every hour of every day he was pestered by the media for more information. He did not even have the opportunity to remember Junior as he was; to recall the memories they shared when, plastered on every news channel and on the front of all the papers, Junior's suicide story ran.

It was mainstream. Samuel was disgusted by the hunger and persistence of the journalists for any morsel of information. When he had needed them, when Junior was alive, they barely returned his emails; yet now, in his death, they wanted to raise the rooftops. He ignored their calls, shouted at the journalists who approached him in the street, pleaded for privacy for the family at this difficult time, but they were relentless.

The fact that Junior had always protested his innocence, and then killed himself in prison, raised alarm bells over the protection of suicidal prisoners and the fact that he might have been innocent all along. The media kept plugging away at the stories until they made a breakthrough; they somehow found the couple who were going to testify in Junior's new appeal.

When the news broke about an innocent young man being a victim of joint enterprise and sentenced to life in prison, the community spoke up against it even more. With the press and media coverage, thousands of people were now aware of the serious consequences of miscarriage of justice. Samuel should have been happy with the success of the campaign he had sacrificed university for. Yet, all he could do was grieve for his best friend. The statistics meant nothing. They could not heal his hurt.

In the run-up to the funeral, Jamie was doing everything he could to help with the preparations. However, his horrendous work hours and strenuous activities meant he couldn't invest as much time and energy as he would have liked. Furthermore, he couldn't even concentrate on his tasks. His mind was often away in a daydream, intercepted by the shouts of his short-tempered manager.

Jamie had withstood terrible conditions and still turned up for work every day, often giving overtime at short notice to an unappreciative boss. He requested time off for Junior's funeral, but the manager refused. Jamie's blood boiled. He was appalled that this was how his boss would repay him after all the hours he had slaved away for the business.

All his emotions combusted into an emotional outrage: a fully-fledged verbal attack on his manager in front of a restaurant full of customers. With venom, Jamie spat undiluted truth, a poisonous rant concluded with an inevitable shout of 'I quit', followed by a self-satisfied storm out of the door. Relieved. Only for a moment.

As he walked away from the hell he had been enduring, he knew his decision would have serious ramifications for his mum's financial stability.

Clouds parted to make way for the sunshine. Across the borough, hundreds of people ironed black garments, shined black shoes. Adorning themselves with the fashion of mourning, they made their way to the church for the service. Every pew was full; the church overflowing. Seated, they listened to the calming melody of the organist. Outside, the black vintage cars carrying the family arrived. The hearse was leading the procession; the windows covered with beautiful flowers spelling Junior's name, son, brother and friend.

Wearing a long black dress with matching brimmed hat, Mrs Okoli struggled out of the car, helped by her husband, her makeup already ruined by her tears. The family followed her up the steps and into the church, greeting well-wishers as they walked to the reserved front rows and sat down. Standing proud and tall, Jason, Samuel and Jamie gathered around the outside of the hearse. It was their duty to lift the burden of their best friend onto their shoulders, alongside his dad and two uncles.

It was an emotional task. Mrs Okoli had picked a beautiful mahogany casket for Junior, lined with silk and decorated with the finest silver. On the count of three, they lifted Junior to the heavens. Having set him on their shoulders, supported him in death when they couldn't do so in life, they carried him through.

Each step echoed the seriousness into their chests and Jamie was shaking. This was the same church where his dad's funeral had taken place and the memories outpoured from his soul. The congregation stood in respect as they walked like soldiers, in perfectly synchronised steps, down the aisle to the sound of one of Junior's favourite hymns.

As they made the journey, they saw many familiar faces in the crowd – Samuel's aunt and family were near the front; he saw his dad near the back. In the same row, Jason's mum and dad stood. Jason gasped. It was the first time he had seen his father in over a year.

They lay Junior on the centre of the altar and took their seats next to Junior's family. Just behind them, Malachi and Victoria sat, distraught. Victoria's sobs were heavy as she felt powerless to a system that had robbed a young, innocent man of his future.

As the service started, cries could be heard sporadically in the large church auditorium. The echoes of the sobbing bounced off the wall and triggered others to join suit. Ngozi was sitting next to Samuel; she held him tight as she could not compose herself while Junior's mum and siblings were being comforted by family.

It was a beautiful service, full of love and memories of Junior; his presence could be felt throughout, as if he was watching them from above. There were poems, hymns and a sermon from the pastor, with inserts of love from key family and friends. Junior's younger siblings stepped up to the podium to speak. Gloria spoke faintly as she wiped the tears from her face.

'My brother was the best big brother in the world,' she said. 'I love him so much and I will miss him every day.' She stood by her brother, Matthew, as he addressed the church.

'I do not know how we will carry on without Junior. He always motivated me and wanted me to be a good person. I will miss him so much.'

Samuel had been chosen by the family to give the eulogy; the pressure was evident and he was unsure if he could make it through without breaking down. Aware of his concern as the Pastor called Samuel's name, Jamie stood, too; he was prepared to be his friend's support if he faltered. Clearing his throat, repositioning the microphone and taking a deep breath, Samuel looked to the sky before beginning.

'Junior was born destined to be one of my closest friends; meeting him was like finding my long-lost brother. Our early days were full of mischief. I led us in – Junior always hesitant, warning against it, but following anyway.' Samuel laughed, which was echoed throughout the church by everyone else.

'We have always been so close, me, Junior, Jamie...' He hesitated. 'And Jason. Our parents would tell you we were always together. We grew from boys to men and, as men, we started thinking about our futures together. We said we would always help each other to succeed, no matter what. It was our very own pact. The future is not certain for anyone; the things that happened to

Junior, that led us all here today, are sad and unfortunate. We can never begin to understand what he went through. Let us not judge his last actions; because I have questioned it, I have been mad at him for leaving us. Instead, I have learnt to move past that slowly, by concentrating on the good times we had and celebrating his life. So, this is to my friend and my brother, Junior.'

Soft applause escorted Jamie and Samuel to their seats. The priest said the final prayer and then invited the congregation to say their last goodbyes to Junior as he announced the casket open. The choir sang a soft hymn, accompanied by the beautiful tones of the organ, as people formed a queue and processed down the aisle.

As they walked past Junior, many were overwhelmed, stopping to pay their respects to the family, consoling Mrs Okoli especially. Junior looked peaceful; dressed in a fitted black suit, he looked unusually smart. Ngozi broke down in front of the coffin, almost fainting; light-headed and weak as she saw her love, dead.

Gradually, the church cleared and the immediate family were left alone with Junior; it was a solemn time. Gloria refused to look in the casket, scared of seeing a dead body. Matthew was also anxious, but felt obliged to show what a strong brother he could be. Looking at Junior, he choked up, the whole situation suddenly very real. His chest became tight; holding his breath, he felt physically sick. This was the last time he would see his brother. It hurt. Unleashing his heart, the tears began to shower down his cheeks. Frozen to the spot, his dad grabbed him and pulled him to his chest, rubbing his head tenderly.

Mrs Okoli sobbed as she looked at her son. Her tears couldn't resurrect him, but her pain wanted nothing more than to hold him, kiss him, and see him alive. Tearfully, she managed to say goodbye.

Thirty minutes later, they arrived at the cemetery in Manor Park. The cars entered and parked as the family got out and walked slowly to Junior's spot. The grave diggers were already at work, preparing the ground. Some of the women, their heels trapped in the grass, stumbled as they tried to get a better look, a semicircle forming around the grave. From one area, a song of praise began; someone had brought a tambourine along and they kept the rhythm as others clapped along.

'When we all get to heaven,' they sang, 'what a day of rejoicing that will be. When we all see Jesus we will sing and shout the victory.'

The chorus subsided as the Pastor gathered everyone's attention. In reverence, heads bowed as he shared a final prayer for Junior. There was a sense of peace amidst the heartache. Junior was lowered into the ground, his family at the edge of the pit, looking down at his resting place. Songs sprung up from the dirt as the choruses accompanied the filling of the hole. Roses and other flowers were thrown. Jason threw a replica Arsenal shirt, Matthew threw in his favourite toy.

After the gifts, the strong men rolled up their sleeves and got to work, shovelling the heaped soil onto the coffin. Samuel, Jason and Jamie were among them, getting their shoes dirty and their clothes sweaty in repeated motions until there was a large mound of soil. The ladies began decorating the grave with the beautiful flowers of sprays, sheaths and wreaths until there was no soil to be seen.

Junior was covered in a blanket of gorgeous plants and blossoms. Under the setting sun, they stood, remembering his life, reflecting on the day, singing songs of praise.

CHAPTER ELEVEN

Injustice polluted the air, gripping people's attention. The local community suffered allergies to the pollen of prejudice and were grieved at the lack of action. A local boy had paid the highest price, his life to shed light on the discriminatory treatment, yet the powers remained silent. Desperate for answers, pressure rose from the pavements of New North Road; convinced the authorities had failed in their duty of care, they demanded an internal investigation. The growing whirlwind of protest contrasted against the normality of routine. Raising a stir, they were not going to be silenced until justice was done.

Oblivious to the storm, Jason's footsteps were firmly rooted in routine as he trudged his way into the Jobcentre. His heart was heavy with the burden of being seen as the scum of society; a mesh of desperate jobseekers and lazy bums. He was in the latter category, barely finding the motivation to fill out an imaginary job search. Hands outstretched, he just wanted the money.

Yawning, he looked around the room and felt a sense of déjà vu. Nothing had changed from the previous Friday; the same people tapping away on the same machines. Still jobless. Still signing on. *What's the point of trying?* Jason thought as he watched them.

He'd have more luck getting paid through a roulette machine than scoring a job in here.

As he sprawled himself on the seat, impatiently waiting for his slot, he was interrupted by a security guard who rudely directed him to the machines. Rolling his eyes, Jason reluctantly stood up and went to the nearest one. Watching other people's dreams shatter as they printed out vacancies that turned out to be filled, Jason decided not to get caught up in the gamble. Instead, he blindly poked the screen and printed out anything.

'Jason Burrell,' a soft female voice called.

Thankful his turn was finally up, Jason disregarded his printouts and walked over to the table on the far left, bringing out his jobseeker's book from his back pocket as he sat down.

'Sorry to keep you waiting, Jason, we're running a bit behind today,' Leanne said, head down, searching to find his folder. 'How has your job searching been going?'

'It has been okay,' Jason replied, lying out of his teeth. He hadn't been searching for anything but a free ride.

Finding his paperwork, Leanne sat back and looked at him directly. It had been a long day and she was tired of the non-committal attitude. She had taken the job to help people get back into employment, but she realised many people didn't care. This got to her, and Jason was a definite offender. She flicked through his records, frowning.

'Jason, you have been signing on now for quite a while. You have not been making any effort to find a job, or suitable training that will gain you qualifications to get a decent job.'

'Leanne, can you just please sign me on so I can go,' replied Jason. 'I am not in the mood today.'

'No!' Leanne replied crossly. 'You need to hear this. Being on jobseekers is a lifeline, not something you decide to just live on. You are a smart, intelligent young man and I know you can do better.'

Jason sighed. He didn't come to the Jobcentre for a lecture from some uppity woman; he came to get paid. In and out. He wasn't interested in a coaching session.

'Well, things happen that change our course in life,' he said. 'I do not see the point, to be honest.'

'Why do you have such a defeatist attitude?' said Leanne. 'Have a look at that man standing there by the entrance.'

Jason slowly swivelled his body around.

'That man lost his job two months ago,' explained Leanne. 'He has been in here every day fighting to get a new job. He says he does not want a handout, but just the chance to provide for his family. The thing is, he wishes he gave himself more tools to succeed. Leaving school without any qualifications, he started working and only learnt to do one thing. Now that one thing has been taken away he is lost. But he is not giving up or feeling sorry for himself.'

'I'm sure he is a great guy,' Jason replied sarcastically. 'Can I go now?'

'Yes, you may.' Leanne signed off his book as she shook her head.

Annoyed at his advisor's attitude, Jason hot-stepped out of the Jobcentre and made his way home. Trudging through the streets, he felt isolated and alone. An overnight hermit, his life restricted to the four walls of his room, Junior's funeral had affected his ability to be sociable. Faced with death, he could no longer hide behind fancy clothes and gorgeous girls; instead, he was haunted by the memory of his friend. Sleep tormented him with nightmares; he often woke up in a cold sweat. Stuck in a cycle of misery, Jason's world was closing in on him.

Opening his front door, he crashed on his bed, eyes fixed on the ceiling. The chill of loneliness targeted his spine; in an attempt to shake it off, he grabbed his phone and called Jamie.

'Yo,' Jason said.

'You alright?' replied Jamie.

'Yeah. What are you up to?'

'Nothing much. Samuel is coming over in a bit. What are you doing?'

'Same, nothing,' said Jason. 'I wanted to come over and chill.'

'Usually that would be cool, but you and Samuel are still acting like little girls and I do not want any trouble in my house.'

'Don't worry about it, man,' replied Jason. 'I will come around another time.'

'Okay, mate,' said Jamie. 'Take it easy.'

Rejected, Jason threw his phone on the bed in frustration. No-one. He had no-one. No-one to care about his existence, wanted his company or checked up on his emotional well-being. All alone. Secretly, Jason knew he could call up a girl to come over and make him feel like a king for a couple hours and he contemplated it.

Unable to commit to the process of convincing a female, he left the house instead. Before he knew it, he was back in a familiar space, wasting his benefit money in the betting shop. The machine had become an extension of him; he related to it, missed being around it when he was gone and treasured the moments they spent together. It was an unhealthy relationship, yet Jason continued to maintain it, even though he couldn't afford it.

Feeling left out, Jason kept trying to meet up with Jamie. It was difficult at first, as Samuel and Jamie were hanging around with each other a lot of the time. However, his persistence paid off and, a few days later, Jamie invited him over to catch up. Relishing the opportunity, desperate for human interaction, he rushed over. Like old times, their competitiveness arose over the PlayStation.

'Jason, I keep telling you, you will not win a game.'

'We'll see.'

Sitting on the floor, backs against the sofa, completely engulfed in the game, the banter kept coming. Jason's hands were a blur against the controller, yet to no avail as game after game ended in defeat. Eventually, he became tired of losing. Turning off the game, they repositioned themselves on the sofa, talking with the TV in the background.

'So how are things with your mum and dad now?' asked Jamie. 'I saw your dad at Junior's funeral.'

'Nothing has changed, really,' replied Jason. 'I haven't spoken to him. That day we just looked at each other, there was no conversation between us. Me and my mum were getting on, but I messed it up after she sorted an interview for me and I didn't show.'

'What happened?'

'She gave me money to buy stuff for an interview, but I spent it on roulette.'

Jamie looked at him furiously, angry at Jason's self-centred attitude.

'Mate, you are not fucking serious? You have a mum that can sort you out and you waste your money in the betting shop? You need to sort it out, Jason. Seriously.'

'I know, I know,' replied Jason. 'I need to fix up, but I just feel so weird. Like life is passing me by. Ever since Junior died, I haven't been able to sleep properly.'

'It's hard, mate,' said Jamie. 'I wake up thinking the whole thing is a dream.'

'Jamie, for me it's more than that. I feel guilt inside me. What Samuel says is true. I should have been there.'

'Mate, you need to move on from that,' said Jamie. 'There is nothing that can change what happened. What you *can* do is sort yourself out, stop wasting your money on that stupid machine. Life is too short for all this bullshit. We just have to live for the present.'

They were still talking when Jamie's mum returned from work; surprised to see Jason, she invited him to stay for dinner. Jason was grateful for the support and Jamie's friendship, even in light of how he had acted in the past.

The next morning, Jamie awoke on a mission; sleeves rolled up, vacuum in hand, serious face initiated. Determined to disintegrate dirt and mess from the flat, he worked from room to room, giving each a deep clean. Music blasting from the stereo took his mind off the time as he worked along to his favourite songs. Unemployment meant he was spending more time indoors. Knowing the effect this had on his mum's workload, he was committed to ensuring the house was clean when she got home.

Satisfied his mission was complete, Jamie cooked lunch as a reward, slapping a pizza in the oven. As he waited, he realised cooking for his mum would be an additional help for her; she had a long shift. Culinary skills were not in abundance in his DNA and he didn't want to cook up food poisoning, so he called on his trusted girlfriend. Emma came over enthusiastically, only to open the cupboards and realise all the ingredients were missing. Sighing, she left as quickly as she came to go to the nearest supermarket.

An hour later she was back.

'Did you get everything?' said Jamie.

'Yes, but I had to go Dalston to pick up the sweet potatoes.'

'Thanks,' Jamie said as he gave her a kiss on the lips.

'Let's get started, shall we?'

'Lead the way.'

Walking into the kitchen, Jamie followed Emma, plastic bag in hand. They emptied the contents onto the sideboard and Emma began preparing the meal. Supervising the activities, Jamie stood and watched her intently, reflecting on how lucky he was to have such an amazing woman in his life. Washing the chicken over the sink, Emma looked behind her, caught Jamie staring and smiled.

'Babe, you said you were going to tell me about your gym in-structor course,' she said. 'How is it going?'

Snapping out of his daze, Jamie smiled.

'It is going really well,' he replied. 'Malachi has so many contacts and this is a great opportunity for me. It is basically a work-based training programme. Right now, I am in a classroom-based environment four times a week and in a gym twice. So I get hands-on experience while still learning.'

'How long is the course?'

'It works in three parts,' he explained. 'Nine months altogether. First three months doing what I am doing now, then I will start getting paid being in the gym. More days in the gym and less days in class. At the end of the course, I can apply for a job at a high-flying gym that will pay twenty grand a year.'

In his excitement, Jamie walked behind Emma, held her waist, pulled her in and kissed her neck. Laughing, she pushed him back with her bum.

'Jamie, stop it! You are so naughty. You know what that does to me when you do that.'

Jamie smiled at her and moved back. He took the chicken from her and started to marinate it with the seasoning she'd handed him.

'So, twenty grand,' she said. 'That is a good starting salary. In three months, when you start getting paid, how much will you be getting?'

'Ten quid an hour,' replied Jamie. 'Almost double what I got at that stupid restaurant.'

'I am so happy for you, babe,' said Emma. 'Something is finally working out for you.'

'Yep! I just need to put my head down and work hard.'

Spending the whole afternoon making dinner, Emma tried to teach Jamie the basics of cooking. An eager learner, he paid close attention but wasn't able to recreate the same results. The chicken successfully roasting in the oven, rice, potatoes and veg on the stove, they relaxed.

Opening the front door to a terrific aroma, Mrs Heale was all smiles as she noticed the spotless flat and dinner cooking. Dropping her bags, she hugged them both, thanking them for taking the burden off her. As she went to shower, Emma finished off the gravy and plated the dinner, while Jamie set the table.

They sat together, eating and enjoying each other's company. After cleaning up, Emma made her way home, leaving Jamie with a kiss and a cuddle before waving to his mum. As she left, Mrs Heale smiled at her son, thankful for the man he had grown into.

'Thanks for dinner tonight,' she said. 'I know you didn't make all of that on your own. The sweet potato and chicken were delicious.'

'It's alright, Mum. I just thought I could help you out in another way, since I am not working anymore and paying any of the bills.'

'Jamie, listen to me. It is still my job to look after you, so please do not worry too much. I am just glad you have found something else you are working towards. The money will come. We will find a way to survive.'

'We will,' said Jamie.

'Are you still going to your dad's grave tomorrow?' his mother asked.

'Yes, I will go in the morning before my class starts.'

'Okay, I hope I will have the time to go,' she said. 'It depends on when my shift finishes.'

'Alright, Mum,' said Jamie. 'I will leave you to get some rest. Goodnight. Love you.'

'Night, sweetheart.'

Sunshine beckoned Jamie from sleep and he rose, anxious to start the day. With purpose in each movement, he quickly got ready and headed out. The journey was accompanied by emotional thoughts swirling around his head; attempting to thump them out with his music playlist, he walked subdued. Stopping at the florist, he had purchased a bunch of beautiful blooms before continuing his steps.

Tombstones lay in perfect symmetrical rows in the soil. Memories consumed him as he paused and read the words around him; so many loved ones lost. He took deep breaths as he approached the spot, the fresh pang of sorrow awake in his soul. Kneeling, he pulled out a few weeds that had sprung up since his last visit. Clearing the area of clutter, he opened the bouquet and placed the flowers in the black vase after removing the withered petals. Closing his eyes, he pictured his dad smiling, laughing, and tears began to flow as he hung his head.

'Hey, Dad,' he said softly. 'It's been two years since you left us. I think about you every day. It's so hard without you being here. Money is a myth and Mum's working so hard to keep us afloat. I know you told me to make sure she's okay, and I promise Dad, I'm trying my best. But sometimes, it doesn't feel like enough. Wish I could tell you that I'm a world famous boxer, but there's more bad news. I had to quit. I'm sorry, Dad. All I want is for you to be proud of me. Hopefully, I'll be half the man you were. Struggling at the moment. Junior's gone, Dad. Gone. No disease, no accident, just gone. Overnight. I can't believe it. Hope you're looking after him up there. Tell him I miss him. I miss you, too. Trying my best, Dad. Love you.'

Jamie sat with his father for a few reflective minutes. Eventually getting to his feet, he turned around and left for his course.

Later that day, he headed straight to Samuel's house. He was worried about Samuel's state of mind; since the funeral, he'd been busying himself with planning and delivering workshops. Andre answered the door; Jamie gave him a high five and went into the living room to greet the rest of family. Samuel was in his room.

'Yo, Jamie, I'm up here.'

'I'm coming.'

Jamie carefully walked through the passage, trying to avoid knocking over the stacks of paint cans that were piled dangerously high.

'What's with all the paint?' Jamie asked as he looked for space to sit on the bed. The bed was covered with freshly-washed clothes that were yet to be folded and put away.

'My aunt wants to redecorate the passage,' Samuel said from behind his laptop. 'Which basically means Andre and I have to do it.'

'Good luck with that,' said Jamie. 'I hate painting. Don't have the patience for it, mate.'

'Neither do I,' replied Samuel, 'but still have to help out. Anyway, how is your gym instructor course going?'

'It's going really well. I can't wait until I start getting paid.'

'That's good.'

'What have you been doing?' asked Jamie. 'You seem to be glued to that laptop.'

'I have been looking into suicides in prison,' replied Samuel. 'Trying to find out what causes people to want to end their lives.'

Jamie looked at him and frowned. 'Mate, are you sure about all that?'

'Yeah, I am. I just want a better understanding and to find out if it happens a lot.'

'So, what have you found out so far?'

Samuel swivelled his chair so that Jamie could see the screen on his laptop.

'According to this website, those who are more likely to kill themselves in prison are males. The most frequent way to commit suicide in prison is by hanging. It goes on to say the most fatal hangings are carried out using blankets or bed sheets as ligatures, while windows or beds are used as ligature points.'

'That sounds exactly like what Junior did,' said Jamie.

They both went quiet, the thought of Junior hanging himself flickering in both of their minds. Samuel was the first to break the silence.

'From 1996 to 2005,' he said, 'eight hundred and twenty-four people had committed suicide in prison. Last year, there were sixty-seven in total.'

'Mate, that is seriously messed-up,' replied Jamie. 'They need to do more to help these people.'

Samuel logged off his laptop and put it on the table.

'The more I read, the more depressing it gets, Jay. I know we have buried Junior and said goodbye, but for me it doesn't feel that way. I still have questions. I need to know why. Only then can I move forward.'

'I hear what you are saying, mate,' replied Jamie. 'But what else can we do?'

'Junior shared a cell with someone, a guy called Sanchez, I think. Well, Victoria pulled some strings; she contacted him and asked if it would be okay if I went to visit him. He said yes, so I will be going in a few days.'

'That's good,' said Jamie. 'At least he can tell you how Junior was when he was in there.'

'Exactly.'

'Anyway, are you ready? Malachi is probably waiting for us.'

'Almost,' said Samuel. 'Just need to find my shin pads.'

'I have not played an eleven-a-side game in a long time,' said Jamie excitedly.

'Trust me,' said Samuel. 'I hope Malachi's team is good.'

'Let's just hope we still have our fitness.'

Samuel and Jamie laughed. They then went to meet Malachi to join his football team for a friendly match.

It was the first week of April. The clocks had just gone forward and British summer time had begun. The weather was bright and sunny. Samuel was on a train, heading for Chelmsford prison. His eyes fixed to the glass, he was wondering what type of person Sanchez was.

On arrival, Samuel went through the security checks before he was taken to the waiting room. There, he waited patiently. Number 11 was the table number that was given to him. In the distance, Samuel saw a tall, muscular man walking towards his table.

'Are you Samuel?'

'Yes, that's me,' Samuel said, rising to his feet.

'I'm Sanchez,' the man replied, extending his hand. Nodding, they shook hands before sitting down.

'Before I start,' said Samuel, 'I would like to thank you for agreeing to meet me. I appreciate it.'

'It's nothing, don't worry about it,' replied Sanchez. 'Can I ask you something before you start?'

'Yeah, go ahead.'

'How was Junior's funeral?'

Samuel smiled, remembering.

'It was a great send-off for a great friend,' he replied. 'Hundreds of people turned up to pay their respects. He was surrounded by people who cared and loved him. It was the best way to see him go.'

'I am glad to hear that,' Sanchez said. Samuel shuffled in his seat, anxious for answers but unsure where to start.

'I guess my first question would be this,' he began. 'What was Junior like in prison?'

'Well, to be honest,' replied Sanchez, 'Junior usually kept to himself. It took me a while to break down his barriers, and I was his cellmate! He only really had a few people he talked to. Me, Alim and a couple others...' He paused, looking upwards. 'It was hard for him to adjust, especially knowing he shouldn't have been in prison in the first place.'

'Sounds like Junior,' said Samuel. 'I wanted to reach out to him more, but he was closing himself off. Didn't even want us to visit in the end. Felt like I was losing him. Even still, I was shocked when I heard he'd killed himself. It hurt me deeply and I haven't really been able to concentrate on anything else since. I have been reading a lot about prison suicides, and I've learnt that many prisoners suffer from depression. Did you notice anything like that with Junior?'

Nodding in silent acknowledgement, Sanchez's eyes found the floor. Solemn, his voice was lowered.

'To tell you the truth,' he said, 'I would say he was depressed. He was angry that he was in prison. The only thing he had was hope. He was clinging on to his appeal; set himself up, was ready to go home. And then, when his appeal was rejected, that shit fucked with his mind. It was the final straw. That's when his behaviour changed.'

'When you say changed, what do you mean?' asked Samuel.

'It was like he didn't care anymore. But anyone would feel down after an appeal rejection, so there were no warning signs, if that's what you mean.'

'What type of things did he talk about?'

Sanchez smiled as he rubbed his hands on his thick beard.

'When he did talk, it was always about his friends and family. Junior was a good guy; it was obvious he should not have been in here. People were shocked when they heard what had happened to him. He always had such a low profile. There was a guy called Alim who he spoke to quite often; he was devastated when Junior died. So, even in here, he had a big impact on people.'

'Yeah,' said Samuel, 'he had that effect on people. Did he ever open up to you?'

'I feel like I opened up to him about myself, to be honest,' replied Sanchez. 'The mistakes I've made, things I regret, that kind of stuff. I'm a big talker. Junior was different; he kept his cards close to his chest, but every night he was scribbling away in a journal or something. Went through them so fast, I'm sure he finished four or five, filled with entries about his life in prison. He always hid them, but that's where he opened up. On the page.'

The news about the journals sprung excitement up within Samuel. He knew Junior loved to write. Those journals could contain the information he lacked, the answers he craved, straight from Junior's hand.

'Do you know what happened to those journals?' Samuel asked eagerly.

'He used to hide them underneath his bed,' replied Sanchez. 'But the night I found him...'

Mid-sentence, Sanchez lost his words. His tongue recoiled as he thought about the last time he had seen Junior; the image of him, hanging by his neck, lifeless, haunted him. It was an image he repeatedly tried to forget; the intensity shocking him again into silence.

Samuel watched the emotion flitter across Sanchez's face, unable to imagine how he had coped finding Junior in that state. He allowed Sanchez the time and space to compose himself.

'The night I found him,' began Sanchez, 'he had laid out those journals on his bed. When they took him away, the prison guard took away all of his property. That's all I know.'

Samuel was noticeably disappointed, but grateful for Sanchez's time.

'Thanks again for talking to me,' he said. 'I really appreciate it.'

'It's all good, man,' replied Sanchez. 'I heard about what you were doing for Junior while he was alive, I respect your friendship. That is what I call loyalty. I used to be in deep with all the madness on the streets. We had a twisted view of loyalty, believing true friends were the ones who would watch your back in a fight. Not knowing those same people would stab you in the back in other ways. So now I just do me.' He smiled at Samuel. 'Take it easy, bro. I hope you get the answers you are looking for.'

Samuel woke up and looked at the calendar. 7th April. He sat up in bed and stared vacantly in front of him in silence for a moment. Then, he quickly got up and got ready to go out and headed for Junior's house. Only Matthew and his younger sister were at home. They both welcomed Samuel into the house.

'How are you?' Samuel asked.

'We're good,' Matthew replied.

'Where is your mum?'

'She went food shopping.'

'Okay,' said Samuel. 'Listen, today would have been Junior's twentieth birthday. So I wanted to come and see you guys to make sure you were okay. Is your mum doing anything today?'

'Yeah,' replied Matthew. 'That is why she went shopping. She's going to cook some food. She just wanted us to celebrate his life, say a prayer and that's it. She told me to call you to see if you guys would come.'

'Yeah, that's fine,' said Samuel. 'I will come back later with Jamie.'

'Gloria, go to your room,' Matthew demanded, turning round to his sister. 'I need to speak to Samuel.'

'Is everything alright?' Samuel asked as Matthew moved from the passage and led him into the living room.

'Samuel, even before my brother died, my mum and dad have been arguing all the time. Now, they hardly ever talk to each other, and when they do it's non-stop shouting. I think my mum is angry at my dad for not being there emotionally for Junior. She is always shouting "money alone will not raise these children" and it is starting to affect Gloria.'

'Matthew, I am sorry to hear that,' replied Samuel. 'You cannot control what goes on between your parents. You are fifteen now; it is your job to protect and be there for your sister, like Junior was for you both. Comfort her and reassure her that things will get better.'

Matthew's voice was breaking under the strain.

'I keep thinking they will break up,' he said. 'But some of my aunts and uncles are always here talking to them both, trying to help them with their issues. I hope they sort it out soon because I don't want anything else to happen to my family.'

'Stay strong, Matthew,' said Samuel. 'You are a good brother.'

The house had been transformed to another location: Nigeria, fuelling the streets with the cultural sensations of the motherland. African drums thumped against authentic melodies, a rhythm of joyous celebration for their son. African aunties, in exotic costumes, swayed welcoming vibes throughout the house. It smelt heavenly; mixed spices wafted through the cracks in the walls. Outside, Samuel, Jamie and Malachi were greeted by the delicious aroma. Pounded yam, garri and fufu, moi moi, jollof, stew, fish and soup. The feast was plentiful.

The clink of Supermalt bottle caps filled the room as energetic conversations echoed festive cheer. The contagious atmosphere spread like a wildfire and all those gathered were touched by the memories of Junior. Stories were shared, jokes and anecdotes of the son they all loved and cherished. Laughter erupted as Samuel and Jamie recalled their most amazing memories.

Gloria and Matthew loved the party; they had found it difficult to talk about Junior, as the subject had been the source of great tension between their parents. Today, they were free to poke fun at the pictures of him, toothless and goofy, on the walls, to reflect on the times they had pranked him, and what a great older brother he'd been.

Mrs Okoli was in her element; tired under the strain of hosting, but enjoying the fact her house was filled with love. It had been so sorrowful, but her home was now uplifted with the positive vibes of her friends and family in remembrance of her son.

Hours passed as they laughed and danced, cut cake, raised glasses and made speeches in Junior's honour. Stomachs full and overflowing, Mrs Okoli piled her guests with doggie bags before they left. Always the first for seconds, Samuel managed to secure three boxes of tupperware. There was excess food left as people ate until they could eat no more.

The annoying ringtone and accompanying vibration pounded through the hostel room as Jason searched frantically for his phone. Eventually locating it in the pocket of his dirty jeans he'd worn the previous day, he answered. It was his mum. Pleasantly surprised to hear from her, Jason sat on his bed and talked. She wanted to see him, urgently. Picking up his jeans from the floor, he grabbed a jumper and a pair of trainers and left.

Glad to get out of the suffocating hostel, Jason inhaled the polluted air, wondering what his mum wanted. It had been a while since he had heard from her, but today she had specifically told him to come to the house. They had always met in the community, away from the prying eyes of his dad. As he approached the house, he spied the street; not seeing his dad's car anywhere, he walked up to the door confidently and rapped the door. His mum answered.

'Hi, Mum.'

'Hi. How have you been?' she asked, looking at him from head to toe.

'I'm alright,' he replied as he followed her, closing the door behind him.

'Glad to hear it. So, what have you been up to?'

She walked into the living room, where she had the ironing board set up. Jason followed her and sat down and watched her as she did the ironing.

'Nothing at the moment,' he replied softly.

His mum shook her head in disappointment. She wondered how her son, who had so much promise, was now doing nothing with his life. Her only son, a bum. Hiding his shame, Jason looked at the floor, avoiding the disapproval in his mother's eyes. Noticing his face, she changed the subject.

'Anyway, how have you been since the funeral?'

'It's been tough to accept that Junior's gone, Mum,' Jason replied. 'It was his birthday yesterday.'

'Every time I think of that boy, my heart breaks. Such a sad story.'

Jason could not respond. He was looking down at the ground, deep in thought.

'So, at the funeral, when you saw your dad,' his mother said. 'Why didn't you acknowledge him?'

Jason sprung up in anger.

'I had nothing to say to him! Plus, that day wasn't about us, it was about Junior.'

'Okay, Jason.' His mum sighed, focusing on the shirt she was ironing. 'Well, the main reason I called you here is because I received a package with your name on it. Did you order something?'

Jason looked surprised.

'No, I didn't order anything.'

'Well, it came for you a few days ago, but I only got a chance to call you today to come and pick it up. Go into the kitchen. The package is on the table.'

Puzzled, Jason wandered into the kitchen. On the table was a brown parcel. Lifting it up, he shook it, bewildered as to what it could be.

'Have you seen it?' his mum shouted.

'Yes.'

'Do you have any idea who it is from?'

'No, but when I get home I will find out.' Jason started making his way to the front door.

'Jason, take care of yourself.' She put the iron down and walked over to Jason and gave him a hug.

Heading back to his hostel, Jason stopped at a cash machine and withdrew his Jobseeker's Allowance in full. Pockets full of cash, his urges returned as the local betting shop whispered sweet nothings into his ear, pulling him in to spend some quality time. A sucker for the seduction of potential wealth, he entered like a love-sick puppy, desperate for attention. Pulling out his crisp £10 notes that had barely been in his pocket five minutes, he offered them up to her charm; loading her with promises of love if she treated him right.

Fifty pounds in; he spread his first bet, but paused before placing the bet. Interjecting his urges was a constant bugging ache, his conscience awakening from sleep and pounding his mind with alternative thoughts. Contemplating his situation and struggling between two choices, he weighed up his options. Knowing there was more to life than what he had become, he recalled Jamie's rebuke the last time they were together.

Calculating the money he had lost, thrown away in blind faith in this exact position, Jason realised he had been foolish. Cancelling the bet, he printed off the ticket and went to the cashier to get his money back. She smiled at him.

'Not today, then?'

'No, hopefully not ever.'

'Well done,' she said. 'Stay away from these machines. It's the devil. I have seen it ruin so many people.'

Leaving with a new sense of purpose, Jason thought about the decisions he had made and the impact they had had on his life. Package in hand, he quickened his pace, eager to find out what was hidden beneath the brown paper. Flinging open his hostel door, he threw his jumper down and sat on the bed. Using his keys to pierce through the cellotape, he pulled back the inside flaps and looked inside. A stack of exercise books.

Confused, he took a closer look, peering at the handwriting. Recognising it as Junior's, he quickly opened the first book, flicking through the pages. He flicked through the rest; every page was full of handwriting, Junior's unspoken thoughts. Bemused, Jason closed the books, unable to understand why Junior would have sent these to him; they were truly sentimental and personal. If anyone was going to get access to them, he expected it to be Samuel.

Placing the books into date order, Jason began to read. Transported into the subconscious of Junior, Jason took his time on each page. It was as if Junior was speaking directly to him; a message from beyond the grave. The details and descriptions riveted Jason to the spot and hours passed, his eyes transfixed to the page. Living each moment with Junior, he got choked up at the things Junior had to endure. Guilt rocked him as he realised he could have heard these stories first-hand if he had bothered to visit, or write. So self-centred; the regret consumed him.

As he finished each book, the next became more difficult to stomach, as things seemed to take a turn for the worse. Hope had faded from the inserts and doom and gloom filled the ink. There were blotches and smudges on the bottom of some of the pages; splotches of Junior's tears interfering with his words. Soul-piercing truths.

Two days later, Jason still hadn't moved from his hostel; he was working through each page of the last moments of Junior's life. Emotions from the pages stung his eyes and they responded in the flowing of tears. Wiping his eyes, he picked up a book and went outside for some air.

Sitting under the clear sky, his eyes fixated upwards, he felt Junior's presence; a sense of peace engulfed him. While he wanted to finish the book, it was a reminder of the end; that Junior was gone. In the tranquil evening, he thanked Junior for sending him such a precious gift; one that had changed his perspective, opened his eyes to life. He was grateful he was still breathing. Inhaling deeply and gathering his thoughts, he opened the book and read the last pages of the journal. It hurt.

The next day, Jason's routine fell back into alignment. He was again sitting in the Jobcentre, waiting for his name to be called, observing the locals. Eventually, his name was called.

'How are you today, Jason?' asked Leanne.

'I'm good, thanks,' he said smiling at her. 'And yourself?'

'Wow! I'm fine,' she replied, surprised at Jason's change in attitude. 'You seem cheerful today!'

'I guess you can say that.'

'Well, I'm glad,' said Leanne. 'It makes a change from the sour face you usually greet me with.' She laughed. 'So, as you know, the purpose of this meeting is to find you a training course. One that will give you skills and qualifications for employment.'

'Sounds good to me,' Jason replied with a smile on his face.

Again, Leanne looked surprised. She noticed there was something different about Jason but she could not figure it out.

'Are you sure you are okay?' she asked. 'Normally, when I suggest courses or jobs, you show no interest.'

'I'm good,' replied Jason. 'I'm just ready to move forward now, that's all.'

'Good to hear,' she said. 'Like I was saying, the purpose of this course is to teach the difference between skills and qualities of employment. It is a short course that is aimed to motivate you. Hopefully, from there you will decide what you want to do.'

'How long is the course?'

'It is a two-week intensive course, four days a week.'

'When do I start?'

'Next week, Tuesday.'

'Okay,' said Jason. 'Great, thanks.'

'Jason,' said Leanne, 'I have to say, I am liking this new attitude of yours. Keep it up and you will go far. Remember, this course has been paid for and you not turning up will be unacceptable. If for any reason you cannot make it, please let me know in advance so I can let the lecturer know.'

'I will definitely be there.'

Sitting quietly in uniform rows, the whole of year 11 were waiting for the speaker to arrive. Clearing his throat, Samuel stood to address them all.

'First and foremost,' he began, 'I would like to thank Mr Christie for inviting me here today. I've had a good day working with you all. If you are to take anything from what I have said to you today, I would want it to be this: do not make decisions based on what other people think of you. Remember that peer pressure is the downfall to many people's success; if you let it consume you, then you will fail. Think for yourself; do not let negative people influence you. Besides, you are at the age where you will be making new friends in a few years. Some of the people you call friends now might not be your friends next year, so don't make a decision that will impact your life on uncertainty. So, thanks again for having me. It has been a great day.'

Samuel walked off the stage as all the students and the teachers applauded him. Bombarded with questions from staff members interested in his work and campaigns, Samuel stayed behind to answer their questions. He was pleased that so many people were aware of his work. One particular staff member caught Samuel's eye; radiance and beauty exuded from her curvaceous frame.

Boldly he approached her and began a conversation about the school. Eva was a teaching assistant and locked eyes with Samuel, mesmerised by him. Immediately liking her, Samuel did not want to waste an opportunity to further their friendship. With gentlemanly charm, he connected with her and exchanged numbers; he walked away grinning from ear to ear. As he left, his mobile began to ring.

'Hello?'

'Samuel, it's me.'

'Hello, Aunty.'

'Are you on your way home?'

'Yes, I just finished at the school.'

'I just wanted to call and give a heads up. Your dad is here. We don't want a repeat of what happened last time he came here.'

'Tell him to wait,' said Samuel. 'I'll be there soon.'

Knowing his dad was waiting for him, Samuel's mood changed slightly. Finding his keys, he opened the front door with a heavy heart. Walking into the living room, he greeted his aunt and exchanged an awkward acknowledgement with his dad. Nodding at him, Samuel ignored his outstretched hand, and left the room to drop his bag in his bedroom.

'David, don't worry about it,' his aunt said. 'He will come around.'

'I hope so,' replied Mr Wise.

Samuel came back to the living room.

'You should both go for a walk and get out of this house,' suggested his aunt. 'It's a beautiful day outside.'

'Are you up for that?' Samuel's father asked, looking at him.

'That's cool. Let's just go,' Samuel agreed.

They walked, the silence deepening. His dad spoke first.

'So, I am going to go straight into it. I understand your aunty told you what happened that night your mother died? I wanted to speak to you earlier, but with the death of your friend I thought it was not the right time.'

'Yes, she did,' Samuel responded, not making eye contact with his dad. He was focused on looking straight ahead and walking.

'The reason I didn't tell you exactly what happened is because I did not want you to have a bad memory of your mother,' Mr Wise continued. 'That is why I asked your aunt not to tell you, but she thought it was time you knew.'

'Why would Mum be seeing someone else?' asked Samuel. 'I don't get it.'

His father sighed. 'You see, son, things were not great between your mother and I. Our marriage was falling apart and we were no longer making each other happy. We were stuck in a loveless marriage.'

Samuel stopped and turned to his dad.

'Didn't you try to make things work?'

'Yes, I was trying to make sure our family would not be split,' he replied, 'but there was no attempt on your mother's side to try. That is when I suspected she was already seeing someone else. To make matters worse, I think she was in love with this person. Your aunt already knew. I asked her what she knew, but she told me nothing; however, her reactions told me a whole different story.

'At that point I was furious; that was the night it happened. When I got home, I confronted your mother. She didn't deny it, which made it real to me. That is when I lost my temper and hit her. I'm ashamed to admit it. I know I should not have hit her, but we both made a mistake and I regret mine every single day.'

Samuel had his head down as they continued walking, unable to find the right words. They had walked all the way to St John the Baptist School, Samuel's old primary school. He remembered the days his dad would collect him from school and he would beg him to play in the small park inside. They walked in together and sat on a wooden bench. Samuel looked around at his former playground, his younger years flashing before his eyes.

'Why did you not tell me?' Samuel shouted, his memories reminding him of the time that had passed. 'Why did you go on letting me think it was just your fault our family broke up?'

'For me,' his father replied. 'A son should always remember his mum in her best light. I was willing for you to hate me; in some way, you were right to do so, because if I hadn't hit her she might still be here today. As time went on, I could not bear knowing my sons were growing and living without me. That is why I have been trying to reach out to you.'

'Hold on,' said Samuel. 'Did Mark know all of this?'

'Yes, your brother knew.'

Leaping up from the bench, the fury wrapped up in his veins, Samuel began pacing up and down in front of his dad.

'So how come I was the only one that didn't know the truth?'

'You were only thirteen at the time,' his father explained.

'Mark is almost ten years older than you, so he could handle it.'

'I just wish things could have worked out differently.'

'So do I.'

Samuel sat back down.

'I remember when I was eight,' he said, calmer now. 'You used to take me to school every day and I would always beg you to let me play in the park before we went in. Remember that day I got chased by the dog and I ran away screaming!'

'Ha ha! Yes, I remember,' his father replied. 'You were shit scared. Your fault though, I told you not to pet him. Good times. I think about those days every time I walk past this park.'

Recollecting the times they had spent together, Samuel and his dad sat talking for an hour. Glancing at his watch, Samuel realised time had run away and he needed to rush to the youth project. Thanking his dad for their talk, he stood, momentarily thinking about giving his dad a hug. Hesitating, he said an awkward goodbye before walking away without any physical contact.

Four hours later, Samuel was on his way home from the youth project. He was in good spirits, happy with the way the day had gone. The workshops at school had been great; he had met a pretty girl and finally got some answers from his dad. Satisfied, he walked home. Suddenly, his phone rang. Not recognising the number, he answered.

'Hello?'

'Who is this?' Samuel replied.

'It's Jason.'

Like the wind, Samuel's good mood vanished, replaced by anger.

'What the fuck are you calling me for?'

'We need to talk.'

'Look, I have nothing to say to you.'

He ended the call.

Later on that evening, Samuel told his aunt about the conversation he'd had with his dad. She was happy that they had made progress, but there was still more work to be done.

Samuel then went to his bedroom, where his cousin Andre had been waiting for him to play a game of Pro Evolution Soccer on his PlayStation. Mid-way through the game, the front door bell rang. Andre was annoyed because he was losing and no one else was going to answer the door. Samuel paused the game and told Andre to go and find out who it was.

Andre went to the door and opened it.

'Samuel, it's for you,' he shouted.

'Who is it?' Samuel shouted back at him.

'Jason.'

Samuel stood up and rushed downstairs to the front door. He told Andre to get back inside. Samuel closed the front door slightly as he stepped out.

'What do you want?'

'Like I said on the phone,' replied Jason. 'I think it is time we talked.'

Samuel clenched his fists and walked right in front of Jason, staring into his face. Jason took a step back, trying not to escalate the tension. Samuel looked around and saw that some neighbours were out on their balconies and could see them.

'Jason, piss off,' he said. 'Seriously, I have nothing to say to you and I want nothing to do with you. Do your thing and I will do mine. If you get in my way, then we will have a problem.'

Samuel walked back into the house and slammed the door shut in Jason's face.

CHAPTER TWELVE

Missed calls. Flashing lights and vibrations alongside a melodious accompaniment. Ignored. Caller ID showed 'Jason'. Samuel, however, had no intention of answering the constant irritating phone calls. This continued day in, day out.

Throwing his phone down after hearing Samuel's voicemail for the umpteenth time, Jason sighed and sat on the floor of his bedroom, legs to his chest, frustrated. Despite his numerous attempts at a reconciliation, he had made no progress, blocked by a refusal to communicate.

In an effort to control his frustration, Jason began his daily 'six pac' routine comprising fifty sit-ups followed by fifty press-ups. Sweating and struggling after his first two sets of ten, his head full of conflicting thoughts, he grabbed his phone and dialled Jamie.

'Hello?'

'Jamie, it's me, Jason.'

'Mate, how you doing?'

'I'm good,' replied Jason. 'Listen, I need you to help me out with something.'

'What?'

'Well, I have been trying to speak to Samuel for the last few days, but he doesn't want to talk to me. I tried calling him. I even went to his aunt's house, but he wouldn't give me a chance.'

'Mate, you know how Samuel is,' replied Jamie. 'He is very stubborn. What do you want to tell him?'

'I just want to put an end to all the bullshit between us,' said Jason. 'I am not asking to get back to how we were, but at least to clear the air.'

'I hear that. Well, I will talk to him and see what he says.'

'Alright, bless.'

'Later.'

In the mood to make wrongs right, Jason turned his attention to other areas of his life. He knew he had been stubborn; distancing himself from those who cared the most about him, especially his parents. All those wrong decisions had led to this. Recognising that he had wallowed in self-pity for long enough, he decided to take action. It was a new day. Straightening up and clearing his throat, his fingers scrolled down to find his mother's number.

'Hi Mum, how are you?'

'Jason! I'm good, son. Nice to hear from you. Everything okay?'

'To be honest, Mum, I'm feeling a lot better about stuff,' he replied. 'There's some things I need to talk to you and Dad about. Are you free this evening?'

'Me and Dad?' His mum couldn't hide her surprise at this change of heart.

'Yeah, both of you.'

'Well, we're going out to the restaurant soon, but we will be back later in the evening,' she said. 'Should I tell your father you're coming?'

'No. I wanna surprise him. See you later, Mum.'

Although he knew it was the right decision, the weight of the issue pressed against Jason's heart. As he made his way to his parents' house, he became uneasy, anxious about the possible consequences. His footsteps slowed as he approached the street and saw his dad's car parked outside. Stopping, he paused, then turned around and began walking in the opposite direction. It was too much, too soon.

Struggling with his thoughts, it took him some time before gaining the courage to make his way back to the house. It was time. Pulse racing, his heart pounding through his chest, he knocked on the door. His palms were unusually sweaty, hoping his dad wouldn't answer the door. It swung open and his grinning mum greeted him with a massive hug before she stepped aside to let him enter.

'Tony!' she shouted upstairs.

'Yes?'

'You have a visitor.'

'Okay. Give me a second. I'll be right down.'

The mood was tense in the living room as Jason sat uncomfortably on the edge of the sofa with great apprehension. He recalled the previous times he had been in trouble, his dad's look of disappointment and the lectures he had given. This was worse; the sinking feeling in his stomach wouldn't shift and the water his mother had fetched him did nothing to calm his fears.

The tick of the clock focused his attention to the time as minutes passed. Upstairs, Mr Burrell was finishing off some paperwork, wondering who could possibly be visiting him. Sensing no kind of urgency and methodological in his approach, he refused to rush his work; taking his time, convinced his wife would play the host. He hated being interrupted. Well-respected for his business mind and enigmatic personality, his presence was felt as soon as he entered a room. Straightening his papers on the desk and organising his pens into their rightful place, he made his way downstairs.

Seeing his son in the front room startled him, throwing his inner equilibrium off balance. Not knowing how to respond, his silence spoke magnitudes as he walked past Jason and sat opposite him. The atmosphere shifted, sucked up by the dramatic entrance. Moving to sit next to her husband, Mrs Burrell waited for someone to break the silence, unsure what this was all about.

Sitting up straight, Jason's dad looked down at his son, waiting for him to speak. Feeling the pressure, Jason put his glass of water down and cleared his throat, hoping some wisdom would come out of his mouth.

'Mum, Dad, I am here to clear up some of the mistakes that I have made. All I want you to do is to hear me out. Firstly, it's been well over a year since I left. Looking back, I know it was my fault how things turned out. I was stubborn and not serious about which way my life was going. You can even say I was spoilt.'

Jason's dad looked at his wife and smirked, folding his arms in satisfaction. He listened to his son as he continued.

'Since I left here, my life has not improved,' said Jason. 'In fact, it has got worse. I admit that this is my own fault, but I am not here because I am finding it hard or because I want to move back home or ask for money. That is not my motive or my intention. I just want to say I am sorry for what I did. I am sorry for being disrespectful. I am sorry for not finishing college. I am sorry for stealing from you.' Jason put his head down in shame.

'Jason!' his dad boomed. 'Look at me.'

Looking up instinctually, his eyes locked with his father's. They connected.

'Son, it takes a real man to acknowledge his mistakes and apologise. I appreciate you coming down to face me. It has been hard not knowing what had become of you. I often felt that maybe I was too hard on you. At the time, I felt I had no choice. When I told you to leave it was due to your attitude, your lack of ambition. Your mother and I worked hard to give you every opportunity to become successful. You threw that back in our faces, squandering your chances. I was disgusted with your actions and felt you needed a taste of reality. Your mother had spoilt you rotten and you refused to work hard. I'm glad that things have changed. Being at Junior's funeral made me realise how short life is and how quickly things can change. I'm proud of you; for maturing and taking responsibility for your actions. And I accept your apology.'

Relieved at his dad's reaction, Jason smiled, thankful that the talk had gone well. Removing his wallet from the back pocket of his jeans, Jason removed a crisp fifty pound note and handed it to his dad. Confused, his dad looked at him.

'What is this?'

Jason's mother smiled. She knew exactly what it was for, but kept quiet, allowing Jason to explain.

'It is the money I stole from you some time ago. I know it was four hundred pounds, but this is the start of me paying it back.'

'Ah, the missing money,' replied his father. 'I knew it was you all along. Nothing else was taken; nothing was disrupted. You didn't even make it look like a real burglary.'

'Yeah, I know, Dad. I am sorry, but I was desperate. I was in a really bad place at that time and stealing was easier than asking you for help.'

'You disappointed me, Jason,' replied his father. 'But mostly I was disappointed in myself. That I had failed at raising my only son.'

'It wasn't your fault, Dad,' replied Jason. 'You gave me all I needed. I screwed up. Like I said, I am here to put things right.'

'Jason, like I told your mother at the time, all you had to do was come and apologise, and then you could have come back home. That is still the case.'

'I appreciate that, Dad, truly,' said Jason. 'Coming here was difficult, but I'm happy with how it has turned out. It has not been easy being on my own, but I have grown as a person. I do not want any handouts. I've got to make my own path in life. I will stay in my hostel and work hard to eventually afford my own place. I am in the process of looking for work. I will then sort out plans for the future while I have some sort of income.'

'I am proud to hear you say that, son.'

Although she had been quiet throughout, Mrs Burrell couldn't contain her emotions. Finally her family was back together. Tears rolled down her face.

'It not all your fault, Jason,' she said. 'I have to admit that, had your father and I been singing from the same hymn sheet while raising you, maybe things would have worked out differently. I am just glad that we are all back together. Every day that we were apart was like a dagger to my heart.'

Jason went over to where his mum was sitting. He sat on the arm of the sofa and gave her a hug.

'Jason, your mum is right,' replied his father. 'We have to take some responsibility. I was more of the tough love parent, while you mum had the soft approach. Maybe if we'd worked together things would have been different.'

'I believe things happen for a reason,' said Jason. 'We are all back here together for a reason.'

They basked in the glory of each other's company that night; reflecting and reminiscing, catching up on old times over a delicious dinner. Jason was glad he came.

City tower blocks, sky-scrapers and houses melted into green, nature, open spaces, bushes and trees. Jamie looked out the train window, noticing the shift in landscape. Sitting opposite him, Samuel reclined in his chair, allowing the fast-changing scenery excite him as they drew closer to their destination. He was the reason for their expedition; although they were arriving by train, they would be departing in style – in his first car!

'Yo, Samuel.'

Oblivious to Jamie's voice, Samuel was locked into his own thoughts; unresponsive. Kicking him slightly, Jamie waited for him to look up.

'Sorry man,' he said. 'I was thinking about my new car.'

'I can see you're excited, mate,' replied Jamie. 'Don't worry, we'll be there soon! I actually wanted to talk to you about Jason.'

'Jason!' Samuel moaned. 'Jamie, please, I am in a good mood right now. I do not want to talk about that prick.'

'Mate, just hear me out,' said Jamie. 'Jason called me yesterday, saying that he has been trying to contact you to talk about something important. Don't ignore him, Samuel. At least hear him out, see what he has to say.'

Samuel rolled his eyes. He had no intention of speaking to Jason and didn't appreciate his good mood being shadowed by this conversation. He tried to nip it in the bud. Looking directly at Jamie, his hands automatically closed into fists.

'Look, Jamie, he tried calling me a few times and I told him I didn't want to talk to him. Then he shows up at my aunt's house. I just told him to piss off.'

'Come on, man, you two have history,' said Jamie, shaking his head. 'Life's too short. Just talk to him, or at least listen...'

'Argh! Man, you're fighting a losing battle,' replied Samuel. 'Like I said, I want nothing to do with Jason. To be honest, I don't even want to discuss it. Anyway, back to my car. I can't wait to finally be on the road.'

'Yeah, I know, mate,' Jason replied, agreeing to change the subject. 'You've been talking about it for ages! So, how much are you spending?'

'I have a grand to spend, but I will try and get a hundred knocked off.'

'A grand, yeah? Nice one. So, you're gonna try barter the price. Is it a private owner or trader?'

'Trader.'

'Boy!' said Jason. 'Good luck trying to get them to come down. Most of them never go down on their asking price, mate.'

'Well, that's why I have you here,' replied Samuel. 'You know all about cars. You can help me check it out, then try get the price down for me.'

Jamie laughed.

'I will do the best I can.'

'Thanks, man,' said Samuel. 'I don't want to spend too much because I've been saving for when I go back to uni. Besides, I am still at my aunt's for now and I'm contributing to the house, so a small decent car will do.'

'Makes sense,' replied Jamie.

'When you joining me on the open road, J? You've had your licence for a while now.'

Jamie sighed. 'To be honest, mate, not any time soon. I'm focused on getting my qualifications, and then hopefully start getting paid. Once me and my mum are on our feet, then I can start thinking about cars and clothes and all that good shit.'

'I hear that, bro.'

Finally, they arrived in Luton and made their way to the dealership, stopping to ask a stranger for directions after taking a wrong turn. Walking through the rows of cars, they spoke to the salesman who took them to the vehicle Samuel was interested in. Trying to look like professionals, Samuel and Jamie walked around the car, inspecting it, kicking tyres and consulting each other about various dents and scratches.

After a five-minute test drive, Samuel left Jamie to start haggling with the salesman. It was evident the business was small; it was owned by two brothers and they couldn't afford to let a sale get away. With £150 knocked off, both parties were happy. Samuel went into the office to complete the paperwork, while Jamie stood outside. While he was waiting, he decided to call Jason.

'Hello?'

'Jamie, what's happening?'

'Nothing much, mate,' replied Jamie. 'I gotta be quick. Basically, I just spoke to Samuel, but he is not interested at all in talking to you. I tried to convince him, but he was having none of it, mate.'

'Alright minor,' replied Jason. 'Thanks for trying, though.'

'It's all good.'

'Do you have Malachi's number?' asked Jason.

'Yeah.'

'Text that to me, please.'

'Will do.'

'Speak to you later.'

'Bless.'

A spring in his step, Samuel strutted out of the office like the cat that had got the cream, keys in hand. Grinning, Jamie walked over to him and jumped into the passenger seat of the black, five-door Volkswagen Golf.

'Better put on my seatbelt. Don't trust you, mate!' Jamie laughed.

'Whatever! I got that pink licence, just like you!'

'Yeah, yeah, that don't mean nothing yet,' replied Jamie. 'The proof is in the pudding.'

Starting the engine, Samuel excitedly put the car into first gear. In his eagerness, he missed the biting point and he stalled, causing the car to jolt forward. Laughing, he looked over at Jamie before restarting the engine.

'Erm, remember to do your six-point check, mate,' Jamie mocked.

Looking over his shoulder, readjusting his mirrors and waving to the car salesman, Samuel pulled off skillfully. Jamie tried to find a suitable station on the radio, fiddling with the knob, hearing white noise.

'Jamie, thanks again for coming to help me check the car and saving me some money,' said Samuel. 'I owe you.'

'That you do,' replied Jamie. 'Dinner is on you, then?'

'Yeah, no problem. So... I hope you know the way back, because I haven't a clue.'

Jamie laughed.

'You amateur drivers, mate! We just jump on the M1 then straight to junction 2. Get off and cut through Archway and Holloway, pass that scum Arsenal stadium, then we are back in the bits.'

'You are not serious?' said Samuel. 'Always looking for a chance to have a pop at Arsenal. If Junior was here, you two would be going back and forth about Spurs and Arsenal. Man United all day, every day.'

'Mate, you Man United fans are nothing but glory hunters. Oi, left mate! Turn left!'

Samuel swung the car round the corner in third gear, taking the corner wide. Another driver tooted his horn in fury.

'That was close,' he muttered.

There were quite a few near misses on the journey as Samuel got used to being back behind the wheel. Roundabouts were the biggest headache; he got distracted as Jamie argued with him about football while directing him back to London. The traffic was terrible in some parts and it took a while before Samuel finally pulled up outside Jamie's flat.

Clouds loomed like a curse over the city; misery echoed on the faces of local commuters. The android movements of people, packed like sardines in the train carriages, irritated Malachi as he was in a rush to get into Central London.

As he tried to navigate his way through the sea of gloom on the platform, he felt a vibration in his pocket; searching for his mobile, he reached it too late. There was a missed call from a number he didn't recognise. Losing connection on the underground, he ignored it and continued his journey.

Across the city, Jason heard Malachi's voicemail; he had tried a number of times without success, so decided to leave a message. A few hours later, his phone rang.

'Hello?'

'Is that Jason?'

'Yes, it is.'

'It's Malachi. I got your message. Sorry I could not call you back straight away, only I was running late for a meeting and I had to take the underground. I've literally just come out of my meeting.'

'It's cool, thanks for returning my call,' replied Jason.

'So... What's up? Long time! I am surprised to even get a call from you.'

'Yeah, it's been a while,' said Jason. 'I was in a really low place, stuck in my own head. Crazy. Right now, I'm just trying to sort my life out.'

'I hear that,' said Malachi. 'So how have you been? What's new with you?'

'I'm good,' Jason replied, trying not to go into too much detail. 'I just have a few things I need to sort out and I need your help.'

'Me? Okay. How can I help?'

'I wanted to know when your next Y.A.M. session is with Samuel and Jamie.'

'This Friday coming. Why?' Malachi sounded suspicious, knowing there was a rift between the three friends.

'I just need to talk to everyone together,' replied Jason. 'It is very important and I have to do it. I just need you to do one thing for me. Please do not tell any of them I'm coming. If Samuel found out, I know he won't show.'

'Okay, Jason, you have my word,' said Malachi. 'I'm intrigued about what you need to say so urgently, but I guess I'll have to wait and see.'

'Thanks, man.'

'No problem. See you on Friday.'

Motivation had overtaken Jason and, over the next four days, his ambition, persistence and initiative was second to none. Epiphanies graced his unconscious thoughts while he slept and he woke up with a zeal for life and a desire for change. Desperate to review his situation, make steps for change and put himself in a better situation, he poured himself into job-hunting.

Finally finding the time to complete his Curriculum Vitae, he used the library facilities to print out fifty copies. Determined, he set himself a goal of distributing at least ten a day at various retail shops, warehouses and factories in the local and surrounding areas. Many companies informed him there were no vacancies; however, he continued the search, allowing nothing to shadow his goals. His days spent walking and talking, he spent the evenings in a meditative silence, re-reading Junior's journals and allowing the words to wash over his soul.

His hard work eventually paid off; by Thursday night, he had received responses from a factory and a warehouse who were both willing to interview him for positions. The joy spread across his face as he knew things were finally looking up.

He awoke with a new sense of purpose. Taking care with his clothes and appearance, he felt proud of the reflection that greeted him in the bathroom mirror. Hot-stepping towards the Jobcentre, his attitude had been transformed. Looking around at the resident unemployed, he knew this was not his future. Yes, he had needed the help. Yes, he had even taken advantage of the handouts while refusing to do the minimal job-searching they required. Not anymore. This was a new day.

As his name was called, he walked towards the table and smiled at Leanne before sitting down. This would be the last time he would ever submit to this situation; he was sure of it.

'So Jason, how have you been?' asked Leanne.

'I have been good,' he replied. 'Things have definitely changed for me over the last few weeks. I won't be coming here anymore.

This is the last time I'll be signing on.'

Leanne looked up, surprised.

'Why is that?' she asked. Jason grinned.

'I don't need your services anymore. By this time next week, I will be working at my new job, no longer looked down upon as the scum of society. I have spent the last few days handing out CVs and have had two callbacks.'

'That's amazing!' said Leanne smiling. 'Well done you! See, I have been trying to drum that into you all this time. You have great potential when you actually put your mind to it and stop feeling sorry for yourself.'

'Yeah, it was about time I got serious and stopped all the excuses,' said Jason. 'Thanks for putting up with me! I know I've been a pain in the arse! Right now, neither one of these jobs will be my career, but I need some income while I figure out what I want to do with my life.'

'You were definitely a pain!' agreed Leanne. 'Well, I wish you the best of luck, Jason. Make sure you come in and see me to let me know how you are getting on.'

'I will. Thanks for all your help.'

'It's my pleasure.'

As Jason left the Jobcentre, he vowed never to step foot in it again.

That evening at the youth project, Malachi and Samuel were waiting for Jamie. The centre was deadly quiet. When Jamie arrived, he was confused as to why he wasn't greeted by the usual bunch of screaming kids. He made his way to the room where the others were waiting.

'Are you alright, Jamie?' Malachi asked as he walked up to him and shook his hand.

'Yeah, I'm fine, mate.'

Jamie walked up to Samuel and touched fist with him.

'How come it's so quiet here tonight?' he said. 'It's the Easter break – where are all the young kids?'

'They all went on a daytrip to Alton Towers,' replied Malachi. 'Their coach should be back around eight-thirty this evening.'

Just as Jamie was about to say something in reply, a shadow appeared by the doorway. Jason walked into the room, his head down, hands in his pockets. Unsure of how they would react to his presence, he was unusually shy and anxious. Looking up to Malachi, he sought affirmation that he would be welcomed.

'What the hell is he doing here?' Samuel yelled, jumping up from his seat and flinging his hands aggressively in the air.

Noticing the potential uproar, Malachi took control of the situation. Walking towards Jason, he shook his hand.

'Calm down, Samuel,' he said. 'Jason will be joining us for today's session.'

Incensed, Samuel scowled and walked menacingly towards Jason, barging his shoulder as he walked towards the door.

'If he's staying, I'm gone. It's that simple.'

Jamie sprung up to Samuel's side, grabbing his arm.

'Mate, just sit down and stop being so hard-headed.'

Malachi agreed.

'Samuel! Would you just hear him out?'

Coming out of his shell, Jason realised this was a good time to interject. He turned to face Samuel, keeping a safe distance.

'Look, Samuel,' he began. 'I know we've got unresolved issues and, after today, you can cut me off completely. But I've got something important to tell you. Just give me a few minutes and it'll all make sense.'

Contemplating the situation, Samuel decided to give him the benefit of the doubt; he could always leave if it was pointless. Jamie caught his eye and nodded, signalling he should stay. With a straight face, Samuel turned back and sat down; the others followed, forming a semi-circle. Malachi stood up to speak to them all before they started.

'For today's session, I have kept it open. There will be no format; we will deal with things as they come up. Jason called me earlier this week and told me he would like to be involved in the session today. I agreed and told him he could come down and address the group. Jason, over to you.'

Malachi took his seat as Jason got up; he had a rucksack with him. He looked them all in the eye before he started talking. Public speaking was not his forte, and he felt uncomfortable. He took a deep breath; this was important.

'Before I start, I would like to thank Malachi for setting this up. I know I have messed up, especially while Junior was alive. There is not a day that goes by that I wish I had acted differently while he was with us. I missed the opportunity to help him when he needed me most, but I was too stubborn and arrogant to admit it. Samuel, most of the things you said about me were right and the reason why we ended up fighting is because I could not handle the truth.'

Samuel kissed his teeth, slouching on his seat and looking uninterested in what Jason had to say. Jason continued.

'I was so submerged in my own problems that I couldn't see anyone else. Even still, there's no excuse for how I acted and I'm ashamed of myself. The day Junior called me, I expected an earful. I deserved it. I wanted to feel his wrath. Yet, he was so forgiving, holding no grudges; it just highlighted what a great person he was. I couldn't handle that reaction when he was alive; it almost ruined me when he passed away. The guilt overwhelmed me, piercing my pain with salt. The reason I am here now is to try to clear things up. This is something I just have to do.'

Glued to every word, Malachi and Jamie were transfixed by Jason's speech. Samuel, on the other hand, was doing his best to ignore him; eyes on the ceiling, face blank. Feeling slightly overwhelmed,

Jason collated his thoughts and pulled his rucksack open, emptying the contents on the table.

'I got a package last week, at my mum's house. As you all know, I haven't lived there in ages so I was surprised and confused. I opened it when I got back to my hostel and inside were a load of books. Journals. From Junior.'

Astounded, Samuel looked directly at Jason, suddenly attentive.

'When I went to see Junior's cell mate,' said Samuel, 'he told me about the journals. When I asked the prison what had happened to them, they wouldn't tell me.'

Jason looked at him. 'To be honest, I didn't understand why he sent them to me. If anyone, I thought you would get them, Samuel. That's why I've been blowing up your phone. I wanted to share it with you. You were ignoring me, that's why I turned to Malachi, to give us all a chance to discuss it properly.'

'Are all those books full?' Jamie asked.

'Yeah,' replied Jason. 'Cover to cover. All his thoughts.'

'Have you read them?' Malachi asked.

'Every single one, multiple times,' said Jason. 'I think it's something we all should read. It took me so close to Junior's heart; everything he thought and felt. It has ultimately changed my perspective on life. If you'll allow me, I'm gonna read a few entries to give you a taste of what this is all about.'

Looking down, Jason flicked through a few pages of one of the journals. Samuel was on the edge of his seat, completely engaged and desperate to hear more about Junior's writings. His impatience caused him to tap his foot on the floor as he waited for Jason to start. Malachi and Jamie were still stunned, unable to speak, exchanging looks. Jason cleared his throat.

'10th January 2007. This cell has become the bane of my life. I see it all day, every day. I know the number of cracks in the ceiling, the steps to the door and the number of bars at the window. I have often looked at the sky and fantasised about breaking free. I just saw a bird. I envy its freedom, I covet its wings. It's no wonder so many people go crazy in here, captivity will drive you insane. There are not enough exercises in the world to take your mind off being incarcerated. I now understand why Gloria's hamster used to run away every time we took it out to clean the cage. It was not born to be imprisoned. What cruelty to take an animal and lock it away for your own entertainment.'

Jason paused to turn a page before continuing.

'I shouldn't even be here. That's the joke. No ha ha. As I sit here, contemplating my situation, I pause and recall that day. Where was I coming from? Why did I stop? Why did I run with them? My life could have been so different if I hadn't been there at that exact moment. I have to snap myself out of this mindset because going around in circles can't change reality. My appeal is going through anyway so I have to stay positive; I'll be out of this dump soon.'

Again Jason paused to turn over a page.

'Today at the canteen I saw Runner and Mo. Their faces piss me off. I told them to stay the hell away from me because I don't want to get involved with their gang bullshit. I've worked out how to survive in this place; staying under the radar, not bothering anyone. These lot, on the other hand, are kicking up a storm on the wing and trying to drag me into it. I am not involved. Sleep is taking me and my hands are tired. Sanchez is snoring, it's about that time. When I sleep, I get to rearrange reality; I'll be back in my own room as soon as I fall asleep.'

Jason flicked through the pages and started reading again. The others were listening intently, deep within their own thoughts.

'27th January 2007. It's freezing. The piercing cold has been pinching my skin and these cheap, flimsy sheets couldn't warm an ant, let alone a human being. As I write this, my hands are shivering; almost blue with cold. On top of that, my stomach keeps interrupting these sentences, angrily condemning me for ignoring its plea. I'm losing weight, soon I'll be a bag of bones. All I'm surviving on is oats. The other crap they serve couldn't tempt me at all. It just looks like dog food. Oh, how I long for my mum's cooking. Counting the days till I get out of here, hopefully I won't even get the time to finish this notebook. Everyone keeps telling me I'm getting out; especially Sanchez. I wasn't sure about him at first, but we've grown to be really close. I don't tell him everything; I'm guarded, but he's always got my back. Supporting me a hundred per cent. Got cramp in my legs; wish I could just go for a walk and stretch my legs but the locks on the doors prevent that. All I have is my pen. Hate being locked up, drives me crazy and I don't think anyone understands. Time to sleep and let my dreams take me to the place I want to be the most. Home.'

The room was silent as Jason prepared to read the next excerpt. Turning over the next page, he continued.

'7th March 2007. Life sucks. Everything sucks. I can't even fully put into words the hatred I feel towards people that are in high positions of power, who view me as another stereotype rather than seeing me for who I am. As I write this, my teeth are clenched and my pulse is racing. I deserted my book for a while as I wallowed in the muck of my reality. This place is home now. Forever. Might as well be.

'My hope was cemented in my appeal process. The day Victoria came, she left with broken fragments of my soul as her words cut into the very essence of my being. Rejection. Failure. Disaster. Stuck; labelled as a murderer, condemned to eternal hell and societal judgement. I couldn't even put pen to paper as the rage took over and I used my fists to punch my feelings into the wall.

'Everyone felt sorry for me, but that didn't compare with what I felt inside. My heart bled horror and misery as my lungs collapsed under the weight of prison and I couldn't breathe. Visitors. Malachi and Samuel came down and I had to fake it; suppressing emotions because I couldn't afford to break down. I closed up. Shut down. Told them no more visits. I had to. It was too painful.

'I even called Jason. He acted like Judas, betraying me when I needed him the most, but I haven't got time to hold grudges. Life is too short for resentment. He sounded so ashamed of himself, the guilt penetrating the phone. He hurt me, he knew that, but I was just glad to finally talk to him. I've missed him throughout this process and am glad he is doing okay.'

At this point Jason's voice began to tremble. However, he took a deep breath and continued reading.

'Alim and Sanchez have been really supportive ever since my appeal was rejected; they felt so bad for me, knowing the circumstances of my case. Even though they are the only two people I really talk to in this place, there are things I cannot tell them, which is why I write. It was only through a conversation with Alim that made me want to write. I feel lost inside and I need to escape; no one truly understands my pain and how I feel. I have to keep a brave face on and pretend I am alright. I have to pretend that I can live with the fact I have to spend fifteen fucking years in this shit hole.

'The only time I am not pretending is while everyone is asleep and I write in this book. I often cry myself to sleep; some of the pages have my tear dots on them. The hardest part is trying not to show weakness in here. The mention of the word hope has no meaning to me. I can never accept this will be my fate, I cannot live like this. Unlike before, as I put this pen down and sleep, I have no hope of waking up at home in my own bed. This is where I will be tomorrow and the day after...'

Jason stopped reading and looked up. He saw that Jamie and Samuel both had their heads down, staring at the floor in silence. Malachi's eyes, too, were downcast. Jason turned to another page.

'I am going to read one more section and that's it,' he said. 'This particular part does not have a date on it. I think he wrote it just before he died.'

Jason read the words in the journal to himself first before reading aloud.

'These words signal my success; it means I am no longer here with you, but my words are. I guess I have some explaining to do. The internal pain is too difficult to describe, clogging my chest, making it hard to breathe. I have tried to survive, but it has become impossible. I hope you can forgive me.

'To my family, I love you all so much; your faces and memories have been a comfort to me in this dungeon. I need you to understand my heart; hopefully, one day, you will read these journals and feel my hurt. Matthew, Gloria. Please forgive me.

'Mum. Words are not enough. Knowing the impact this would have on you has caused me to rethink my plan many times. I never meant to cause you this pain...'

Jason stopped reading. 'Sorry, I think that page should be left for Junior's family to read. This bit is directed at us.' He flicked to the next page and continued reading.

'My brothers. Samuel, Jason and Jamie, don't hate me. I had to do it this way, I couldn't bear it anymore. I'm sorry to leave so abruptly, but that's not the focus of my message. Read this carefully, all of you. We are more than the stereotypes, more than statistics, more than people expect us to be. Over these years, we have experienced so much together. We all know it hasn't been easy, but we always came out stronger with the support of each other.

'Many people treat us like we are beneath them, because of where we grew up; they call us the socially deprived. In school, no one believed in us, but we came through that together. Friendship is one of the most important things we have; it is what keeps us going, knowing there are people that care for us. I do not want what happened to me to be the cause of the breakdown of the friendship. Fix it before it is too late.'

Tears were beginning to form in Jason's eyes and he was finding it difficult to control his emotions.

'Let's not forget the ambition pact we made,' he continued. 'Make sure that it continues until you all reach those heights of success we once talked about. Samuel, Jamie and Malachi – I appreciate all the work you put in to trying to get me out. Jason, like I told you over the phone, I hold no grudges. We are all family.

'Regardless of what happens, it is always better to stick together and make sure you grow together. I met some amazing people in here who gave me a different outlook on things, but the majority of them have regrets. Remember, success no matter what!

'Finally, continue to keep an eye on my younger brother and sister. Much love, Junior.'

Samuel had a bleak look on his face as his tears fell down. He tried to wipe them away with his sleeves, but he could not help the flow. Jamie was lost in a distant gaze. Malachi stood up to flick through the journals that were on the table. Jamie shook his head, snapping himself out of his thoughts.

'Junior went through a lot,' he said. 'More than we could ever understand.'

'You can feel the passion and pain in his words,' Malachi stated.

Malachi then left the room to get some refreshments. They had already been in there for an hour and he knew they would not be leaving any time soon. Jason was still standing. He waited until Malachi returned with the drinks.

'I was surprised when Junior sent his journals to me,' he said. 'I asked myself why many times. I guess he wanted me to be the one to fix what I helped break. Looking back almost two years ago, it was Junior who first came to this Young Ambitious Minds session and then convinced us all to come. Now, even in death, he has managed to bring us all back together again. I just want to say, again, I am sorry for the part I played in fucking everything up.

'Knowing Junior didn't have a grudge made me feel better, but I wish I could have said sorry properly. Like Junior said, it is all about us sticking together. I want us to keep that ambition pact alive. I am still trying to figure out what I will do with my life, but I am making progress and I can't do it alone. Jamie, you are the most talented boxer I know; you should pick up those gloves again, as well as carrying on with your gym instructor course. Samuel, you are already on your way to achieving your goals. I just hope we can move forward together.'

With that, Jason sat down on his chair.

Jamie walked over to Jason. Extending his hand, he lifted him up and gave him a hug.

'Mate, that was emotional, thank you.'

Malachi then walked up to Jason and shook his hand.

'Well done, that was inspirational,' he said. 'This is a unique situation, but I have never been so inspired. The initiative and the actions you took are incredible.'

Samuel, his face expressionless, was still sitting down on his chair. Hesitating, he stood up and walked over to the others. They all watched as he approached. Without saying anything, Samuel reached out his hand and gave Jason a hug. They stood there for a moment. Samuel said no words as tears continued to flow down his face.

After a minute or so, the friends all sat back down except for Malachi, who stood to speak to them all.

'Anything I say now will never compare to what we have heard today,' he began. 'I will simply reiterate what has already been said. To remember to always be there for each other during the good and the bad. So, it seems the ambitions of the deprived are still alive and well, until you all succeed in your different ventures.'

'Yes, you are right,' Samuel said as he cracked a smile for the first time in the session.

'Junior is gone, but he is never forgotten,' Jamie declared.

Jason looked at them. 'Jamie, Samuel, I think you should both read the journals in full. Then, when you have both finished, I think we should give them to Junior's younger brother. They will give him a better understanding of what his brother went through.'

'I agree, mate,' replied Jamie. 'And Gloria can read them when she is old enough to understand.'

Sunlight peeked delicately through the cracks around Jamie's window. The early morning birds danced dangerously on the roof, singing a chirpy song, rousing Jamie from his sleep. His eyes peeled open as he embraced the dawn, his mind focused and clear. Motives for the next few hours pranced to the forefront of his cranium and he smiled, ready for a new challenge.

Stretching his arms towards the ceiling, he yawned loudly before shaking himself awake. Locating a pair of shorts and a T-shirt, he rummaged under the bed for his well-worn running shoes. His feet nestled into the familiar tread of the soles and his toes uncurled, ready for exercise.

Bursting through the front door, energised by the thunderous bass of his musical playlist on his iPod, he allowed the breeze to flow through him as he prepared to jog. The streets were dead, no cars, no people; a ghost town. Enjoying the moment of solitude, his feet pounded to the rhythm, his heart in overdrive.

A new day meant a new route and he allowed his soul to direct his feet; he was out of practice and felt the burn after twenty minutes. Pausing, bent over to catch his breath, he took in the sights and realised he was on the Hackney side of the Olympic construction site. As the workmen entered the site, Jamie greeted them, smiling as he imagined what the site would look like once completed.

This was confirmation of his dream; it was no accident that he had decided to take this route and rest here, at this point. Taking in the atmosphere, he saw himself winning Gold and imagined the grin on his mum's face as she cried with pride. He knew it was pretentious; but he could dream. Enthused and in awe, he proceeded to jog back home, a new spring in his step.

'Morning, Mum.'

'Morning, sweetheart. I was wondering where you'd gone.'

'I couldn't sleep,' said Jamie, 'so I went for a quick jog.'

'Okay, have a good day. I am running late for work.'

'Thanks Mum, love you.'

'Love you, too.'

Table full of steaming dishes, the empty plates and cutlery eagerly awaited their individual portions. Samuel peered across the feast with joy, knowing his aunt's seasoning had, by now, fully infused into the meat that had been stewing for most of the evening. Attempting to steal a morsel from the pot, Samuel's knuckles had been rapped by his aunt as she scolded him and looked on disapprovingly. He laughed, awaiting his father's arrival.

The house free of his cousins and uncle, his aunt had prepared a banquet especially for this new relationship to blossom. She knew her food would bring out the best in them; love went into every dish. They sat expectantly as his aunt dished, Samuel and his dad in cahoots about who would get the biggest piece of meat. Laughter and good conversation interrupted intense chewing and satisfied swallowing. Stomachs murmured in appreciation.

'Felicity, you have outdone yourself again,' Mr Wise commented. 'Dinner was delicious.'

'Oh, David, you are too kind.'

'Aunty, on a serious note,' said Samuel. 'How come you do not cook like that every day?'

'No time, my dear,' she replied. 'It takes good preparation to make meals like that. I am glad you both enjoyed it.'

Reclining in their chairs, both Samuel and his dad looked like stuffed animals; they were barely able to move. Allowing the food to settle, they relaxed with Samuel poking fun at his dad's expression. As his aunt started to clear the table, she glanced at Samuel, who immediately sprung up and began to help, hoping this would save him from having to wash up.

Before long, Mr Wise prepared to leave.

'Felicity, thanks again for a wonderful meal,' he said, putting his blazer on.

'You are welcome. See you again soon.'

Samuel walked his dad to his car.

'Have you spoken to your brother recently?' his father asked.

'Yes, I spoke to Mark the other day,' replied Samuel. 'He told me his wife/girlfriend is expecting a new baby. I will probably go and see them before I go back to uni.'

'Good, it is important that the family stays in contact,' said his dad. 'I know we have only just started talking again, but it means so much to me. After all this time, there is so much I want to know about you.'

'We will take it a day at a time, Dad.'

They both paused, simultaneously shocked by Samuel referring to his father as 'Dad'. Those words hadn't been uttered in years. His dad smiled, thankful for the change. Trying not to focus too much on it, Samuel broke the silence before it became awkward.

'Oh yeah, that's the car I bought,' he said, pointing across the road. 'The one I was telling you about over dinner.'

'The black Golf?'

'Yes.' Samuel smiled proudly; the car reflected his age and maturity. His dad looked at the car in more detail.

'Not bad for a first car,' he said. 'Maybe one day you'll take me for a spin.'

'If you're paying for petrol... of course!' said Samuel. They both laughed as his dad unlocked his car door.

'Hmm, we'll see! Hope to see you soon, son. Take care.'

'Bye, Dad.'

Knocking at the front door, Jamie, Samuel and Jason waited anxiously outside. Each chest heaved with the pressure of what was about to occur. A week since Jason had dropped the bombshell of the journals, both Samuel and Jamie had read them from cover to cover. It had been a bittersweet experience; they felt privileged to have a piece of their friend still with them, yet the pain and the ending was hard to swallow. It was now time to return the journals to Junior's family.

Unaware of their plans, Mrs Okoli opened the door, happy to see them. Her tight embraces were shared amongst them as they greeted each other. She showed them into the house.

'Well my dears, this is a nice surprise! How have you been?'

'Good, thank you,' Jason replied. 'And you?'

'It has been difficult, my love, but I am trying to take each day as it comes. Sometimes, I wake up and I forget he is gone.'

The boys looked sorrowful, unable to imagine the emotional rollercoaster Junior's mother was facing on a daily basis. Jason removed one of the journals from his rucksack.

'We came to show you this,' he said, turning her attention to the book.

'What is it?'

'Junior was documenting his thoughts and feelings in notebooks and they were sent to me after he passed. We have all read them, but they belong here.'

Grasping the book with shaking hands, Junior's mum struggled to comprehend the magnitude of what Jason had said.

'Oh my!' she exclaimed. 'This is such a precious gift. My son's heart on paper.' She clutched the book to her chest. 'I can't read his secrets. It wouldn't feel right.'

'That's okay,' Jason replied. 'We wanted to talk to Matthew and see how he feels about reading them.'

'Yes,' replied Mrs Okoli. 'That would be good for him. I think he feels somewhat troubled about what has happened and needs closure. This would help him understand. He is upstairs. Let me go and get him for you.'

A few minutes later, Matthew entered the living room sheepishly, wondering what they all wanted.

'Matthew!' Samuel called. 'How have you been?'

'I'm cool,' replied Matthew. 'Just enjoying the Easter holidays.'

'That's good,' Samuel smiled. 'You look nervous. I'm sure you're wondering why we're all here.'

'That's okay,' Matthew responded. 'What's going on?'

'Well, it's about Junior,' explained Samuel. 'When he was in prison, he wrote some of his thoughts down in journals; about how he was feeling, what happened on each day, all the things he didn't say to us. We have all read them and now we think you should, too.'

Matthew looked shocked. He listened keenly.

'Hopefully, it will help answer many of your unanswered questions about Junior,' said Jamie.

Jason joined in. 'When you feel Gloria is old enough to read them, give them to her as well.'

Handing over the journals to Matthew, Samuel hoped it wasn't too soon to bombard Matthew with these emotionally charged books. He, himself, had faced each page with difficulty.

Stunned, Matthew took the books, desperate to start reading. The loss of his brother had left a void no one could fill and he was finding it hard to settle into the role of older brother. The responsibility felt too heavy and he needed and wanted his brother back. He knew this wasn't physically possible, but felt the journals would soothe his soul as he communicated with his brother from beyond the grave.

Understanding that Matthew would need some time alone, they all made their way out, stopping at the kitchen to say goodbye to Junior's mum. Matthew followed them to the front door. Samuel was the last to leave. He turned to Matthew.

'Where is Gloria?'

'She is playing outside somewhere.'

'Make sure you look after your mum and your sister. When your dad is not around, you are the man of the house.'

'I will. Thanks again for the journals.'

'You're welcome,' said Samuel. 'Some of them are pretty heavy going. If you need to talk, just give me a call, okay?'

'Yeah. Defo. Thanks, Samuel.'

Three pairs of hands gripped three bouquets of flowers, as three pairs of legs paused at their destination. Shiny shoes scrunched autumn leaves, decorating their well-tailored suits with colourful splashes of seasonal changes. Samuel, Jamie and Jason stood, heads bowed in reverence, at the designated resting place of their closest friend. Things had changed and they wanted to update Junior on their progress. Surrounding his headstone, they stood quietly, each reflecting on the impact Junior had made on each of their lives. Samuel spoke first.

'Hey, Junior. Today's been such a brilliant day. We had to come share the news with you, coz you're the reason. I hope you're proud of us. We've all been feeling your presence during this journey... It's done, J. Officially. We all put our heads together and made it happen. The Junior Okoli Charity Foundation is here! The launch went amazing – hundreds of people turned up to hear our message. We will speak on your behalf, continuing to fight against joint enterprise. Your words, your message, have fuelled our desire to raise awareness about suicides in prison. We won't stop. It's all for you, bro. Miss you like crazy.'

Samuel walked closer to Junior's headstone and placed his flowers on the earth.

It was Jamie's turn next. 'Mate, I know you and my old man are up there watching over us. Words can't even explain how much I miss you both.' He placed his flowers down next to Samuel's.

Jason took a moment to collect his thoughts before he stepped forward.

'J, at first I didn't understand why you sent me your journals, but now I do. You have always been the glue that has held us together. In your name, we plan to make a real difference and to keep our pact going. Miss you, fam. Continue to rest in perfect peace.'

All three stood in reflective silence before they made their way out of the cemetery. On the way home, they continued talking about the launch and the future of the charity.

'I am really glad we decided to set up the charity,' Jamie said.

'Yes, it has been hard work, but definitely worth it,' Jason replied.

'You two, with the help of Malachi, will have to oversee things because I will be back at uni in three weeks,' said Samuel. 'But I will be down here helping as much as I can, especially now I have a car.'

'Are you looking forward to going back to uni?' Jamie asked.

'Yes, I am, actually,' replied Samuel. 'But I will still be here for your big return to the ring. How are you feeling about that?'

'Mate, I am buzzing,' said Jamie. 'I have never felt so good. Now I am part-qualified as a gym instructor, I get paid to help people keep fit. When I finish working, I can concentrate on my own fitness. So, money is coming in, my mum's not working as much and I am itching to get back in the ring. London 2012, here I come!'

'I feel sorry for whoever you are going to be fighting, Jamie,' said Jason. 'They are going to get knocked the hell out.'

'Jamie "the Menace" Marker is back!' Samuel roared.

Jamie laughed. 'Can you believe, it was just over two years ago we were watching London win the bid. So much has happened since then.'

'Trust me, time flies,' Samuel replied.

'This cemetery is huge,' exclaimed Jason. 'We have been walking for ages and have only just got to the exit.'

'Yes, it is, mate,' replied Jamie. 'Every time I come here to see my dad, I say the same thing.'

'What are we doing? Cab, bus, or are walking to the tube station?' Jason asked.

'Let's just walk, man,' Samuel suggested. 'So, Jason, how is your new flat coming?'

'I'm so glad I am finally out of that hostel,' replied Jason. 'I can't really call it a flat; it's more of a bedsit. It is coming along well, though. Just need to paint it and get some furniture and I am good to go. I just need some more money before I can finish it; it's a good thing I get paid weekly from my warehouse job. Then back to college in a few weeks.'

'You've done well, mate,' said Jamie. 'What are you doing in college?'

'Business and economics.'

'It seems like we are all back on our journey towards success,' Samuel said.

'Looks that way,' replied Jamie. 'Let's just keep it going.'

'Only one more thing left,' said Samuel with a cheeky grin on his face. 'That's for Jamie to propose to Emma.' All three laughed, but Samuel laughed the longest.

'Mate, you've kept your movements with that Eva chick quiet,' retorted Jamie.

'Don't worry about me, bro,' Samuel replied as he gave Jamie a wink.

'You have been with Emma for years, fam,' said Jason. 'Just pop the question, man.'

'When the time is right, mate.'

Walking along the path, they discussed and reminisced on their journeys. Much had happened and yet still there was more to come. With a new sense of purpose, and with the support of their friends, they were ready to take on the world. These were their dreams. The ambitions of the deprived.

The End